£13:92   NW03001575   MCGEN/05

Term... ...pening h...

WITHDRAWN

N 0120655 9

CHILD PSYCHOLOGY IN ACTION

CHILD PSYCHOLOGY IN ACTION

Linking Research and Practice

Edited by
JOHN HARRIS

NEWMAN COLLEGE
BARTLEY GREEN
BIRMINGHAM B32 3NT

CLASS 155.4
BARCODE 0120 6559
AUTHOR CHI

CROOM HELM
London & Sydney

BROOKLINE BOOKS
Cambridge, Massachusetts

© 1986 John Harris
Croom Helm Ltd, Provident House, Burrell Row,
Beckenham, Kent BR3 1AT

Croom Helm Australia Pty Ltd, Suite 4, 6th Floor,
64-76 Kippax Street, Surry Hills, NSW 2010, Australia

British Library Cataloguing in Publication Data

Child psychology in action: linking research and
    practice.
    1. Child development
    I. Harris, John
    155.4   BF721

    ISBN 0-7099-3750-4

Brookline Books, PO Box 1046,
Cambridge, MA 02238
Library of Congress Cataloging in Publication Data

Main entry under title:

Child psychology in action.
    Bibliography: p.
    Includes indexes.
    1. Child psychology.   2. Child psychology—Research.
I. Harris, John, 1951–
BF721.C516   1986   155.4   85-22405
ISBN 0-914797-19-0

Typeset by Words & Pictures Ltd, Thornton Heath, Surrey
Printed and bound in Great Britain by
Biddles Ltd, Guildford and King's Lynn

CONTENTS

List of Figures

Preface   1

Introduction   2

PART ONE: FAMILIES   9

1. The Parental Empowerment Process: Building on
   Family Strengths *Moncrieff Cochran*   12

2. Presenting Psychological Knowledge to Mothers of
   Young Children *Pam Harris*   34

3. Advising Parents of Young Deaf Children:
   Implications and Assumptions *Susan Gregory*   50

4. Ways of Increasing Parental Involvement in Children's
   Development and Education *Sheila Wolfendale*   73

PART TWO: SCHOOLS   99

5. From Psychology to Instruction *Leslie Smith*   103

6. Developmental Psychology and the Pre-school
   Curriculum *Kathy Sylva*   127

7. The Contribution of Developmental Psychology to
   the Education of Mentally Handicapped Childen in
   Special Schools *John Harris*   143

8. The Derbyshire Language Scheme: Research to
   Practice in Remedial Language Teaching
   Mark Masidlover   171

9. Political Constraints on the Use of Research Findings
   in Schools: Experience in England and New Zealand
   David Galloway   191

PART THREE: PROFESSIONAL TRAINING   205

10. Developmental Psychology Applied to Teacher
    Training *Charles Desforges*   208

11. Evolving Clinical Practice from Research Findings:
The Problem of Professional Education *Kay Mogford*   220

12. Service-based Research *Roy McConkey*   235

Overview   255

Contributors   260

Author Index   264

Subject Index   270

FIGURES

1.1 Degree to which Family Matters Met Empowerment
    Criteria   26
4.1 The Portage Structure   86
7.1 A Model of the Processes of Translating Child
    Development Research into Educational Practice
    in Special Schools   163

PREFACE

This book is a collection of articles by psychologists who are involved at the interface between research and practice. Its prime objective is to establish the relationship between research and practice in child development as a problematic area which deserves consideration in its own right. This involves a critical analysis of past research, and the ways in which attempts have been made to modify practice to match new research findings and new theories of child development. It also involves questioning the assumptions behind established views of the research–practice relationship, and suggestions for modifying that relationship in the future so that research has a more powerful and productive impact on practice. Finally, it involves illustrative examples of the ways in which research can be effective in the systematic development of good practice. The book is divided into three parts concerned with the impact of child development research in the family, the school, and the training of professionals who work with children and their families.

The book will be of interest to those whose prime interest is in carrying out child development research, as well as those who, as professionals, see themselves as 'consumers' of research. It is addressed to developmental psychologists, professionals whose work brings them into contact with children, students who study child development as part of a professional training course and those who teach child development on professional, vocational and academic courses. I would like to think that it will make researchers more sensitive to the problems of conducting research which has implications for practice, and provide practitioners, students and teachers of child development with a clear understanding of the advantages and limitations of research findings. Over and above this, a long-term objective is the emergence of new and better links between research and practice and researchers and practitioners.

This book has been a collaborative exercise. However, in addition to the other contributors there are a number of people whose help I should like to acknowledge: Jill Lewis and Graham Upton for their helpful suggestions and comments in the early stages of the preparation of the book; David Middleton for his continuing interest and lively comments; and Carol Grant for her speedy and efficient typing of parts of the manuscript.

1

INTRODUCTION

Social science, and psychology in particular, have since their inception sought not only to increase knowledge but to provide the basis for improved social policy and the alleviation of social problems through systematic intervention. In its own way, child psychology has accepted a role in the generation of knowledge relevant to the improved care and education of children. However, in contrast to the widely held assumption regarding the applicability of much research in child psychology, relatively little attention has been paid to the mechanisms by which research impinges on practice and the extent to which practice has implications for the conduct of research.

This book does not fit easily into any of the usual categories which developmental psychologists use to describe their particular areas of interest. It is not concerned with any one aspect of development, but with the relationship between two related areas in which developmental psychologists work: psychological research and professional practice.

The central theme, which each of the contributors address, may be simply expressed: to what extent and in what ways does research on child development influence practice; how might research and practice be changed so that research becomes more relevant to practice and practice more closely in tune with research? These questions are considered in relation to three areas of activity in which child psychology directly impinges upon practice; the family, schools and professional training of those who will work with children and their families.

There are a number of different perspectives from which the research practice relationship may be viewed. The different perspectives tend to focus attention upon different aspects of the relationship and give rise to different interpretations concerning the central issues. The perspectives tend to be implicit rather than explicit and, for this reason, they are not always easily identifiable. Furthermore, authors may employ a combination of the perspectives when describing a particular example of research and practice. Nevertheless, the perspectives do give rise to different kinds of analysis, the description of different problems and the advocacy of different solutions. These views are not necessarily incompatible but, like the products of a triangulation research method, they each provide a valid and complementary view of a single process.

The aim of this introduction is to make explicit some of the perspectives which have been adopted by the various different authors within this volume. The task of relating the different perspectives and drawing out the common themes and major issues will be left until the Overview.

Perspectives on Research and Practice

First, it should be pointed out that 'Linking Research and Practice' has been deliberately chosen as a title for this book in order to emphasise the inherent ambiguity of the relationship; it is not necessarily a case of research being translated into practice (although this accurately characterises one perspective from which the relationship may be viewed) since it is not unreasonable to expect the demands of practice to influence research, or indeed for practice to act as a testing ground for theories conceived within research settings. The relationship between research and practice is complex and this title makes it possible to accommodate the different interpretations which reveal that complexity. Four perspectives from which the research practice relationship may be viewed are summarised below.

Research is the Process of Generating Knowledge; Practice is the Process of Applying Knowledge to Solve Problems

The traditional view of research and practice, heavily influenced by the distinctions which have evolved in the physical sciences, is that research gives rise to factual knowledge and a set of theories about the world, which can then be used as a basis for intervention. The intervention process is seen as being analogous to the classical laboratory experiment in so far as it is the means by which induced changes in an independent variable are used to create desired changes in a dependent variable. Accurate information and valid theories provide the basis for predicting which independent variables can be influenced in order to effect changes in specific dependent variables. For example, Susan Gregory describes in her chapter how in the 1960s existing theories of child language acquisition gave rise to the view that deaf children could be helped to acquire the rules for the generation of linguistic structures if they heard large amounts of adult speech. Subsequently, the increasing significance attributed to the modifications in the adult language addressed to young children produced a shift in the focus of intervention away from the amount of speech which deaf children heard towards deliberate fine tuning of language by parents and teachers talking to young deaf children. Gregory argues that recent developments in the theory of a language acquisition indicate yet another shift in the focus of intervention, to the functional communications systems which evolve between mothers and children prior to the onset of speech.

Another example of research having a direct effect on innovations in practice comes from the chapter by Mon Cochran in which he describes how the concept of parental empowerment has been derived from an ecological view of human development. Cochran argues that there are environmental factors, operating outside the influence of the developing child, which may inhibit or distort developmental progress. 'Empowerment' is a form of compensatory intervention designed to provide those families who are vulnerable to such environmental influences with the means of influencing the individuals or institutions in the community at large which exercise power and control over such things as welfare services and education. If the wider ecological conditions for development can be improved then, it is suggested, the possibilities for individual growth and development will follow in the form of better parental care, a more stimulating environment, higher quality social interactions and better learning opportunities.

In reviewing the effect of child development research on educational practice, Charles Desforges argues that the observable effects of research being translated into practice are negligible and, furthermore, that an examination of contemporary child development research suggests that there is very little which is applicable within the context of education. In the light of this depressing conclusion, Desforges urges the need for the forging of alternative and more productive relationships between those who conduct research and those who might be regarded as potential consumers of research knowledge.

Research as Technology

A second view of research and practice sees research as a technological instrument by which appropriate intervention can be achieved. The most obvious examples concern attempts to establish normal appearing behaviours in those individuals who have been identified (or have identified themselves) as deficient or deviant with respect to specific skills or abilities, and strategies for changing the environments of socially and educationally disadvantaged children. In a recent article, Argyle summarises the rationale for this approach with respect to social skills training: 'The traditional logic has been to compare groups of effective and ineffective performers, discover how their social behaviour differs, and teach the good skills to others.' (Argyle 1984: 405) The research technology provides the means by which those aspects of behaviour which characterise normal functioning are identified and described so that similar behaviours can then be taught to the client/patient. Hopefully, the newly established part of the behavioural repertoire will be indistinguishable from that found in the 'normal' model. This perspective makes no demands for a theoretical interpretation of the significance of behaviour, since the sole objective is to make the recipients of intervention 'appear more normal'. The chapter by John Harris examines the ways in which this kind of approach has been applied to intervention with mentally handicapped children. Since normal development can be characterised as a sequence of progressively more complex behaviours, some intervention programmes have attempted to move mentally handicapped children towards normal functioning by teaching the behaviours that make up normal development. He suggests that such an approach encounters problems when one questions the criteria which are used to identify some behaviours rather than others as representative of a normal developmental sequence.

Practice as a Research Activity

The third view of the relationship between research and practice sees research as a characteristic of good practice and practice settings as indispensable to the conduct of applicable research. First, it has been suggested that practitioners ought to extend and elaborate their role so as to include the research functions of systematic evaluation and dissemination of results. Sheila Wolfendale documents the way in which a variety of schemes have arisen to encourage parental participation in the teaching of reading, and the ways in which reports of individual schemes have circulated to provide models and a stimulus for other similar projects, albeit in slightly different local settings. As Wolfendale expresses it, 'the link is not one of pure research preceding practical applications, but of research on practical applications; research and practice thus become two interrelated aspects of the same scheme' (Chapter 4, p. 84). The study of parental empowerment by Cochran, and Pam Harris's chapter on teaching child development to parents can both be seen as examples of research which seek to examine the ways in which an innovatory strategy can best be organised and implemented in community settings. In both cases research results indicated the need for significant change in the way in which community services were provided.

Another result of using practice as a research heuristic is that the conditions are created whereby it becomes possible to evaluate theories in the light of success or failure of the forms of intervention which they generate. Kathy Sylva expresses a view similar to that of Desforges, in so far as she argues that theories of cognitive development have had very little impact on practice in the pre-school. However, she goes on to describe one example in which implementation of a theory-based intervention scheme in American pre-schools provided the context not only for the evolution of more appropriate practice but also for the elaboration and modification of the original theory.

In describing the development of the Derbyshire Language Scheme (DLS), Mark Masidlover argues that child language research and the experience of language teaching in the special school provide two complementary sources of ideas for intervention and two different possibilities for evaluation; ideas which seem to work in the classroom need to be examined in the light of research, while intervention based on research must be exposed to field trials before it can be incorporated within the DLS. As a result, the DLS is neither an innovation derived solely from research, nor simply a summary of good classroom practice, but the product of a research study which has used practice as an additional resource to achieve practical objectives. Interestingly, neither existing classroom practice nor research findings emerge from this exercise unscathed.

Like Charles Desforges, both Roy McConkey and Kay Mogford see a problem in the gap between traditional research practices and the work of practitioners who are actively engaged in helping children and their families. As part of the solution, McConkey advocates institutional reform so that the barriers which have in the past emphasised the distinction between research and practice are broken down. McConkey suggests that in future there should be a greater recognition of the value of service-based research of the kind described by Sheila Wolfendale in relation to parental involvement in the teaching of reading. This would involve 'practitioners', especially professional psychologists working in the community, becoming researchers and developers of their own services. McConkey's chapter provides a rationale for this approach and gives examples of the way in which research and practice might be successfully combined within existing local authority services and organisations.

Meta-theory on Research and Practice

A fourth view of research and practice seeks to elucidate the relationship between 'scientists' who observe phenomena objectively, those who make decisions about intervention, the individuals who act as subjects of scientific psychology, and those individuals who become the objects of intervention. It is concerned with the assumptions which constitute the ideology of scientific enquiry and thus legitimise the exercise of power whereby those with access to knowledge are able to make decisions and control the less powerful in the name of education and social reform. It involves a consideration of research in the light of government policy, scientific and social ideology and personal values. Much has been written on these topics (Ingleby 1974; Rose 1979; Henriques, Holloway, Urwin, Venn and Walkerdine 1984; Sinha, in press) and this book does not set out to explore the implications of this kind of analysis in detail. However, two chapters in particular address relevant issues. Les Smith emphasises that the link between research and practice is never direct because the shift from what *is* to what *might be* introduces the subjective element of values and value judgements. Intervention is concerned with the creation (and by implication the denial) of opportunities for those receiving intervention. Smith's point is that if research is to be used as a basis for improved educational practice, then those who are concerned with intervention must be clear about their values and intentions; they will then be in a better position to use research which is relevant to their objectives and ignore research which is not.

David Galloway examines the wider social and political context in terms of making research more effective with regard to changing policy and practice. He argues that researchers must be aware of the limitations and limited effects which any piece of research *per se* is likely to have in the short term. Acceptance of research findings and widespread implementation will depend, Galloway suggests, as much upon social and political factors beyond the researchers' control, as upon the validity or intrinsic worth of the research and the significance of the social and educational problems which implementation might alleviate.

Each of the contributors has addressed the problem of linking research and practice in child psychology in the light of their own experience. Three areas of activity, where research and practice intersect, form the basis for the organisation of the chapters into sections. These are concerned with the family, the school and the training of those who will become practitioners within the fields of child health and education.

References

Argyle, M. (1984) Some new developments in social skills training, *Bulletin of the British Psychological Society*, *37*, 405–12

Ingleby, D. (1974) The psychology of child psychology in M.P.M. Richards (ed.), *The Integration of the Child into a Social World*, Cambridge: Cambridge University Press

Henriques, J., Holloway, W., Urwin, C., Venn, C. and Walkerdine, V. (1984) *Changing the Subject: Psychology, Social Regulation and Subjectivity*, London: Methuen

Rose, N. (1979) The psychological complex: mental measurement and social administration, *Ideology and Consciousness*, 5, 5–68

Sinha, C. (forthcoming) Psychology, education and the ghost of Kasper Hauser, *Educational Psychology*

PART ONE: FAMILIES

Families provide a universal context for child rearing and one which has been considered as having a crucial influence on the development of children. Since families clearly vary both in the kind of care they provide and in terms of the quality of care, it is not surprising that psychologists have taken a particular interest in the relationships which exist between aspects of family life and developmental progress. It is also understandable why families have become one of the key areas for intervention designed to influence developmental outcomes.

The Family Matters Project, described by Mon Cochran in Chapter 1, sets out to test the proposition that a particularly effective way of helping children is to help their parents to be more confident and skilful in utilising the resources available in the community for coping with the problems and stresses of family life.

In Chapter 2 Pam Harris elaborates the distinction between what psychologists and other professionals think parents ought to know about child development and what parents see as useful and helpful information, when provided with the possibility of making an informed choice. Interestingly, there is relatively little agreement between the two.

Sue Gregory in Chapter 3 considers the implications of research on child language for early intervention within families of young deaf children and in doing so she argues for a move away from a concern with spoken language and the need for a greater sensitivity towards the communicative, as opposed to linguistic, needs of the deaf child and his family.

The final chapter in this section is by Sheila Wolfendale who provides an overview of recent programmes in the United Kingdom which have been designed to increase parental involvement with children and different aspects of their formal and informal education.

1 THE PARENTAL EMPOWERMENT PROCESS: BUILDING ON FAMILY STRENGTHS

Moncrieff Cochran

'Empowerment' is a term very much in vogue in the United States at the moment, especially among 'revisionist' thinkers and practitioners in the human services. What is empowerment? Is the concept new, or simply a rehash of old ideas? How might it be manifested in a workable programme of family support? What basic challenges to standard practice in the delivery of human service programmes are presented by the empowerment approach? The chapter which follows will begin with some discussion and a working definition of the empowerment concept. The principles embodied in the concept will then be illustrated with the use of a case study, a programme of support for young families called Family Matters. Following presentation of the case study there will be a systematic effort to measure the programme against specific criteria contained within the definition of empowerment. The chapter will conclude with a discussion of several issues raised by the Family Matters example which have special significance for those who would apply the social sciences in the service of individuals, local communities and the larger society.

The Empowerment Concept

While no comprehensive attempt to trace its roots has yet been undertaken, the concept of empowerment appears to have emerged in the United States during the early 1970s in response to the social and economic power struggles of the previous decade. With such lineage it can be assumed that political ideology played a part in shaping the meaning of the concept. In that context it is interesting to note that the term empowerment has been used in the past decade by thinkers on the political right (Berger and Neuhaus 1977) as well as the left (Freire 1973; Solomon 1976). This breadth of utility can be thought of as testament both to its possible significance and to its lack of clear definition.

A comparison of various efforts to define empowerment reveals both similarities and differences. One commonality is an underlying assumption – not shared by traditional human service providers – that individuals understand their own needs better than others are able to understand them (Berger and Neuhaus 1977; Rappoport 1981; Whitham 1982; Cochran and Woolever 1983). Implied in this assumption is another shared element in these conceptualisations; that individuals should have the power both to define their own needs and to act upon that understanding (see also Baker-Miller 1982).

Differences in definition involve whether empowerment is a state or a process, and whether empowerment as a process involves only change in individuals and mediating structures or also in controlling structures. Berger and Neuhaus (1977) imply – the title of their book notwithstanding – that individuals are more or less empowered, as if empowerment were a state (like anger or wealth). Other authors refer quite explicitly to empowerment as a process. Baker-Miller says that to empower is to foster growth in others. Cochran and Woolever refer repeatedly to a process, and suggest that it may contain a predictable series of identifiable steps. Rappoport introduces the term 'collaboration' to describe the nature of involvement by the helping professions in the process of empowering others. Whitham begins with the process involved in Freire's largely cognitive concept of 'critical reflection', and extends it to include the interpersonal processes which provide the conditions for such reflective appraisal.

Those defining empowerment as a process are themselves in some disagreement over which unit(s) of society should be the focus of efforts to empower. Baker-Miller and Rappoport have the individual as their focus, although Rappoport is also concerned with the part played by the helping professional in the process. Cochran and Woolever are also concerned with a process involving changes in individuals, but include as change agents in that process para-professionals and informal peer support groups. Whitham gives special emphasis to the interpersonal aspect of empowerment, arguing that the collective dimension permits individuals to risk change and ensures that structural changes in institutions and organisations retain human dimensions. Berger and Neuhaus (1977: 7) focus on what they call 'mediating structures' – family, neighbourhood, church, voluntary association – arguing that these 'are the principal expressions of the real values and the real needs of people in our society'. They propose that these structures will, if empowered by the public policies of society, in turn empower the individuals embraced within them. Donald Barr, whose principal interest is in the politics of power and human services, proposes that the empowerment process gives special attention to knowledge about power as it relates to the controlling structures in society; schooling and employment in particular (Barr, Cochran, Riley and Whitham 1984). One implication to be drawn from Barr's concern with key controlling institutions is that the empowerment process could include, or even emphasise, efforts to alter power relationships between those governed by and governing such institutions, on behalf of more equal distribution of power in the community as a whole.

Virginia Vanderslice has recently (1984) presented an evolving definition of empowerment which takes into account the writings of those referenced earlier in this chapter. She refers to empowerment as 'a process through which people become more able to influence those people and organisations that effect their lives and the lives of those they care about' (p. 2). In addition to the assumptions common to all those working with the empowerment concept Vanderslice stresses as a goal the making of 'meaningful changes in institutions', and argues that in order for such a goal to be reached the empowerment process must include people working together on behalf of something greater than themselves as individuals.

Vanderslice refers to empowerment as a developmental process, and even identifies some steps in that process. Yet empowerment must involve more than the normal course of development if it is to make a unique contribution to practice in psychology and improvement in the human condition. What distinguishes the empowerment process from those engaged in by individuals in the normal course of living? Developmentalists are interested in understanding how individuals proceed from one developmental stage or phase to another, and the changes that occur throughout this life course. Those involved with the empowerment process assume that development occurs, but recognise and systematically acknowledge those obstacles to development which operate outside the spheres of influence of the developing individual. Such obstacles include social class structure, structural differentiations by race and gender, and perhaps even the influences of bureaucratisation upon individuals and groups. An entire 'school' of theorists has emerged during the 1970s and 1980s around the general thesis that schools and work-places are organised to maintain power differentials based upon historically and physiologically defined differences in class, gender and race (see, for example, Willis 1983; Anyon 1980). For individuals assigned less value by those criteria the unequal distribution of resources based upon such discrimination represents an obstacle which stands in the way of full development throughout the life span. Developmental psychologists do not, as a rule, give such impediments to development a central place in their enquiries. They are more likely to 'control them away'. The proposition offered here is that such obstacles are indeed central to the empowerment concept, although not always explicitly acknowledged as such. The proposal is that empowerment only becomes germane to the developing individual when barriers to the normal course of development are encountered, the removal of which are beyond the present or future capacity of that person as an individual. These obstacles are the *raison d'être* of the empowerment process, and therefore progress in overcoming them must be seen as the basic purpose underlying that process.

Useful for understanding the concept of empowerment in this context is the theory of 'resistance', which 'celebrates a dialectical notion of human agency that rightly portrays domination as a process that is neither static nor complete' (Giroux 1983: 289). Giroux argues that in all societies where structural inequities exist there is resistance to those structures. It follows that the empowerment process must, to be complete, provide an outlet for those energies of resistance in the service of overcoming obstacles to the realisation of full developmental potential.

A case study, presented in the next section of this chapter, will be used to identify some of the implementing issues and programmatic challenges involved in applying the empowerment concept at the local community level. The reader needs criteria with which to judge the success of the empowerment process described in the case study. As a way of establishing those standards the following definition of empowerment has been distilled from the previous discussion:

> **Empowerment** – an interactive process involving mutual respect and critical reflection through which both people and controlling institutions are changed in ways which provide those people with greater influence over individuals and institutions which are in some way impeding their efforts to achieve equal status in society, for themselves and those they care about.

A Case Study: The Family Matters Programme

In 1976 three Cornell University professors, Urie Bronfenbrenner, William E. Cross Jr and the author, set out together to study 'the capacity of urban American environments to serve as support systems to parents and other adults directly involved in the care, upbringing and education of children' (Bronfenbrenner and Cochran 1976). They wished to include as part of that study the development and testing of a modest set of supports for families with young children. While at that time empowerment had not evolved as a unified concept, these thinkers were aware that they wished to develop a programme designed as a clear alternative to what they viewed as the 'deficit model' characterising most social programmes for individuals and families in American society. The assumptions, goals and workings of the home-visiting and cluster-building programme which emerged over the five years of the project, and the ecological orientation which framed the undertaking, provide the material for this case study.

Sample, Research Method and Conceptual Framework

The study involved 276 families in the city of Syracuse, in western New York State. Each family contained a three-year-old child. The families were evenly distributed among 18 Syracuse neighbour-hoods, and family incomes ranged (in 1978) from about $US5,000 to $US50,000 per year. About one-third of the families were Afro-American, and the families were also about one-third single parent in structure.

The families in ten of the 18 project neighbourhoods, 160 in all, were offered the family support programme. The control group consisted of the families in the remaining eight neighbourhoods. Prior to programme assignment the parents in all 276 families participated in a series of in-depth interviews, which provided demographic data, perceptions and descriptions of the neighbourhood, world of work and personal social networks, perceptions of family members, and descriptions of the child's daily activities. These data constituted the baseline phase of an evaluation strategy designed to provide information about the impact of the Family Matters programme upon the performance of children in school. Since then, the programme has been completed and follow-up data collected. The measures used for collection of that follow-up information paralleled those administered at baseline, but also included additional information about children's school performance and contact between home and school.

What was the conceptual basis from which we approached the tasks of examining family stresses and supports, and the development of a family supports programme? The ecological perspective takes as its starting point the view that human behaviour is explained not only by the biological characteristics of the individual and the influences associated with the immediate setting containing that person, but also those external settings that have indirect impact through their effects upon the mental health and general well-being of the individual (for example, the legal system, welfare system, system of governance). Thus, growth is conceived as a series of encounters *across* as well as *within* ecological systems that both include and are external to the home environment. One can imagine a set of concentric circles, with the family at its centre (Bronfenbrenner 1979). Each circle represents an ecological system. From this perspective interest in development extends beyond, for instance, parent–child or husband–wife relations in the centre circle. The goal is to learn more about how the developing person transitions in to and out of involvement with systems beyond the immediate family, and how these larger systems might support or impede those transitions. One such encounter, the transition from home to school, is a major event in the life of a child and was one of the major focuses of the family support programme.

Although the ecological framework incorporates a number of systems through which human behaviour may be influenced (mass media, education, employment, etc.), one such system has characteristics that combine to provide it with special potential for mediating between forces more distant from the family and the relationship between parent and child. The personal social network provides every parent with social links to others outside the home who can provide a variety of supportive services to both parent and child (Cochran and Brassard 1979; Wellman 1981; McLanahan, Widemeyer and Adelberg 1981; Cochran, Gunnarsson, Grabe and Lewis 1984; Riley and Cochran 1985). These relationships may serve as bridges to other major ecological contexts, like the school and the world of work.

Programme Assumptions and Goals

Five assumptions beyond those implicit in the ecological perspective had a discernable impact upon the goals and design of the Family Matters programme. First, there was the conviction that all families have *some* strengths, an assumption that ran counter to the deficit perspective which is one of the basic tenets of service provision in the United States (Grubb and Lazerson 1982). From this deficiency perspective has come the requirement that one clearly demonstrates inadequacy or incompetence before becoming eligible for community-based, family-focused programmes. This perspective has led, in turn, to the 'blame the victim' syndrome in which the poor or unemployed person is viewed as the instigator of the very circumstances that he or she is enduring (Ryan 1971).

A second assumption central to the Family Matters approach was that much of the most valid and useful knowledge about the rearing of children is lodged among the people — across generations, in the networks, and in the historically and culturally rooted folkways of ethnic and cultural traditions, rather than in the heads of college professors, trained professionals, or books written by experts. This did not mean that individuals necessarily knew all they needed to know in order to raise children successfully. It did imply that a given parent knew more about her or his child than anyone coming in from outside the family, except perhaps a close relative or friend, and that in that sense parents were experts.

A third premiss was that a variety of family forms are not only in operation but are also legitimate, and could promote the development of both healthy children and healthy adults. The factor determining the capacity to rear a child successfully appeared to be not personal or family characteristics *per se*, but rather the number and types of resources that parents could marshal and bring to bear upon the child-rearing process (Keniston 1977). Thus, one very important goal for this project was to understand better what really constitute 'resources', and how different types of supports and stresses interact to make parenting easier or more difficult.

Just as mothers contribute to the strength of the family unit through work for pay outside the home, so fathers can help by playing an active role in activities with the child and in household tasks. This fourth assumption was buttressed by recent research documenting the contribution made by fathers to child development (Lamb 1976).

The final assumption underlying development of the programme was that cultural differences are both valid and valuable. Assuming that families have strengths, and that the parental knowledge that is the basis for those strengths is rooted in historical and social ties and in the rituals and traditions associated with those ties, then there must be value in the cultural and ethnic heritages that embrace those traditions and rituals.

The goals of the programme were all related broadly to the parenting role, and ranged from simple engagement and awareness to more active initiation and follow-through. In the first instance, the aim was to find ways to recognise parents as experts. Another goal was to exchange information with family members about children, the neighbourhood, community services, schools and work. The emphasis on the exchange rather than the dispensing of such information reflected our aversion for the deficit approach and our assumption that much of the important knowledge is 'out there'.

Reinforcement of and encouragement for parent–child activities was a third goal of the programme. A fourth goal involved social exchange beyond rather than within the immediate family: the exchange of informal resources like babysitting, child-rearing advice, and emotional support with neighbours and other friends. Finally, there was a desire to facilitate social action where parents deemed such action appropriate. A neighbourhood-based community development process was envisioned, in which needs assessments carried out by the parents of young children would lead to the identification of issues of common concern, and to change efforts related to those issues.

Programme Processes

What did this programme, designed to build upon family strengths, actually look like? Initially, two separate approaches were used to involve families in activities related to their children. One, a home visiting approach, was aimed at individual families and made available to all participating families in five of the programme neighbourhoods. Families in the other five neighbourhoods were asked to become involved in group activities with clusters of other Family Matters families in their own neighbourhoods, in an effort to emphasise mutual support and co-operative action, with family dynamics and the parent–child dyad as a secondary (although still explicitly acknowledged) focus. While methods were used to encourage participation by eligible families (cards and letters, home visits, telephone calls, newsletters), attendance was not required, and the participants themselves ultimately determined their own individual levels of participation. Families were involved with programme activities for an average of 26 months, and the programme itself came to a close early in the summer prior to first grade entry for most of the target children included in the study.

The home- and family-focused strategy took the form of home visits to parents and their children designed to give recognition to the parenting role, reinforce and enrich parent–child activities, and share information about child care and community services. Para-professionals hired from the Syracuse community were trained to exchange information about child rearing with parents and, when appropriate, to provide examples of parent–child activities geared to the developmental age of the child. The starting point was to be with the parents as experts about their own children, and so initial home visits were spent learning the parents' view of the child and seeking out examples of activities that were already being carried out with the child and defined by the parent as important for the child's development. While these interactions between worker and parent involved both participants in the process of defining success and importance, every effort was made to emphasise the parents' definition whenever possible.

Once parents began to sense that the workers were serious in valuing the parental point of view, they identified a wide variety of activities that they were doing with their children that they felt made a difference both to parent and child. Our workers brought such activity examples back to the office, wrote them up in a standard format, and returned them to the parent along with a request that other project workers be permitted to share the activity idea with other families in the programme. This process accomplished two goals: first, it further recognised the parent as important and productive, and second, it was a way of gathering parent–child activity information *from* parents *for* parents, rather than relying upon the 'professional as expert' model, which many of our parents had come to expect from outside agents.

As time passed and a strong trust relationship was forged between home visitor and family, some parents began to ask for information beyond parent–child activities. This included requests for information about other families in the neighbourhood who were themselves participants in the programme. This pressure pushed us to consider permitting (or not preventing) clustering in 'home visiting' neighbourhoods.

In the cluster-building neighbourhoods the goals were to reduce feelings of isolation by bringing the families together at the neighbourhood level, to encourage the sharing of information and informally available resources among families, and, when parents voiced a need to have changes made in the neighbourhood, to facilitate action in pursuit of those changes. The initial home visits in the five cluster-building neighbourhoods were limited to a process whereby worker and family got to know each other and the worker could learn from parents how they felt about the neighbourhood as a place to bring up children. After this relatively brief initial period of familiarisation with individual families, the worker set out to arrange a first group meeting, the purpose of which was to introduce neighbouring families to one another in a friendly and supportive atmosphere, and begin to get a sense from the group of what changes in the neighbourhood might contribute to making life easier for families with children living there. Child care was provided at all Family Matters gatherings, and parents were encouraged to bring their children with them. There was always time for parents to socialise with one another, and the worker/facilitator also looked for ways to encourage participants to utilise each other as resources outside the regular group.

The desire by home-visited parents to move beyond the ecological limits of the immediate family for contact with neighbours placed workers in the difficult position of having to resist the constructive initiatives of the parents in order to prevent contamination with the cluster-building approach. There was also an indication in the cluster-building neighbourhoods that the combination might work better than individual elements. Only about half of the invited families in those neighbourhoods could be coaxed out of their homes and into group activities.

Based upon these two sources of programmatic tension, active social initiation by some home-visited parents and passive resistance by parents uninterested in neighbourhood clustering, the decision was made after nine months to merge the two approaches. One consequence of access to both components of the newly integrated programme was an increase in overall programme participation. Initially this increase primarily took the form of more home visits, mainly to families who previously had been offered only the neighbourhood linking alternative. This development was viewed as an indication that a trust-building process conducted within the security of their own homes was required before some parents would seriously consider venturing out into neighbourhood oriented cluster group activities. With more time came involvement by more families in clusters and groups, and some who participated simultaneously in both home visiting and neighbourhood-based group activities.

As the children associated with the programme grew older and approached the age of entry into kindergarten and first grade, increased emphasis was also placed on programming related to the transition from home to school. The focus of these activities, prepared for delivery in both home-visiting and cluster-grouping formats, included topics like the value orientations of home and school, how to evaluate kindergarten and first grade classrooms, preparation for a parent–teacher conference, understanding the child's report card, and parent–child activities for school readiness. The emphasis in each of the activities continued to be on the parent as the most important adult in the life of the developing child.

The Effects of Family Matters

More than two years were spent by neighbourhood workers in regular contact with 160 families, helping parents identify their strengths and their needs, and working towards improvements in their life circumstances. What had begun as an effort to gain a deeper understanding of parental stresses and supports was increasingly being referred to as empowerment by the time the programme finished. What did we mean by the term 'empowerment' at that juncture? First, there was the sense that empowerment was a process rather than an end-state. Parents didn't 'achieve empowerment'; rather they changed over time in what appeared to be systematic ways. Second, there was anecdotal evidence of what seemed to be steps or stages in the process of change. The initial step appeared to involve change in perception of self; some of the mothers who, when first visited, viewed themselves quite negatively, showed signs over time of beginning to believe in and care for themselves. Another step seemed to involve relations with others; new efforts to reach out to spouse and child, and also to relatives, neighbours and friends outside the family. A later step involved social action on behalf of the child. A number of neighbourhood groups were formed around plans for neighbourhood improvement, and some parents got involved with the schools their children were attending. Thus there appeared to be several different aspects of empowerment, beginning with the way in which individuals viewed themselves and progressing through relations with others nearby to interactions with more distant organisations and institutions.

When the time came to evaluate the effects of the empowerment programme it was carried out with this emergent process in mind. Consequently findings in three areas will be reported; mothers' feelings about themselves, their relations with relatives and friends, and their contacts with the school of the six-year-old child. There will also be brief mention of how the programme affected the school performance of the children in the project.

Mothers' Perceptions of Themselves as Parents

Mothers were asked what they liked and disliked about themselves as parents, and to rate their own performance on a seven-point scale. Findings indicate that the programme did affect parental perceptions. This was especially the case for white single mothers, whose control group scores were especially low, and black married mothers, where the women in the control group had unusually high scores. The programme appeared to raise the lower perceptions of the Caucasian mothers to a reasonable level, and somewhat reduce the unusually positive self-perceptions of the Afro-American mothers. The lower programme perceptions in the latter instance should not be thought of as negative. The scores of the black women in the programme were still well on the positive side of the scale, and so might perhaps be thought of as somewhat more realistic than those unusually positive feelings in the control group.

Changes in Mothers' Social Networks

The term social network refers to those relatives, friends and neighbours whom parents feel make a real difference to the way in which they live their lives and raise their children. Family Matters parents were kind enough to discuss those relationships during a social networks interview, and from that information social maps were constructed for each of them. The maps were divided into three social zones based upon how deeply involved network members were with the mother. Those most distant were placed on the periphery, those more involved were put in the functional zone, and those described by the mother as 'most important' were put in her 'primary circle'. Interest was in the size of the networks, the activities going on with network members, whether the network is dominated by relatives or non-relatives, and whether the relationships are supportive or stressful. Because distinctions by race and family structure proved to be so crucial to an understanding of the data, this summary is framed in those terms.

Unmarried Mothers. The findings indicate that single mothers were especially responsive in network terms to programme involvement. White, unmarried mothers in the programme reported a greater increase in the number of non-relatives in their networks, overall and at both the functional and primary levels, than did their control group equivalents. A closer look at the content of exchanges revealed involvement with larger numbers of non-kin people in relation to borrowing, work-related and emotional support. At the primary level, change mostly consisted of the addition of non-relatives who had not been present in the network three years earlier. With black unmarried mothers, the increase in the new primary membership due to the programme was also significant, but differed from that for single whites in that it was almost as likely to include relatives as non-relatives. This reflected a more general tendency by black than by white women to rely upon kinship ties.

Married Mothers. With married women, programme effects were much less pervasive than for single mothers, and effects were confined to relations with kin. In the case of married, Afro-American women there was an increase at follow-up in the number of relatives reported in the primary network, many of whom were people not included in the network at any level three years earlier. White married mothers involved with the programme reported a decrease in overall network size in comparison with the appropriate controls. But this decrease was limited to non-relatives, and it was balanced at the primary level of the network by an increase in kinfolk.

It is safe to conclude from these findings that the patterns of change in network resources as a function of inclusion in the Family Matters programme were not simple. Mothers in certain socio-ecological circumstances were affected more than those in others, and the aspects of network structure manifesting change were also influencd by those 'niches'.

Contacts Between Home and School

Communications between home and school, which was initially of interest for understanding the child's transition into the school setting, could also be thought of as reflecting a step in the empowerment process; the willingness to interact on behalf of the child with institutions somewhat distant ecologically from the family. A parent interview and a teacher questionnaire were used to generate data about the frequency with which parents and teachers were in contact via conferences, notes and telephone calls.

The most powerful finding to emerge from examination of these parent–teacher contacts was that communications of any kind were contingent upon the perception of the child as having school-related difficulty. Only in the cases of children having school-related problems was there any appreciable communication between home and school, and only under those circumstances were contacts greater for programme than for control families. While the fact that negative perceptions of child performance are a precondition for home–school communications is not surprising, we were disappointed by the manifest inability of the family support programme to influence this association. The reward for that 64 per cent of our families whose children were 'doing fine' in school is that they received significantly fewer notes, telephone calls, or conference invitations from the teacher.

The Child's Performance in First Grade

Performance in first grade was assessed with the use of a questionnaire completed by the child's teacher, from which were distilled variables called personal adjustment, interpersonal peer relations, relationship to teacher, cognitive motivation, and average report card score (cognitive). Analyses of these data indicated that involvement with the programme did indeed have a positive impact upon childrens' school performance, but that this impact was limited to certain kinds of families. A direct, positive impact was found for the children of married couples where those parents had no more than a high school education. There was also a positive impact for the children with only one parent living at home, but only when accompanied by other changes; increases in non-kin at the primary network level, higher perceptions of self as parent (whites), and joint parent–child activities involving household chores (blacks). A feature common to all of the subgroups for which positive school effects were found was those families' relatively less advantageous position in the social structure. Positive school outcomes associated with the family support programme were indicated for those children with less educated parents, including some two-parent and most one-parent families.

Family Matters and Empowerment: Lessons Learned and Issues Raised

Up to this point the reader has been exposed to a number of the theoretical dimensions involved with the concept of empowerment, and then introduced to the workings and impact of a family support programme which has, at least in retrospect, been referred to as 'empowering'. Now theory and reality will be tested against one another, primarily to gauge the adequacy of the programmatic effort but also to assess the utility of the concept. The chapter will end with discussion of several other issues raised by the Family Matters experience.

Did Family Matters Empower Parents?

The Family Matters programme espoused a number of specific goals, enumerated earlier, which ranged from the provision of positive recognition for parents to facilitating their efforts at social action. There is evidence to indicate that a number of these changes occurred for a good many of the parents in the programme. But can it really be said that these families were engaged in an empowerment process? To address this question it is useful to return to the definition of empowerment provided earlier, and test what is known about Family Matters against the criteria contained within it.

Figure 1.1 below provides an overview of the success with which the Family Matters programme met the empowerment criteria posed in the earlier definition.

Figure 1.1: Degree to which Family Matters Met Empowerment Criteria

Fully	Partially	Not At All
Interactive – home visitors	Not all exchanged with peers	
Process		
Mutual respect		
	Unclear how much critical reflection	
Change in participants		No change in controlling institutions
Greater influence by child	Little demonstrated increase in influence by adults	

Seven empowerment criteria were drawn from the earlier definition and are reflected in Figure 1.1. The first requirement, that social interaction play a central role, was fulfilled at the one-to-one level through regular involvement of the para-professional home visitors. However, only certain of the families participated in the neighbourhood-based peer cluster groups, and so the programme was only partially successful at the broader social level.

Family Matters was unusually successful at documenting the extent to which empowerment-related change took place on a process continuum. Evaluation of programme effects suggests that individual parents entered into transactions with the programme at different points in their own involvement with the empowerment process, and so were affected by the programme in different ways. Mothers with very low self-regard seemed to begin with changes at that level and then proceed in the direction of relations with family and network members. Women and men already confident about their own self-worth and secure in relations with others were more likely to move more quickly into individual or group actions involving the neighbourhood or school. Thus our strong hypothesis is that empowerment is a process which involves a series of changes, and that the order in which these changes occur is relatively stable.

The issue of ensuring that a high level of respect was accorded the families participating in the programme was addressed squarely by Family Matters, as the case study description indicates, and the result was a great deal of trust and respect accorded the neighbourhood workers in return. This aspect of service provision – identifying and building upon existing family strengths – was absolutely indispensable, and its importance cannot be emphasised enough.

Much less clear was how much the interactive processes sponsored by Family Matters encouraged parents to engage in 'critical reflection'. Freire (1978: 56-7) says of critical reflection that

> groups take their own daily lives as the objects of their reflection in a process of this nature. They are required to stand at a distance from the daily lives in which they are generally immersed and to which they often attribute an aura of permanence. Only at a distance can they get a perspective that permits them to emerge from that daily routine and begin their own independent development.

Certainly some of the parents in the programme engaged in this process at one time or another. But neighbourhood workers were not systematically exposed by the programme director to the importance of such a process, nor were they taught skills with which to introduce or maintain critical reflection through home visits or cluster group meetings. For that reason critical reflection is shown in Figure 1.1 as a criterion only partially met by the Family Matters programme.

Criteria five and six from the empowerment definition stipulated that 'both people and controlling institutions are changed' by involvement in the empowerment process. Data bearing upon changes in the 'people' were presented as part of the case study. They indicated that changes did in fact occur in some participants' perceptions of themselves, in their relations with network members, and under certain circumstances in their communications with the schools attended by their children.

Those data also suggest that prevailing ideologies compete with efforts to initiate new relationships with 'controlling institutions'. Parents did not respond to encouragement for (and practice in) increased contact with the schools of their children until those children were defined as 'having difficulty'; parent involvement in the normal course of events was not a part of the ideologies of either parents or schools. And Family Matters workers did not become directly involved with the schools with the aim of changing the attitudes or behaviours of teachers or school administrators. One can safely conclude, then, that the Family Matters programme did not attempt to bring about changes in the relevant school systems as part of its effort to provide families with support, and so did not meet that criterion. It is worth noting that the idea was raised as a support strategy by Programme staff, but was vetoed by one of the funding sources underwriting the project. More recently a home–school communications in-service programme for elementary school teachers has been developed and pilot-tested by Family Matters (Dean 1984), and is now receiving nationwide distribution.

The final criterion contained in the definition of empowerment was that the process 'provide . . . people with greater influence over individuals and institutions . . . impeding their efforts to achieve equal status . . .' Evidence was presented earlier to indicate that a number of the children who had been a part of the programme were performing better in school than their control counterparts, and that these tended to be those children with relatively less educated parents. Such children would normally be thought of as at risk in their efforts 'to achieve equal status', and so there are grounds for arguing that the programme fulfilled that criterion for these children. However, little attention was paid by those assessing the programme to whether participating parents could show evidence of being better able to influence key individuals (bosses, local politicians, teachers) or institutions (school, city government, social services). While there is some anecdotal evidence to suggest that such changes did occur in individual cases, no baseline measures of such behaviour were gathered at the outset, indicating that those designing the programme had not given high priority to that sort of impact.

Perhaps the most accurate conclusion to be drawn about Family Matters as a programme of empowerment is that it was incomplete. While successful at interacting with families in a non-judgemental way, and changing certain attitudes and even behaviours of some of those constrained by socio-economic circumstances, the programme was only partially able to stimulate peer interaction and critical reflection, and failed to address the question of changing the balance of power between families and controlling institutions.

Who Shall Define My Needs?

The Family Matters example has served as a useful device for applying a largely theoretical definition of empowerment to practice in the real world. The Family Matters approach also raises several other issues for practice which, while related to empowerment, deserve attention in their own right. One of those issues involves the question of how needs are determined and to whom services are provided. The preponderance of the evidence from evaluation of the Family Matters programme indicates that families with fewer resources, who were in general experiencing higher levels of stress, were more likely to show significant positive changes along the empowerment continuum than those richer in personal resources. This general finding held for both parents and children in the programme families. The greatest changes were seen in black and single-parent families, which together made up about 45 per cent of the programme sample.

If it is possible to predict with some certainty which families will show the most positive effects from programme participation, why not limit eligibility to such families? Surely it would be possible to identify and target families in which parents are relatively uneducated, with low opinions of themselves and small support networks?

This client-oriented, categorical approach to programme eligibility and delivery is typical of human services in the United States. Experiences with Family Matters strongly suggest that it is self-defeating, primarily for two reasons. First, the approach attaches a stigma to the service; potential consumers immediately realise that to be associated with it they must accept an arbitrary, public definition of themselves as insufficient. Those with self-respect stay away from such a service, and those who do enlist begin by being put down rather than uplifted. Second, such labelling takes the responsibility for identification of needs away from the consumer and places it fully in the hands of the provider, shifting the consumer's role from active partner to passive recipient. This shift makes no psychological sense, if the ultimate goal is to foster independent, self-supporting individuals and families.

It is not surprising, given these concerns, that those committed to providing empowering opportunities for individuals and groups favour a universal entitlement approach to such services. One primary argument against universal provision is cost. The thought of neighbourhood workers being made available as supports to all families with young children carries with it visions of great expense in salaries and transportation. In fact, there is reason to believe that supports of the sort offered by Family Matters could be made universally available to families on a relatively cost-effective basis. Clues to a possible strategy for cost containment are to be found in data regarding use of the several programme options offered to Family Matters families. Cluster groups, which had a relatively low per-family cost, were most appealing to families outside the centre city, where there was little fear of violence in the neighbourhood and neighbours were perceived as benign or supportive. The home visiting option, which involved much higher per-family cost to the service provider, was most attractive to families in inner-city neighbourhoods, who were likely to be afraid to venture out to night meetings and often suspicious of their neighbours. Thus it was possible, within the same overall programme, to provide different amounts of support to families expressing varying amounts and types of need, and in differing personal and family circumstances. The expense of making repeated home visits to that relatively small number of families expressing high need would be balanced by a far greater number of families interested in only one or two initial visits and then monthly meetings with other parents. In this way middle resource families could be included in the service at little added cost, while at the same time providing the benefit that a stigma-free programme would bring to those with high need and low self-regard. And, if as is proposed, a non-judgemental approach to eligibility produces more rapid movement to independent action and away from dependence, then it would also shorten the overall duration of the high intensity home-visitor service required by the person with high initial need, and so further reduce the long-term 'per-family' cost of the service.

Standardisation vs. Respect for Differences

It must be obvious by now to the reader that there are a number of good psychological and social reasons for making a programme available to families which offers them a number of options regarding ways of becoming involved. This approach respects the different background characteristics, strengths and needs that families exhibit, and it places the responsibility for defining those needs and identifying appropriate supports squarely in the hands of the consumer. But there are other forces which create a press in favour of fewer options and greater standardisation of offerings. Not the least of these is the rush to document effects; to provide quantitative evidence of impact. One can argue persuasively that in order to clearly understand how families in differing life circumstances respond to a service, the input from workers to families should vary as little as possible from one family to the next. In that way, these critics argue, it is possible to avoid the claim that differences in the responses of the families to the service are attributable to variations in the supports provided rather than to differences among the families themselves.

From the Family Matters perspective, this kind of thinking reflects misplaced priorities. The future emphasis in research and evaluation related to programming for families should not be on demonstrating that families differ along a number of dimensions, but in showing how supports tailored to reflect those differences are helpful to different kinds of families in different ways. Differences in families are obvious. In the Family Matters sample there was an Irish neighbourhood, a middle-income black neighbourhood, a white-collar suburb, a blue-collar and a public-housing area. Within neighbourhoods 30 per cent of the parents were not married; some lived alone with one or more children, others lived with a boyfriend, and still others lived with their own parents. In some of the families the three year old was the first, or even the only, child; in others there were teenagers whose needs, from the parents' perspective, far outweighed those of the pre-schooler. Employment patterns in the sample varied tremendously: two parents, one working full- and the other half-time; two parents, both working full-time; two parents, one working one and a half jobs and the other at home; one parent, working full-time, or half-time, or unemployed. These differences were easy to identify, and their effects upon parental perceptions and expectations became increasingly obvious as time spent with families increased. The challenge was to find ways in which to provide supports which respected those differences, and then to evaluate the impact of a programme which delivered differing services to different kinds of families. That challenge must be met by anyone committed to providing supports for families from an empowerment perspective.

Acknowledgements

For their ideas and encouragement the author is indebted to the following members of the 1983-4 Empowerment Work Group: Don Barr, Christiann Dean, Herb Engman, Kathy Fox, Dave Riley, Dorothy Torre, Ginny Vanderslice and Michelle Whitham. Special gratitude is expressed to Jill Lewis for her insight, enthusiasm and courage.

References

Anyon, J. (1980) Social class and the hidden curriculum of work, *Journal of Education, 162,* 67–92

Baker-Miller, J. (1982) Women and power, *Work in Progress,* No. 82–01

Barr, D., Cochran, M., Riley, D. and Whitham, M. (1984) Family empowerment: an interview, *Human Ecology Forum, 14(1),* pp. 4–13

Berger, P. and Neuhaus, R. (1977) *To Empower People: The Role of Mediating Structures in Public Policy,* Washington, DC: American Enterprise Institute

Bronfenbrenner, U. (1979) *The Ecology of Human Development: Experiments by Nature and Design,* Cambridge: Harvard University Press

Bronfenbrenner, U. and Cochran, M. (1976) The comparative ecology of human development: a research proposal, Ithaca, New York: Cornell University

Cochran, M. and Brassard, J. (1979) Child development and personal social networks, *Child Development, 50,* 601–16

Cochran, M. and Woolever, F. (1983) Beyond the deficit model: the empowerment of parents with information and informal supports in I. Sigel and L. Laosa (eds), *Changing Families,* New York: Plenum Press

Cochran, M., Gunnarsson, L., Grabe, S. and Lewis, J. (1984) *The Social Support Networks of Mothers with Young Children,* Gothenburg, Sweden: University of Gothenburg Research Bulletin, No. 25

Crockenberg, S. (1981) Infant irritability, mother responsiveness, and social support influences on the security of infant–mother attachment, *Child Development, 52,* 857–65

Dean, C. (1984) *Cooperative Communication between Home and School,* Ithaca, New York: Cornell University Media Services, Research Park

Fischer, C. (1982) *To Dwell among Friends: Personal Networks in Town and City,* Chicago: University of Chicago Press

Freire, P. (1973) *Pedagogy of the Oppressed,* New York: Seabury Press

———— (1978) *Pedagogy in Progress: The Letters to Guinea-Bissau,* New York: Seabury Press

Giroux, H. (1983) Theories of reproduction and resistance in the new sociology of education: a critical analysis, *Harvard Educational Review, 53(3),* pp. 257–93

Grubb, W. and Lazerson, M. (1982) *Broken Promises,* New York: Basic Books

Keniston, K. (1977) *All Our Children: The American Family Under Pressure,* New York: Harcourt Brace Jovanovich

Lamb, M. (ed.) *The Role of the Father in Child Development,* New York, Wiley

McLanahan, S., Widemeyer, N. and Adelberg, T. (1981) Network structure, social support and psychological well-being in the single-parent family, *Journal of Marriage and the Family,* August, pp. 601–12

Rappoport, J. (1981) In praise of paradox: a social policy of empowerment over prevention, *American Journal of Community Psychology, 9(1)*, 1–25

Riley, D. and Cochran, M. (1985) Naturally occurring childrearing advice for fathers: Utilization of the personal social network, *Journal of Marriage and the Family*, in press

Ryan, W. (1971) *Blaming the Victim*, New York: Pantheon Books

Solomon, B. (1976) *Black Empowerment*, New York: Columbia University Press

Vanderslice, V. (1984) Empowerment: a definition in process, *Human Ecology Forum, 14(1)*, 2–3

Wellman, B. (1981) Applying network analysis to the study of support in B. Gottleib (ed.), *Social Networks and Social Support*, Beverly Hills, California: Sage Publications

Whitham, M (1982) Women's empowerment: a word of our own – a work of our own. Report to the Conference on Empowerment: Strategies for Education and Action with Paulo Freire, 3-6 December 1981, Ithaca, New York

Willis, P. (1983) Cultural production and theories of reproduction in L. Barton and S. Walker (eds), *Race, Class and Education*, London: Croom Helm

2 PRESENTING PSYCHOLOGICAL KNOWLEDGE TO MOTHERS OF YOUNG CHILDREN

Pam Harris

> *Tutor of course on child psychology:* 'What difference if any do you think this course has made to you?'
> *Sally (a mother):* 'It stopped me losing my marbles.'

The above quotation takes pride of place for its function in placing the somewhat abstract title of this chapter in a more concrete perspective. By looking at the relevance of psychological research to the practice of bringing up children, I am in reality addressing the question 'What was it that stopped Sally losing her marbles?' To put it in a more academically acceptable form, this chapter aims to answer the question 'Which areas of psychology can parents usefully exploit in the quest to make life easier with young children?' Such an approach places the emphasis not upon the direct benefits accruing to a *child* from psychological research, but rather upon benefits experienced by *a parent*. It does not include consideration of community programmes designed to foster early cognitive and behavioural development such as Head Start, Follow-through and Home Start in the United States and similar British projects such as that described by Harrison (1981) (for further discussion of such intervention schemes, see Wolfendale, this volume). Programmes for intervention are primarily intended to help parents to become more effective in promoting the development and education of their children, although of course parents themselves may accrue some incidental benefits. To this extent psychological research is being used as a vehicle to promote the achievement of certain abilities which are valued by the community as a whole, for example, literacy and numeracy. The beneficiaries of such forms of intervention are, in the first place, children, and secondly the community at large; the benefits to the parents themselves are seldom considered. In contrast, the focus of this chapter will be the needs of mothers of young children, not from the point of view of what psychologists feel mothers *should* know in order to maximally facilitate the development of their children, but in relation to what mothers *choose* to take from psychology in order to cope better with the problems and issues which they confront as caretakers of young children.

34

A logical starting point is to consider what psychology has to offer, and the discussion therefore begins with a necessarily brief look at psychological research; what is known about child-rearing practices, child development and intervention? The second section of the chapter looks at courses on child development for parents, with particular reference to the development over nine years of one particular course, where changes where made as a direct result of feedback on content and methods from all the mothers who attended. The changes in course content can be conceptualised in terms of a transition from research into practice, and the extent to which research survived unscathed will be the major theme. The chapter concludes with a discussion of what parents really want from psychology. It will be suggested that mothers did not primarily gain knowledge, or understanding in the courses discussed, but rather the contents of a survival kit, and furthermore that the survival kit as described is incomplete. It will be argued that the psychology of the parent may be as important as the psychology of the child and thus any professional involved in presenting psychology to parents, whether in therapy or education, must look beyond the traditional boundaries of child psychology research to find workable implications for practice.

To begin with, it is necessary to look at what child psychology has to contribute to a curriculum for courses for parents.

Research on Children

Child-rearing Practices: What Is A 'Good' Parent?

It is customary to begin discussions about child psychology for parents with the observation that an increased number of children are now guaranteed physical survival, allowing us the luxury of considering their mental well-being (for example, Newson and Newson 1974; Pringle 1975). 'Luxury' may not be the best word to employ; Grotberg's (1979:217) observation that 'parents in fact have been discovered as critical to the education and development of their children' suggests that 'duty' may have the more accurate implication. If it is argued that parents should provide an environment for their children within which 'optimal' development can take place, those members of society who undertake research into child development should be able to provide guidelines to aid parents. The form of such guidelines might be based on an account of what child-rearing methods are in current use by parents, which of these are successful in terms of the needs and aspirations of the members of our particular society, and lastly a clear formulation of methods for changing the behaviour of parents whose practices are not conducive to optimal development. After all, professionals still talk about or at least imply the existence of 'good' and 'bad' parents with the implication that there must be a list of qualities belonging to 'good' parents which can be taught to the 'bad' ones. Burton (1979) categorised the parenting functions of 'effective' mothers into three groups:

1. Design – this involved creating safe environments where resources for child play and child use are accessible and safe.
2. Consulting – the mothers made themselves constantly available to their children as sources of comfort, imparters of information, resolvers of issues and answerers of queries.
3. Authority – the mothers within loving and supporting environments set clear limits for acceptable/unacceptable behaviour.

Wolfendale (1983: 155-6) provides the following 'List of Parenting Functions':

   (i) provide means of survival (meet 'primary' needs);
  (ii) provide emotional support and endorsement (meet 'secondary' needs);
 (iii) provide the setting in which personal development takes place;
 (iv) provide an environment in which exploration and hypothesis-testing can take place;
  (v) provide a frame of reference against and in which exploration outside the home can take place;
 (vi) provide a protective environment for their young;
(vii) provide opportunities and direction for the growth of independent functioning and self-organisation;
(viii) act as models (of language, social/emotional behaviour, etc.);
 (ix) train and guide their young towards understanding of, and adherence to, social norms (controls and restraints);
  (x) act as possessors and transmitters of knowledge and information about the world;
 (xi) act as decision-makers and arbiters of decisions, minute by minute and in the long term.

Such attempts to fit the functions of parents into some kind of theoretical framework are of limited use to those involved in the practice either of bringing up children or of advising parents and other caregivers. For one thing, they provide no clear behavioural descriptions and therefore leave us with queries such as 'What is a supporting environment?', 'how do you provide a setting in which "personal development" takes place?', 'will any setting do?', 'is any development OK?'. In addition, as Wolfendale herself points out, little is known about the relations between child-rearing methods and their effects in terms of aspects of development such as patterns of growth, social behaviour and skill learning. Little long-term research has looked into what actually goes on in the home. Even the remarkable long-term data on parents' aims and methods in child-rearing provided by the Newsons' work in Nottingham (Newson and Newson 1963, 1968, 1976) can only provide that information which parents are willing and prepared to part with. The interview schedules for this project were designed to encourage openness and honesty, and although the data thus acquired may be as accurate as is currently feasible, it is almost certainly not the whole story; however 'naturalistic' any research attempts to be, things go on between parents and their children that will never be witnessed by others. Without this kind of data, and without a clear idea of what a 'good' parent does, it would be wiser to regard statements about one type of caretaker being 'more effective' than another as predictions rather than as empirically supported conclusions.

Child Development

I have argued that global attempts to define a 'good' parent are unsatisfactory, at least as a basis for teaching parents. Can we instead obtain ideas for a potential curriculum from research into specific aspects of child development? If so, how much is reaching parents at present?

There is over half a century of systematic empirical research and research-based knowledge available. Much is known about the visual world of infants (Bower 1977); about the cognitive processes which lie behind a child's un-adult understanding of the world (beginning with Piaget) or perhaps more recently how un-childlike (in Piaget's terms at least) this understanding is (Donaldson 1984); psychologists have emphasised the child's active role in socialisation (Ainsworth, Bell and Stayton 1974) and documented children's relationships with their siblings (Dunn 1984); bonding became an 'in-word' for a while,

'critical periods' came and went and came again and, in the area of
child language, research has led from a syntactic, through semantic to
a functional or pragmatic description of the 'what' of child language,
and a host of questions about the 'why' (in the motivational sense).
With regard to play, information has varied from theories about the
cathartic function of play, through the educational value to the use of
play in assessing the many and varied aspects of the child.
Developments in techniques to modify children's behaviour
systematically cannot be ignored in a quick run-through of key areas.

In terms of research evidence, psychologists clearly know a great
deal more about children than they used to. The research evidence is
available in undiluted form in research journals and books intended
for students and professionals who work with children. By the time
parents (unless they are also students or professionals) acquire the
information, it has been diluted in some way either in a book written
for parents, or in a magazine, or from the mouth of a professional who
has been consulted by a parent. There are of course many parents who
learn about child development from their own parents, from looking
back at their own childhood and from watching their own and their
friends' children, but here I am concerned with printed sources of
information about child psychology such as can be found in
pamphlets, baby books and child-care manuals. Wolfendale (1983)
lists three major disadvantages of typical baby-care books. Firstly,
the norms of child development are set out in a simplistic format,
causing unnecessary worry to parents of children who do not happen
to conform to the average. Secondly, she points out that the writers of
child-care books cannot resist the temptation to exhort parents to hold
the 'right' attitude and use the 'right' method to cope with both the
normal humdrum of life with children and with the little surprises
children have a habit of springing upon them. If the methods do not
work (as they often do not) parents feel it must be their own fault.
Lastly, Wolfendale accuses the authors of these leaflets and
textbooks of claiming to offer a blueprint for successful rearing and
effective parental involvement. In spite of (or possibly because of)
these properties of child-care manuals, the better ones continue to sell
tremendously well, and it would be churlish to blame the authors for
becoming complacent regarding what parents want to know. It cannot
be denied that these books are read, and often enjoyed, along with
newspaper articles and television and radio programmes. While it is
not safe to assume that the knowledge gained from popular books
actually changes parental behaviour (there is very little information

on this), those of us who are responsible for imparting child psychology to parents must take this knowledge base into account. Whenever psychologists teach or advise parents, almost invariably someone else has got there first.

In concluding this section on the availability of child development credit should be paid to Douglas and Richman (1984a, b) whose concise guides to coping with young children will hopefully herald a new approach to translating research findings for parents. Their two handbooks avoid the faults listed above, and also provide references for those parents who wish to read more about the research upon which the advice is based. For example, in *Coping with Young Children* many problems are discussed from both child and parents' point of view. The chapter on separation begins 'Many parents, especially mothers, are surprised how difficult it is for them to be apart from their young baby' and continues 'From about nine months your baby may become more clinging and attached to you or to the other people who look after her regularly. This is a normal phase of development, although children vary in the amount of upset they show. Some never go through this stage at all.' (1984a: 65) The remainder of Douglas and Richman's chapter gives practical, and, more importantly, flexible suggestions for dealing with separation in many different situations and taking account of individual differences in temperament and past experience.

Intervention

Reviews of research relating to parental involvement in children's development (such as that provided by Grotberg 1979) reveal that the major focus has been on low income families. Metzl (1980: 583) also makes this point: 'While most research has focused on the effects of intervention on children at risk due to biological, emotional or environmental factors, few studies have considered the effects of providing parent education and emotional support for middle-class families.' Metzl investigated the effects of a specific parent-administered language stimulation programme, beginning at birth, on the development of normal middle-class first-born infants. She concluded that such intervention was beneficial not simply in terms of the children's language scores, but also in terms of making the mother-child interactions more rewarding for the mother, and encouraging greater involvement on the part of the father: 'it appeared that the more alert and responsive the baby, the more the father became interested in continued interaction' (ibid.: 585). This introduces a new element to the discussion. Recent evidence shows that knowledge about child development enables parents to enhance their children's development (for example, Tizard and Hughes 1984) but, more importantly in the context of this chapter, Metzl's conclusion brings in the notion of parental 'enjoyment'. Her findings are encouraging, particularly since her research concentrated only on increasing parental knowledge about language development. They are also unusual in documenting a relationship between particular parental activities and particular outcomes. It may be that transmitting to parents wider knowledge about social, cognitive and perceptual development would further increase the enjoyment parents can gain from child rearing. Wolfendale (1983: 161) emphasises that 'the interest and involvement of participating parents is evident in many research reports' and Stern (1977) maintains that a caregiver's role can be enhanced by knowing more 'about the process and finding it easier to create and perform in and enjoy it more thereby'.

The idea of parent education and support to increase the enjoyment of parenthood is intuitively satisfying, but it is clear that there is insufficient evidence regarding the efficacy of such intervention schemes, not only because the required research is patchy but also because we do not have suitable research-based criteria by which to evaluate them.

The discussion so far reveals an emerging concern in the literature for improving the experience of child rearing to the presumed benefit of parents, children and society. One means of improving parent–child relationships, not yet mentioned, is by 'minimising deviant behaviour', 'reducing non-compliance' (Forehand and Peed 1979) or, more simply, stopping children being naughty. 'Deviant' appears to be an inappropriate word in this context, since children's non-compliance with parental demands is an extremely widespread occurrence (Forehand and Peed 1979). In this area at least, the research evidence is clear; reviews of the literature (for example, O'Dell 1974) indicate that parent behavioural training programmes are effective in teaching parents to modify behaviour problems of their children in a clinic setting, although the evidence on transfer and maintenance is less encouraging. For example, Forehand and Peed's (1979) programme for training parents to modify non-compliance in their children was successful, and claimed to demonstrate effective maintenance and transfer of training. However, the claim was based on home observations, and their method of conducting these is quoted here not only to suggest that the claim of transfer may not be justified but also to illustrate further a point made earlier in this chapter, namely that what are reported as 'naturalistic' observations may be far from natural:

> The mother was instructed to remain in 2 adjoining rooms with the child, to ignore the observer, and to avoid having visitors, telephone calls, or the television on during the observation. The observer, equipped with a cassette tape-recorder, earphone and coding sheets, stationed himself so that he could observe the mother–child interaction in either of the 2 adjoining rooms.
> (Forehand and Peed 1979: 173-4)

Forehand and Peed claim to have demonstrated transfer of training by such a method, but a more realistic interpretation would be that they had merely succeeded in transferring the clinic to the home.

The major contribution of research into teaching parents behavioural methods is that it allows parents the luxury of 'controllable' children by providing detailed instructions based on principles of reinforcement. The problem of maintaining the *parental* behaviour remains, but it is undoubtedly reassuring for parents to know that they can achieve control of their children if they really try.

Courses on Child Development

Provision of information and support to parents through courses on child development has a recent and patchy history. Work by the National Children's Bureau (Pugh 1981) demonstrates a concerted attempt to clarify and organise the hazy information on parent participation and support, with the aim of providing a national service of the kind recommended in the Court Report on Child Health Services (1976), but this is a complex and long-term project. A co-ordinated service of provision does not yet exist, and consequently courses may appear as a part of health education (in schools and antenatal clinics for potential parents), in adult education departments, or in correspondence form from educational institutions such as the Open University.

Turner (1980) identifies four types of courses in developmental psychology: short courses, service courses, minority subject courses in colleges and universities, and full-length specialised review courses. At first consideration, courses for parents come under the heading 'short courses', which Turner defines as those which are 'intended to inform but do not lead to any formal qualification' (p. 153). She lists three aims of short courses:

> to provide the students with information directly relevant to their area of interest; to give sufficient information to the students concerning the methods of developmental psychology for them to be able to put the information they are given into perspective; to give the students the opportunity for some practical experience, if only in observation.

Parents are not mentioned as potential students but it is clear that the third aim would be unnecessary in their case, since they have plenty of practical experience; indeed, it is likely to be the nature of that experience which sent them to the course in the first place.

Anyone wishing advice on teaching parents will find more appropriate material in Turner's section on service courses. The definition of a service course does not immediately appear to 'fit' parents ('provided when the students are preparing for a non-psychological qualification ... but require a psychological component' (p. 153)), yet the job of parent implies the need for just this kind of material, and the acknowledgement of student requirements in relation to a service course is certainly appropriate to parents:

> When planning such a course the teacher has a choice, either he can consider growth and change in the people with whom the students will have to deal . . . or he can concentrate on growth and change in the students themselves, so that the experience of the students becomes the content of the course. This second approach involves such notions as development to date and the students' changing sense of identity as they become aware of the demand of the professional role for which they are preparing. (p. 155)

The assertion that viewing courses for parents as service courses is more appropriate than viewing them as 'short (interest) courses' is based on the experience of a series of such courses over a period of nine years, and it is to this experience that the discussion now turns.

In considering teaching psychology to parents, it is clear that at once we have a departure from traditional psychology teaching carried out in a psychology department of a college or university. There are two major differences between students registering for a full-time degree in psychology and those who enrol for adult education classes. The latter normally do so for different reasons to those, usually younger, students in full-time education. Some adults may choose to study child psychology for professional reasons, but for most the driving force will be the desire to benefit either themselves or the children under their care. The other notable difference between traditional full-time students and those studying in evening classes is that the latter may attend or not, as they please. Adults can, to put it bluntly, vote with their feet. The psychology taught to adults *must* be seen by the students to be directly relevant to whatever needs brought them to the course in the first place. They will not justify the hassle they go through to attend the course in the way some traditional students will, on the lines of 'some of it is a bit tedious, in fact I find a lot of it deadly dull, with no relevance to anything or anybody I know, but . . . well at least at the end I'll have a degree'. For adult students in extra-mural departments of universities or adult education centres, the course must be its own justification. Falling attendances are a sure sign to the tutor that either tutor or course or both are failing somewhere. This is not to say that this should not be the case in traditional psychology teaching; clearly it should be, but it often is not. At any rate, adults attending part-time unassessed courses can afford to be more selective.

A Course on Child Development for Parents

The particular series of courses under discussion here began as a short course entitled 'Understanding Children'. I 'inherited' the course and was five years into teaching it, and had three children of my own before I realised that neither I nor anyone else 'understood' children in any real sense of the term, and the inherited and presumptious name was changed to 'Living with Young Children'. The course began somewhat inauspiciously in 1974 and was divided into two parts. The first ten-week unit covered pregnancy and the first two years of life; topics included physical and emotional changes in the mother in pregnancy, physical development of the baby from conception to two years, the physiology and psychology of labour, and genral topics, such as babies' needs for play, were discussed. The second ten-week unit covered the ages from two to seven years, and included child-rearing practices, physical and cognitive development, play, pre-school provision, reading, socialisation and intelligence. The sessions were two hours long, at weekly intervals. Mothers came from a variety of backgrounds, most were married and living with their husband and their children varied in number from one to five and in age from three months to twelve years. At the end of the course the 25 or so mothers who attended were given the chance to provide anonymous feedback about the course to the director of adult education at the University. They were asked to comment specifically on the following three areas:

1. Organisation of content; did they prefer a developmental approach or a special topics approach?
2. Discussion; was there too much discussion (as opposed to straight lectures) or too little?
3. Duplicated notes: were they useful? (Handouts were provided for every lecture in the first ten-weeks and for only three in the second, so it was possible to compare the two. Since they were time-consuming to prepare, it was relevant to discover if they were actually useful to the parents.)

The comments were invaluable, so much so that the practice of requesting feedback became a regular occurrence providing comments on 15 separate courses from 250 mothers. The organisation of each course changed less and less over the years as the customers gradually began to get what they wanted. Pointers to what mothers really did want from psychology were to be found in comments on the first two areas; organisation of content, and discussion. Firstly, related to organisation of content there was overwhelming support for a special topics approach, rather than a developmental, sequential description of children. If development was covered stage by stage, interest varied according to whether mothers had children close to the age/stage being discussed, whereas special topics (such as language development or sleeping difficulties) very often spanned a range of ages. The desired topics varied with each class, so after the first year a 'List of Possible Topics' was handed out, which the class members ranked according to their interests and the characteristics of their particular children. Each time the course was presented, it changed slightly in response to the votes of the class members. As an interesting bonus, this ranking system produced some fascinating data on the preoccupations of mothers with young children. With the exception of one particular year, the topic on dealing with behaviour problems was always ranked the most important. The reason for its movement down the ranking in that one year, where 'behaviour problems' were ousted by 'language and communication', became apparent on looking at the relevant children. Most unusually that year all the children from the class were under two years of age. Behaviour problems, apart from not sleeping enough, had just not become an issue. Clearly, after about two years, interest in children's language development can become submerged by an overwhelming feeling of lack of control over children's behaviour. I was rather intrigued by the fact that language and communication was ranked second on twelve separate courses, and as a psychologist felt somewhat uplifted that theoretical psychology did hold some interest for mothers – until I discovered that it was the word 'communication' which was attracting people, reflecting thoughts on the lines of 'If I could only *communicate* with him he might do what he was told now and again.' So we were back to the behaviour problems. Overall, what appeared to matter most was getting through the day with the least misfortune, and with the odd bonus now and again, particularly if there was more than one child in the family. This can be illustrated further by a description of the way in which the content and presentation of some of the topics developed, following presentation and feedback of a number of courses.

'Play' began in 1974 with theories of why children play, what they gain from play (educationally or emotionally), the different types of play and the use of play in therapy and assessment; in 1983 it was 'Entertaining your children at home'. General discussion of learning theory in 1974 became in 1983 'How to write a behaviour modification programme'. The 1974 theories of bonding, separation and attachment became a discussion in 1983 of when, how and where to leave a child with the least upset to both child and parents. Theoretical discussion about reading became over the years 'teaching pre-schoolers to read'. Theorising aloud about the importance of peers to young children became translated into the practical problems of how to stop them poking each other's eyes out, and general theories of and evidence about development became a run-through of particular problem areas such as bed-wetting, toilet training, sleeping difficulties (difficulties of course for the parents; their children rarely found lack of sleep a problem), fears and phobias, inability to make friends, jealousy, tantrums, stubbornness, defiance and clinging behaviour. Feedback comments provided the information that, were the course longer, mothers would like to hear more about the theory, but within the time limits they would prefer the time to be spent on practicalities. On later courses an annotated reading list was provided to cover theoretical and research aspects of child development, and the course itself was built upon unashamed pragmatism.

The second area in which feedback was provided was 'discussion'. It was more difficult to achieve consensus on this one. The first year the comments suggested that there had not been enough time for discussion, so there was less direct lecturing during the second course. That year the feedback was that the class members would have liked less discussion, and so it went on. There was consensus, however, over the topics for discussion. At the start of every course after the first, class members were asked to write down *why* they had had children. Every year this request was greeted with blank stares, followed usually by furious writing, and everyone appreciated discussion of this topic, if in a somewhat horrified way. Many mothers had not thought about this question before, and discussion revealed that the realities of being a parent came as a not always pleasant surprise. Most had had children because it was 'expected' (both by the mothers and by others around them) without being fully aware of the implications in terms of loss of privacy, identity, career and temper. It is unlikely that any other such life-disrupting decisions are made with so little awareness of the consequences, and with so little training, and this alone could provide the explanation as to why coping skills became such a focus of class requirements.

Another universally popular area for discussion was child-rearing practices in different cultures and in different ages; perhaps the popularity of this lecture and discussion was the emphasis on the transient nature of child-rearing fashions. Mothers found it somehow reassuring to know that if they did not agree with some of the contemporary ideas on child rearing, or if they found them unworkable, other methods were probably popular somewhere else, and may become popular in our own culture in a generation's time. A third popular area for discussion was sex differences and sex-role stereotyping. Presumably this reflected current popular thinking and the responsibilities that lie upon parents regarding their role in the maintenance and possible modification of sex-role stereotypes. It was evident from comments on discussion topics, as with lecture topics, that mothers were interested in discussion relevant to their day-to-day existence looking after young children, rather than in theories regarding *why* children behave as they do, or research on long-term *effects* of particular practices.

The final area of feedback was the provision of duplicated notes. There was general agreement that these were not only desirable but essential for two main reasons: firstly, to keep for later reference (when the child was older or had entered into some particular problem 'stage'), and secondly because a feature of these courses was a crèche. The crèche itself may have been the main attraction of the course initially, but there were occasions when children did not settle in the crèche, and mothers had their children on their laps during a lecture/ discussion; in keeping their own child relatively happy, they missed much of what was said.

Such was the development of the course. Is it a tale of theory into practice, or is it just practice? For example in the area of 'play' there may appear to be no identifiable psychology-based educational ideas behind the lectures on entertaining young children. The aim was to keep children happy and interested (and, it must be said, preferably out of the way) for as long as possible. Yet devising activities for children requires a knowledge of developmental stages, so the 'theory' must be in the tutor's head somewhere, even if rarely seen naked in class. To this extent, courses for parents have links with therapy. A speech therapist does not tell a mother all she knows about language; a psychoanalyst does not tell a client all he knows about psychological processes. A therapist is expected to give theory-based advice because he or she is trained in dealing with the particular problem with which the child/patient is presenting. But the mothers in these courses were not coming with a problem in the way they might take their child to a therapist. Mothers of 'normal' children are not allowed to see a therapist (at least under the National Health Service) when their children are just doing the things all children do. They are not supposed to have a problem. Although it is generally accepted that bringing up children can be wearing, it is not seen as a problem to be treated; the implication is that if parents do see it as a problem, then they must be failing somewhere.

This kind of analysis leads to a view of the tutor on parent education courses as a therapist to people who are not allowed to admit they have anything to treat, and to a view of the class members as providing the type of support typically associated with group therapy. The feedback comments on the courses under discussion here would support such an interpretation, but this would be neither a complete nor particularly constructive conclusion to this chapter. There are wider implications for the teaching of parents that arise from the preceding account.

Conclusions

The feedback comments suggested above suggest a prevalent desire for a pragmatic approach in parent education, an emphasis not so much on *why* children and parents do and feel particular things, rather upon ideas for preventing or coping with such behaviours and feelings when they arise. Theory is pushed into (or remains in) the background, or at most used as a starting point for discussion about things that really concern mothers. At the beginning of the chapter desirable course content was described as constituting a survival kit and a number of suggestions have been given in this chapter as to the form of such a kit. It was also suggested that such a kit is incomplete, and it is in discussion of this that I would like to conclude.

When presenting psychological knowledge to mothers of young children, what is normally presented is child psychology. But since short courses for parents appear to fit the category of service courses, the notion of growth and change in the students (in this case parents) is as important as growth and change in the people with whom they have to deal (children). In all societies, becoming a parent is a major life event which creates special problems and responsibilities. The nature of Western industrialised society has tended to isolate families, particularly mothers, and to create special problems and areas of stress for parents. I would suggest that any parents, whether their child is developmentally normal, or handicapped in some way, would find their role easier to manage if psychologists offering advice on parenting shifted the focus away from the question of how to help the child towards optimal development towards a solution to the incipient psychological and social problems faced by parents. There is a considerable body of psychological knowledge which to date seems to have received little attention in respect of the needs of parents. I have in mind work in the field of social psychology — interpersonal perception, attribution theory, typical reactions under stress, social needs and, under the circumstances in which many mothers bring up their children, I do not feel that studies of prisoner behaviour would be out of place. The volume of research on the self-image must provide some valuable insights to people who, as many class members admitted, appear to have lost their identities somewhere between pregnancy and the present. And where situations cannot be changed knowledge of methods of cognitive restructuring would surely be valuable.

References

Ainsworth, M.D., Bell, S. and Stayton, D. (1974) Infant–mother attachment and social development: socialisation as a product of reciprocal responsiveness to signals in M. Richards (ed.), *The Integration of a Child into a Social World*, Cambridge: Cambridge University Press

Bower, T.G.R. (1977) *The Perceptual World of the Child*, Cambridge, Mass.: Harvard University Press

Burton, L., White (1979) Critical influences in the origins of competence in J. Oates (ed.), *Early Cognitive Development*, Milton Keynes: Open University Press

Court, S.D.M. (1976) *Fit for the Future: Report of the Committee on Child Health Services, Vols. I & II*, London: HMSO

Donaldson, M. (1984) *Children's Minds*, London: Fontana/Flamingo

Douglas, J. and Richman, N. (1984a) *Coping with Young Children*, Harmondsworth: Penguin

———— (1984b) *My Child Won't Sleep*, Harmondsworth: Penguin

Dunn, J. (1984) *Sisters and Brothers*, London: Fontana

Forehand, R. and Peed, S. (1979) Training parents to modify the non-compliant behaviour of their children in A.J. Finch and P.C. Kendall (eds), *Clinical Treatment and Research in Child Psychopathology*, New York: Spectrum Publications

Grotberg, E.H. (1979) The parental role in education and child development in S. Doxiadis (ed.), *The Child in the World of Tomorrow: A Window into the Future*, Oxford: Pergamon

Harrison, M. (1981) 'Home start' *Early Childhood, 1(5)*

Metzl, M. (1980) Teaching parents a strategy for enhancing infant development, *Child Development, 51(2)*

Newson, J. and Newson, E. (1963) *Patterns of Infant Care in an Urban Community*, Harmondsworth: Penguin

———— (1968) *Four Years Old in an Urban Community*, Harmondsworth: Penguin

———— (1974) Cultural aspects of childrearing in the English-speaking world in M. Richards (ed.), *The Integration of a Child into a Social World*, Cambridge: Cambridge University Press

———— (1976) *Seven Years Old in the Home Environment*, Harmondsworth: Penguin

O'Dell, S. (1974) Training parents in behaviour modification: a review, *Psychological Bulletin, 81*, 418–33

Pringle, M.K. (1974) *The Needs of Children*, London: Hutchinson

Pugh, G. (1981) Parenthood: towards a framework for education and support, *Early Child Development and Care, 7(2, 3)*

Stern, D. (1977) *The First Relationship: Infant and Mother*, London: Fontana

Tizard, B. and Hughes, M. (1984) *Young Children Learning*, London: Fontana

Turner, J. (1980) Developmental psychology in J. Radford and D. Rose (eds), *The Teaching of Psychology*, Chichester: Wiley

Wolfendale, S. (1983) *Parental Participation in Children's Development and Education*, New York: Gordon and Breach

3 ADVISING PARENTS OF YOUNG DEAF CHILDREN: IMPLICATIONS AND ASSUMPTIONS

Susan Gregory

Most deaf children are born into hearing families where no other member of the family is deaf. It is unlikely that the parents will know much about the problems and difficulties of prelingually deaf people, or even have experienced deafness first hand, other than the deafness of an elderly person who has gone deaf with age and has totally different problems. Thus, most families with a deaf child find themselves in an unfamiliar situation and feel that they need help and advice.

This chapter looks at the guidance that is currently given, and the change in the content of the advice over the past 20 years. This is considered within the context of the changes in developmental psychology over this time, particularly in the study of language and language acquisition. It also examines the implicit assumptions behind the notions of giving guidance and the values underlying the actual structure and content of the advice.

The Diagnosis of Hearing Loss

Deafness is a handicap that effects about one child in 1,000, but it is a disability that is rarely detected and diagnosed at birth. Although it is feasible to screen for it in the first 48 hours of life, using a microprocessor-based system such as the Crib-o-gram or Auditory Response Cradle, and confirm the hearing loss using more sophisticated and expensive procedures of electrical response audiometry within the first three months of life, only a tiny minority of children are currently diagnosed this early in their lives. It is more likely that diagnosis will be made following health visitor screening tests at around ten to twelve months of age. Unfortunately, not all children are detected by this stage. It is difficult to give up-to-date information on the age of diagnosis of deafness as inevitably any study must be retrospective. In a comprehensive project undertaken by the EEC and published in 1979, reviewing children born in 1969 in the United Kingdom, it was found that of 919 deaf children, 99 were diagnosed

50

before 12 months, a further 231 before 24 months, and a further 182 before 36 months, leaving 407 for whom no diagnosis was made until after 36 months. It seems likely that the position is gradually improving, but there can be no complacency as all too often diagnosis is made after the first year of life, sometimes after a long period of stress and anxiety for the family who may have suspected something was wrong for quite some time.

The reactions to the diagnosis of deafness are complex and varied. For some families, as well as the dismay or despair or confusion, there are elements of relief. These can either be because the diagnosis means a confirmation of their existing suspicions, which were therefore not neurotic, or relief that the problem for the child is deafness, not mental handicap, which parents often dread much more.

Whatever the reaction though, most parents find themselves in a position where they are not sure what to do, or what the implications of the deafness will be. There are medical questions to be answered concerning the cause of the deafness, whether or not it can be cured, and whether there is a genetic basis for it which would increase the likelihood of further children in the family being affected. There are technical questions about how hearing-aids function and how they should be used. Then there are the more general questions as to how the child can be helped, how he or she will be educated, and what the future will hold. Nowadays most families of pre-school children will receive visits from a peripatetic teacher of the deaf, who will offer advice or guidance or counselling.

The Origins of the Advisory Service

The peripatetic service began in 1948 when a teacher was appointed to the Deafness Aid Clinic in London to work with those children not in special schools. At the same time, in Lancashire, a peripatetic service was established to work towards making educational provision for all children with a hearing loss. These, however, were teachers dealing with children of school age but gradually their duties were extended to deal with children of all ages with any degree of hearing loss. The impetus for a comprehensive pre-school service came in 1961 with Circular 23/61, issued by the Ministry of Health, which stressed the importance of the early care of deaf children. This was really the beginnings of a full peripatetic service where the present emphasis is on work with pre-school children, but which also has some responsibility for older children.

It is important to recognise that this service for pre-school children stemmed from earlier educational provision for school-age children. In practical terms, the educational aspect is currently reinforced by teachers working in school terms only; thus there are no visits during the holidays, including the long summer break, even for the youngest children. I will argue later that the framework of educational practice, and the goals and assumptions underlying it, are not necessarily the best or most appropriate ones for work with very young children, particularly as deaf children are being diagnosed at a younger and younger age. Moreover, working with families in their homes, or occasionally in a clinic setting, is very different from working with children in a classroom. It was noted in the Warnock Report (1978: 82) that teachers of the deaf are not trained for this: 'Moreover, very few peripatetic teachers of the deaf have had any special training in working with parents or in the development of young children.' It is not unknown for a teacher to finish work in a partially-hearing unit for secondary age children on a Friday evening and start work as a peripatetic teacher working with young children on the following Monday morning.

This is not a criticism of peripatetic teachers. Most parents value the help they receive from them. In my interview study of parents of young deaf children, 66 per cent spoke positively about the peripatetic service, and only 6 per cent expressed serious reservations (Gregory 1976). The educational nature of the work has been stressed in order to provide a context within which to examine the practices of peripatetic teachers. If for some reason the history of the pre-school services had been different, perhaps being instituted by the medical or social services, the nature of the resulting provision might have been very different.

In order to look at the relationship between theory and practice, I have chosen to look at the advice given over the past 20 years, as this covers the period when a full peripatetic service was being established. The advice to parents cited in this chapter will all be taken from books and pamphlets readily available to parents, and commonly recommended. The analysis of this advice will appear critical, but this is not the point of the chapter; rather the aim is to analyse how the advice comes about, how it relates to the psychological approaches of its time and more general trends within society. Most people who work with the deaf do not feel totally happy with all aspects of the present system and look for ways of improving the service.

Advice on Language Acquisition

One of the expressed aims of those involved in the peripatetic service, and something which is abundantly clear from the advice that they give, is that their main aim is the facilitation of the development of spoken language. The problems of the deaf have largely been construed in terms of the difficulty they have in developing language, as this is the most obvious manifestation of their difficulties.

First, I wish to look at the advice which has been given over the past 20 years concerning language, to examine changes in the content of the advice, and to show how these reflect the study of language and language acquisition in academic psychology. The study of language within psychology has shown a rapid expansion over the past 20 years. However, academic psychologists are not usually concerned with practical applications of their work, and have not sought to make their findings relevant or even accessible to those working with children developing language, or, more specifically, children who have problems in language acquisition. Moreover, the questions that academic psychologists ask about the process of language acquisition are not necessarily those questions that are relevant in considering an individual child learning language, and this creates problems for practitioners in their attempts to use these findings.

Inevitably in any study of theories of language acquisition, the effect of the work of Chomsky is crucial, so much so that there is a division into a pre- and post-Chomsky age. Chomsky's seminal works were published in 1957 and 1965, yet his influence on the study of language development in psychology only really came in the late 1960s and early 1970s as researchers working in the field of child language acquisition attempted to elaborate and validate his ideas.

The Study of Language in the 1950s and 1960s

If one looks at basic psychology texts of the 1950s and 1960s, a relatively small proportion of them is concerned with language acquisition, compared with texts of the present day. For example, in the textbook by Krech and Crutchfield entitled *Elements of Psychology* published in 1962, only 20 pages out of a total of 700 deal with language, and of these only four consider language acquisition, describing it in terms of learning the sounds of speech, building these into words, and words acquiring meaning by association and reinforcement. This is typical of books of this period. If one looks at books specifically about language, such as George Millar's

Language and Communication (originally published in 1951, but made more generally available by being published in paperback in 1963), it seems that the questions that were being asked were about speech perception, and the types of experiments being carried out reduced speech to its smallest discernible parts to see how they were discriminated.

Language acquisition was thus discussed at this time in terms of seeing how children built up words from smaller elements, sounds, and finally combined words into sentences. Much was made of the reported finding that children make all possible sounds in the first year of life, but only those relevant to the particular culture remain, the others fading away. The actual process of acquisition was dominated by behaviourist theories and seen as an uneasy combination of associating words with objects, through reinforcement, and some learning by imitation.

The influence of this in practices with deaf children can be seen by considering a standard textbook for teachers, *Teaching Deaf Children to Talk* by Ewing and Ewing (1964), in which much space is devoted to the topic of articulation. In fact, there are whole chapters devoted to such elements as 'Phonation and Vowels' (Chapter IX) and 'Consonants' (Chapter X). Specific suggestions are given on how to encourage children to make the various sounds of speech. In order to show how to make the long and short vowel sounds, it is suggested that teachers clip paper strips into confetti with the child, and the child will, by analogy, work out how to clip the vowel sounds s/he is making. Specific advice is also given for consonants:

> Sometimes a child can be helped to say S by holding a spill of paper (or a lemonade straw) between his teeth in such a way that the tip of the tongue just touches the end of the spill, which he inserts and holds between his teeth and keeps there while he hisses out breath. The tension, necessary to hold the spill steady between the teeth, secures the tension that is required for the correct articulation of S. The fact that the tip of the tongue touches the spill brings the tip into the right position, behind the opening of the teeth but not touching them. An alternative method, involving a hand analogy, is to hollow the palm and extended [sic] fingers of a hand lengthways and then to hiss the breath along the midline. (Ibid.: 227)

It is, of course, all too easy to be critical with hindsight. To give these examples only with a view to pointing out their inadequacies would be unfair since, by focusing attention on the needs of deaf children, by stressing the need for special training for teachers of the deaf, and by encouraging the development of hearing aids, the Ewings have made a major contribution to the welfare of the deaf in this country. Rather, the examples serve to illustrate a serious point, and that is to do with the relationship between psychological theory and practice. The fact that psychologists were dismantling language, to see how it was made up, does not mean that in the process of language learning the child needs to do the same thing. Such questions about speech perception are not necessarily relevant to the study of language development; yet, because language acquisition was couched in those terms, it was almost inevitable that practitioners would also adopt the same model.

The Study of Language Acquisition after Chomsky

In 1957 and 1965 Chomsky published two books which changed the way linguists and psychologists thought about language. He made the distinction between the surface structure of a language, which is the simple arrangement of the words in an utterance, and the deep structure underlying this, that is, the actual relationships conveyed by the sentence in terms of its meaning. If we consider the classic example

John is easy to please
John is eager to please

in terms of the surface structure, we cannot explain how we understand in one sentence that it is John who is doing the pleasing and in the other sentence it is John who is being pleased. The relationships between the elements of the sentences cannot be explained in terms of the simple, associative rules which had previously been cited. Instead, it is necessary to consider the deep structure of the sentence. This in turn leads us to Chomsky's notion of transformational grammar, that there are rules which relate the deep and surface structure of a language. Chomsky's aim was to specify those rules which enable the speaker of a language to generate all the sentence forms considered acceptable in that language.

It must be said at the outset that as a linguist Chomsky was concerned with language as an object of knowledge; not with its function within the communication system, but as a body of knowledge with internally consistent rules. He was not attempting to write an empirical account of how a child acquires language, but rather a description of the rules that characterise that language. However, psychologists took over these notions and attempted to work out how children learned the rules which made them able to create language. They then attempted to write grammars for the early speech production of children.

Arising from this a further question seems to be posed by the work of Chomsky concerning the way in which children develop language with its complexity from the speech that they hear. Adults' (usually mothers') speech to young infants has been studied and its features described, and attempts made to relate these to the process of language acquisition in young children. This focus on mothers' speech to hearing children resulted in an increasing concern that deaf children, because of their handicap, are not exposed to the same amount of speech as hearing children. This concern was realised in practices with deaf children as an emphasis on quantity of language, sometimes expressed in terms of the need to 'get enough in'. At a conference for teachers of the deaf on Parent Guidance (1976), H.C. Glendenning said in his introduction, 'Even if the profoundly deaf child could have the undivided attention of a teacher throughout every school day, this would still be equivalent to no more than three months of the normal child's opportunity to acquire language.' In a National Deaf Children's Society pamphlet of advice to parents in 1971, there is a section 'Feed the brain' in which it says:

> No, I don't mean you to give it more eggs, steak etc. I am talking about the amount of knowledge that is fed into the brain. It is as simple as this – when we hear a noise, we put it into our brain store (memory) and with it we usually associate the meaning of the word. When we speak we repeat the sound that we were able to put into our memory – it had to be fed in before it could come out.
>
> Let us assume that the brain is a tank that can receive water by one tap and give out water by another tap. It is fair to say that:
>
> (a) the tank can only take as much water as will fill it – in this case a normal hearing child can only hold as much knowledge (water) as a partially deaf child.
>
> (b) the tank will take in knowledge as quickly as the tap will allow it – in this case, with two equally intelligent children, AT THE BEGINNING ONLY, the normal-hearing child will take in knowledge more quickly; however as time passes, the effect of training and extra powers that only the partially deaf child will develop, will be that they can both take in knowledge at the same rate.

(c) the tank will give out knowledge as quickly as the tap will allow it – in this case there is no difference between a normal hearing child and a partially deaf child. (Whitehill 1971: 12)

The idea that sheer quantity of talk was critical became toned down in later advice as psychological studies of mothers' speech to their children became more detailed. It became clear that mothers' speech, or 'motherese', has particular qualities whereby mothers use simplified forms of language with their young children, which is not only highly repetitive, but also largely refers to the here and now. As research proceeded it was established that mothers' speech varied in relation to the competence of the child, that mothers were adjusting or 'fine tuning' their language to the linguistic competence of their child. Also, studies began to emphasise the pragmatics of the communication situation, that language was understood by children because it was appropriate to the situation.

Thus, in considering language learning by deaf children, a more sophisticated model was advanced. It was not the amount of talk, but also the content of the language that was felt to be important. Moreover, this speech had to occur within meaningful contexts. In a recent book, intended for advisors of parents of deaf children, Tucker and Nolan (1984: 324) say: 'the total amount of talk is not the most important feature of linguistic input although obviously a certain amount of minimum exposure will be necessary'. Much of the emphasis is on mothers tuning their speech to the child's capacity: 'Parents learn quite naturally to tune their use of language to the child's language level and the child learns the rules of language without them being made explicit and without the need for force or drills.' (page 317) The current emphasis is thus clearly on talking normally and relating the language to the child's experience.

Assumptions Underlying the Advice on Language Development

Most of the advice to parents of deaf children is concerned with ways of facilitating the development of language in the child. Inevitably this advice is based on assumptions, many of which are never made explicit, as to what are the desirable achievements of deaf children, and how best these should be realised. In the sections below I wish to draw attention to four of the main issues. Firstly, it seems to be generally assumed, without question, that oral language should be the language of deaf children, and secondly, that they will, with few exceptions, be able to learn to talk. Thirdly, the emphasis on language seems to imply that language *per se* should be the focus of attention. The fourth assumption concerns the advice to parents of deaf children that stresses the need for normal language to be addressed to the child, in order to achieve normal language development from the child, as if notions of normality were non-problematic.

Oral Language and Deaf Children

Possibly the most surprising assumption for the layman is that deaf children are expected to learn to talk; in fact no other possibility is considered in current books and widely available leaflets for parents of deaf children. The 'man in the street' assumes that the deaf use sign language to communicate in the same way as it is assumed that the blind use Braille to read. This is even more the case now with the increasing visibility of sign language on television, in special programmes for the deaf, some news programmes, the Queen's Christmas Speech, Party Political Conferences, etc. When their child is first diagnosed, most parents assume they will have to learn to sign, and are surprised when they are told that this is not the case. The notion generally held by professionals, that parents are against their children learning signing, seems to be ascertained from parents of young children, who have been told that speech is a real possibility. Parents of older children often express a different view.

It is important to state here that when we talk of children with a hearing loss we are talking about a vast range of disability; from minor losses for which hearing aids are not prescribed, to the middle range of losses that are helped enormously by amplification, to very severe and profound losses. If we take into account the whole range of hearing loss, the vast majority of deaf children will develop spoken language skills, but the variation in these skills will be great. Some will develop a facility with language which makes them able to cope in a hearing world, and of these some will be hardly distinguishable from hearing people. Some will develop a competence in spoken language, but it will never be a means of free and easy communication for them, and as they grow older they are likely to use signing as their main means of communication in their social and personal life. Others will not develop spoken language that will allow them to communicate in the hearing world to any useful extent. Conrad (1979) reports that of 331 children of school-leaving age in special schools for the deaf, only 14 per cent were 'wholly intelligible', and 48 per cent were 'very hard to understand' or 'effectively unintelligible'. Although such data is, inevitably, open to the criticism that it is based on children diagnosed some years ago when modern aids and current teaching practices were not available, nevertheless, there is not such a dramatic improvement in language competence of deaf children currently at school to convince one that there has been a radical change in their spoken language skills. Moreover, this finding appears to be universal, and all countries, whatever their form of education, have some deaf people who do not communicate easily by spoken language. Given this it seems strange that in virtually all published advice to parents of deaf children, communication by spoken language is presented as the only possibility.

In emphasising to parents that spoken language is the obvious goal for their child, 'first it goes without saying that you want your child to develop language' (Nolan and Tucker 1981: 143), it is also made clear, by implication, that a child who does not develop spoken language has failed, and is even a misfit in society. In their book they say, 'Many parents tell us that what they want for their child is for him to fit into society, to be acceptable socially: and paramount in their minds is that he should talk.' (Ibid.: 144) Thus, parents may assume from this that a child who does not talk is not acceptable socially. It may be, of course, that practitioners here are only reflecting the view of society at large, with its emphasis on normalisation, but it also may be the case that they themselves are constructing this view in the process.

Certainly, some groups of parents are now demanding information about alternatives to spoken language. A group of parents in Hull got together to compile a report based on interviews with all parents of under fives in their area. In this they say:

> Half the parents interviewed said they would like a policy change for them and their children from natural oralism to a Total Communication approach. This is despite the fact that no information is given to parents about this approach and it's actively discouraged by the Service for Hearing Impaired Children. Such parents have obviously found things out independently, have no help in learning and have to face the disapproval of the Service for Hearing Impaired Children. (Hull and District Branch, National Deaf Childrens Society, undated, probably 1983)

The Possibility of Language Development for Deaf Children

A similar problem to the idea that spoken language is essential for a child to be considered normal and acceptable, though more of an issue in the 1970s than it is now, is that in presenting spoken language as a real possibility there was an implication that if the child did not learn to speak it constituted a failure on the part of the parents. A booklet frequently given to parents and published by the National College of Teachers of the Deaf entitled *You CAN Help Your Deaf Baby* says:

> Helping deaf children to understand what is said to them and to talk themselves is always a job that takes a lot of time. You need faith that in the end many deaf children can talk and can become as normal as possible. They can certainly lead happy and useful lives. . . It's up to you. Will your deaf child fit into the world of hearing people, or will he grow up as a lonely person who can't understand and talk to other people? Of course he'll grow up to live a full and happy life, because you CAN help your deaf baby to talk. (Williams 1972: 12)

Many parents have expressed feelings of inadequacy and ultimately failure because of their inability to meet the sort of demands that seemed to be made of them. Such were the feelings of one parent speaking at a recent conference:

> Sometimes dynamic teachers and the dynamic books dynamic teachers produce can be counter-productive with some parents. The impression which is so often left with a parent is that he should be on the ball all the time. Do not waste any time. In every situation you should be talking to your child. If a parent happens to be someone who is naturally reserved the parent has to make an effort to change. . . This does induce a feeling of inadequacy and one gets the sense that time is being lost all the time. The vital years are between one and five and you are always wrestling and in the end you may feel that you have done nothing. (Collett 1976: xix)

The assumption is that spoken language is normal, attainable and a realistic goal, despite the demands this makes on parents and the real possibility of failure for them. Yet those who write about developing language in deaf children do warn that it may be years of talking to the child before s/he says anything back as the following two examples show:

> We would anticipate that by the time he is three you will have

noted progress in his reception of speech and his own expression, which may by now contain some intelligible words, or may simply be becoming like the rhythmic babble of the normally hearing child at an earlier age. (Nolan and Tucker 1981: 160)

And similarly McCormick (1976: 10) states:

> If you are the sort of person who likes to see immediate results for your work, you could easily become disheartened by your child's apparent lack of progress in speech and language development in his earliest years. This is one of the biggest frustrations facing parents in your position, for the fruits of your toil may appear only after a considerable period of cultivation. It would be a mistake to try to measure the effectiveness of what you are doing by assessing only what your child is giving back in the early years, although human nature tempts us to do this. Some children give back a great deal, and others very little in the early years.

The problem in developing spoken language skills is confirmed in my own interview study of parents of deaf children. In the age group three and a half to five years, of the 42 children, 9 could talk in sentences, a further 16 had a vocabulary of six words or more, 9 had five or less words, and 8 could not speak at all. This means that, at this age, four out of ten of the children had five or less words in their expressive vocabulary, and thus effective communication from the child is dramatically reduced, as none of the children had any form of gestural communication or sign language.

The assumption underlying this, of course, is that normality is the achievement of spoken language, even if it takes many years, rather than normality being the establishment of a 'normal' competence to *communicate* in the early formative years. By normal communication I mean that the deaf child has the ability to express the range of ideas and feelings that most children of his/her age have. It seems from the advice given that, by implication, the richness of communication of the first two or three years is to be sacrificed without comment to the possibility of the achievement of 'normal' spoken language. If this is the case, it is surprising that Nolan and Tucker claim, without qualification, 'it goes without saying that you want your child to develop language' (1981: 143).

It may be that one of the reasons that this has arisen is that advice to parents is given by teachers and thus within an educational framework. Part of a teacher's work in school is to facilitate language development leading to reading and writing skills. Thus, the aims of the educational system are being implemented in the more general setting of the young child in the family, and provide part of the context of this advice. Would it have been the same if advice were given from a different professional basis where the needs of child and family were perceived in another way?

This is not in fact a disguised argument for the introduction of signing for some deaf children in the early years, though it may be the logical conclusion of some of the ideas presented here. Rather, it is a plea to consider the needs of the deaf child and the family in a way that focuses on their need for communication and examines how the early development of communication is best facilitated. The issues of the so-called oral-manual controversy, the argument about whether deaf people should be educated totally orally, or whether some manual/ signing component should be introduced, are too complicated to go into here. In a sense it is the controversy itself and the questions it poses that have created some of the problems. It has construed the difficulties of deaf people in terms of the means, rather than the process, of communication.

Language as an Appropriate Focus for Intervention

This brings us to the third assumption – the idea that the problem of the deaf is linguistic rather than one of communication. Because the difficulties of the deaf are manifest in poor spoken language ability, and because the psychological study of language, at least until recently, was primarily concerned with language production, language in itself became the focus of attention. However, language can only occur within a context and seeing it as an abstracted entity, independent of this, can be counter-productive. Although recent advice has stressed the importance of meaningful language, rather than the 'talk, talk, talk' notions of earlier advice, the focus is still on the language itself. The issue is posed in terms of making the language appropriate, rather than considering how to facilitate communication.

Concepts of 'Normality' in Language Development

The fourth assumption that is implicit in current advice practice is the notion that parents should speak *normally* to their children and thus their children will develop *normal* language. It is assumed that if parents do what comes naturally they will intuitively adjust to the child's linguistic level and thus provide him or her with an appropriate language model. This idea arises from studies of mothers' speech to hearing children which show that they intuitively adapt to the child's linguistic level and competence. Interestingly, some early studies of mothers' speech to deaf children was by those interested to see whether the adjustment to the child's level was to their linguistic or cognitive level, and there is still a controversy as to whether mothers of deaf children do adjust to their child's linguistic level.

Without elaborating on the specific details of the debate, I would like to put the more general question as to what normal, natural speech means with a child whose cognitive and linguistic levels are at variance. Is it likely that a mother speaks to her four-year-old deaf child with an expressive language appropriate for 18-month-old children, because that is the child's apparent language level? Even if 'normality' is only meant to apply to the structure of the sentence and not the semantic content, surely the sorts of things a mother might want to say do not necessarily fit the available structures? What happens if the communication needs of the situation are way beyond the language the child can understand? And surely the actual limitations of the situation, the very fact of it being an abnormal situation, mitigate against one acting 'normally'.

Also, the actual act of communicating with the deaf child is not the same as with the hearing child — it is not simply a matter of doing what comes naturally for conversation cannot as easily accompany activity, and talking may require more effort. One mother of a six-year-old, severely hearing-impaired girl said:

> It's just more difficult talking to her. You do get used to it, but even then it's a bigger strain having her sitting up in the evening than Sharon (her sister). You have to keep talking to her all the time. It's an effort when you're tired to be patient and to talk. (Gregory 1976: 117-18)

This problem is implicitly recognised in the advice given. While much emphasis is placed on normal, natural behaviour, many elements are introduced which are not normal and natural. This becomes clear by contrasting various pieces of advice, all contained within the same booklet, and intended for parents of deaf children. (McCormick 1976: 14)

> If I were to summarise the message contained within this series of articles in just a few words, I should say be natural with your child

and notice how much of his behaviour is typically that of any child of his age. The emphasis is therefore on normality, and your child's only privilege should be that of being exposed to a great deal more talking to than any child with normal hearing.

Nothing should be allowed to interfere with the normal parent–child relationship. You will probably be more natural and successful with your child if you view him as a perfectly normal child whose only problem is that he cannot hear as well as you or I.

Yet, despite all this stress on normality, there are also several sections in the booklet describing how parents should behave in very specific non-natural ways.

It may be helpful to summarise briefly the conditions you should try to create if you are to give your hearing impaired child the best possible chance to make sense of the language he is exposed to, and which results from everyday activity and play experiences. (1) You should be at a reasonable distance from your child (three to four feet is ideal). (2) Your face should be well illuminated and not in shadow. (3) The material being talked about should be brought up to the face so that it is two to three inches from the lips. With larger objects you might have to angle yourself, or the object, so that there is not too much distracting material in view at the same time. If the material is held even six inches away your child might fix on it so much visually that he misses the fine movements of your face as you speak. (4) You should speak clearly and naturally, in full phrases and sentences just as you do to any normally hearing child. The more enjoyment and interest you can secure from each opportunity for speech, the more your child will enjoy these situations, and the greater will be the benefits he derives. (Ibid.: 1)

Thus, within a framework advocating explicitly normal behaviour, the mothers are being asked to behave in specified ways that cannot be normal.

The goal of normal speech to deaf children is normal language development on their part. Despite the optimism of some workers in this area, an examination of the first words of deaf children shows significant differences from that of hearing children, both in content and in the rate of vocabulary growth at various stages (Gregory and

Mogford 1981; Gregory 1983). There is also evidence from recording three-year-old deaf children in interaction with their mothers that they actually treat conversation in a different way from hearing children — as a problem to be solved rather than part of a process of negotiation (Mogford and Gregory 1980). Thus, the assumption that normal language is possible with the deaf child begs many questions and these are not simply resolved by asserting that it should be the case.

Communication and Development: Recent Trends in the Study of Normal Language Acquisition

Recent research on language acquisition has focused on the prelinguistic period. Part of the reason for this has been the increasing dissatisfaction with accounting for children's language development in terms of the language they hear. While research indicated more and more subtle adjustments in mothers' speech to their children's linguistic competence, our common-sense knowledge of the world tells us that not all children grow up in this sensitive language environment, yet virtually all hearing children learn to talk. Cross-cultural studies show evidence of cultures where chidlren are rarely addressed directly, yet they still learn to talk (Ochs and Schieffelin 1983). Within the study of mothers' speech this has led increasingly to an emphasis on the pragmatics of the situation, and to a view that children's understanding of language is facilitated because they understand the situation itself. Parallel to these considerations in the field of language acquisition *per se* have been studies of infant behaviour based on video recordings, which emphasised the sophistication of their prelinguistic communication skills. Thus, psychologists came to look for some of the roots of early language development in the prelinguistic period.

This has implications for counselling parents of deaf children. The problem at this point is that it is not possible to be prescriptive in terms of specific things to do; the issue is rather how to conceptualise the problem. It does reinforce, however, the point that language arises from communication and is not simply a skill that is taught by saying the right thing at the right time. It is of course easy to point this out, but what does it imply in terms of counselling or advising? It means, firstly, that ways must be established to understand the young deaf child. It is not always easy to understand the way in which a deaf child is making sense of his/her world. S/he may focus on different aspects of the environment and may be very aware of visual elements that we disregard, an interpretation which is supported by many failures in screening for hearing loss, where a deaf baby has responded by noting subtle movements of the tester, shadows, changes in light, etc. It seems important that attention should be refocused on the child. What does his or her behaviour mean, what is s/he trying to achieve? One of a number of things that can be particularly useful here is for parents to watch and discuss video tapes of themselves playing with their baby, especially if the sound is turned off. Many studies of mother–baby interaction with handicapped babies have shown these mothers to be more controlling and more directive with their babies than mothers with hearing infants. I suspect this is a 'natural' reaction to a situation that is ambiguous, and it may be necessary to take deliberate steps to redress the balance.

The very way in which an advisor talks to parents is an issue. An emphasis on language leads to questions about what the child can say or what words they can understand whereas an emphasis on communication may lead the advisor to ask more general questions about how the child makes himself or herself understood, and what deaf children are able to understand and predict and communicate about themselves, their wishes and their feelings. Of course, these can only be illustrations of how the guidance situation may be restructured and there is no intention to prescribe a set of new things to do but rather to illustrate a possible reformulation.

This focuses on a general problem in advising on such matters as facilitating language development. I feel that one implication of our current notions of language development is that counselling is essentially giving parents ways of understanding the situation in order that they may best realise its possibilities for themselves. However, advising without being prescriptive or directive is extremely difficult both for teachers who are asked specific questions and parents who would like specific answers. Yet specific prescriptions often mitigate against the occurrence of the very aspects of behaviour that they attempt to facilitate. It seems that it is not just the content of the advice that needs evaluating but the very processes involved in the giving of the advice itself.

Advice on General Issues in the Development of Deaf Children

This chapter has focused on advice concerning language acquisition as this has been the main concern of teachers of the deaf, and until 15 years ago the advice offered addressed itself to little else. Any other problems were seen as arising from the child's poor competence in language rather than from the deafness itself. Thus, Ewing and Ewing (1971: 131) said: 'We are not urging the acquisition of language just for its own sake. Very much more is at stake. Put it quite simply, it is the whole social emotional life of the child.' However, over the past two decades there has been a massive increase in the advice offered to parents in general, via books, magazines and television programmes, and this trend is reflected in sections on more general issues appearing in books and leaflets for parents of deaf children.

One trend in the early advice was to emphasise the overriding importance of the deaf child being acceptable; it was even suggested that deaf children may need to be better behaved than hearing children to achieve this. The following three abstracts from a correspondence course for parents of deaf children, a book and a booklet, all published in the late 1960s or early 1970s illustrate this:

> In order that he may achieve his greatest possible success in life he [the deaf child] must be a little better than his hearing fellows. He needs to be more courteous, more considerate of others, more energetic, more ambitious and more efficient. He must be willing to work harder, to take more pains to do his work well, to be more alert in recognising needs and opportunities. (John Tracy Clinic Correspondence Course, quoted in Dale 1967)

> The most effective discipline is firm, timely and consistent and is tempered with a thorough understanding of the child's problem. If anything, discipline should be stricter than for hearing children in the earlier years because a deaf child's limited vocabulary prevents a parent from reasoning with him. He must learn to obey if he is to fit in socially. (Ibid.)

> Be firm with your deaf baby, though in a kindly happy way. Remember — deaf babies, deaf children and ultimately deaf adults have to live in a world of hearing people, and the more easily they fit in the happier their lives will be. You can see the reason for this, can't you? (Williams, 1972: 3)

Nowadays, such an emphasis would be rare and would seem to most people unrealistic and unnecessarily demanding. The emphasis in current advice is on treating the child normally. To give examples from a book and leaflet currently available to advise parents of deaf children: 'except in the areas of speech and language, you should assume your child's development will be the same as that of a normally hearing child, and then work to rear him and socialise him in the normal way' (Nolan and Tucker 1981: 193). In a leaflet that deals with problems of families with hearing-impaired children, in answer to a question about how to cope with people making concessions for the deaf child the answer is, 'There is only one way and that is to tell them that unless they treat him as they treat normally hearing children his behaviour will never be like that of a normal hearing child.' (McArthur, Tucker, Nolan and Fulbeck 1981: 13)

However, this approach (as in the advice on language development) raises questions as to what is meant by normal. Is it meant that deaf children should be treated as if they were hearing? Does it mean that the expectations for them should be the same as those for a hearing child? Or, does it mean they should be punished to the same extent, as all these alternatives are incompatible? I will give just two examples — there could be very many more. Parents walking along the street with their hearing children may well let them run ahead and explore, confident they can call them back should any dangerous situation arise. Because parents of deaf children cannot call their children back, what would constitute normal behaviour for them? Should they keep them close by and be more protective than a parent of a hearing child, or let them run ahead and hope for the best, or should the children be better behaved so the parent can be certain that they will not run on the road. Likewise, at bedtime, when the deaf child is in bed with his or her aid removed, and the light switched off, s/he can feel very isolated and cut off from the world. Is it normal here to switch the light out, as one would for a hearing child, or leave the light on so the deaf child has some contact with the world? Although these examples may seem trivial, they do illustrate that 'normality' is not possible in a simple way in situations that differ from the usual ones. In interviews, parents made it clear how complex it seemed to them (Gregory 1976):

> I think that because she can't hear you and you can't tell her the first time. Like with a normal child you can say 'you do this again and I'll smack you next time you do it,' but with Wendy, you've either got to let her get away with it or else turn away. (Mother of three-year-old girl) (p. 21)

I mean you can't say, like when Janet (his sister) gets older, we'll say 'now you won't touch the fire because it will burn. Nasty. Hurts.' But all you say to Stephen is say 'no' and that's it. You can't explain why. It's horrible. (Mother of a four-year-old boy) (pp. 20-1)

The advice to treat deaf children normally seems to reflect the trend in advice about language, that is, where parents are told to talk normally. Teachers of the deaf are often in a very difficult position when they are expected to give advice on these more general issues. Firstly, they may have had no training in general problems of development that occur during the early years of life, and secondly, giving guidance on general, rather than educational matters is a very different skill, for which some teachers may be unprepared. To advise a parent on what is essentially how to be a parent involves a consideration of the needs and requirements of the whole family, together with an understanding of their needs and aspirations. The leaflets giving advice to parents, as well as stressing the necessity of a 'normal' approach, do seem to assume that certain values and particular life-styles are the general case, as is apparent in the following quotes: 'everybody needs time away from their children if the husband–wife relationship is to blossom' (p. 23); 'tantrums occur when there is a clash of wills, the parents' and the childs', and it is a necessary part of discipline that the parental will is achieved' (p. 17); 'it is useful to have a bedtime routine, one that you follow each night: children respond well to routine' (p. 18). These are all typical quotes from a current National Deaf Children's Society booklet of advice for parents of deaf children (McArthur, Tucker, Nolan and Fulbeck 1981).

Many teachers, of course, deal sensitively with these issues; some express uncertainty about giving advice on these more general matters because they do not feel they have the necessary expertise. However, this leads to a more basic problem that applies to all of the guidance they give, and that is the expectation of the parents that the teachers have the answers. The very existence of a parent guidance service implies that there are established ways of treating deaf children, which are successful, and which parents will be taught. Immediately a teacher rings the doorbell for the first time, at a home where there is a deaf child, s/he is put in a position where s/he is expected to have some answers. They may, and often do, feel inadequate to deal with some of the issues with which they are confronted, but nevertheless their very presence in that context implies they have some solutions. It does seem that the whole issue of guidance to families with young deaf children is not a simple one. As deafness is diagnosed earlier and earlier, and teachers deal with families with younger and younger children, an approach is needed that puts such work in perspective, rather than seeing it as an extension of the work of teachers in schools.

Conclusion

In this chapter I have looked at the situation of advising parents of deaf children as a way of illustrating some of the problems that arise in putting research into practice. I am aware that within the context of this book this could appear to be a highly negative chapter, as well as being extremely critical of researchers and practitioners. I am also aware that it would have been possible to take the same material and write a very optimistic and positive account, looking at the progress that has been made in the education of the deaf over the past 20 years, and the way theory has been applied in practice. However, in order to understand how theory can inform practice it is necessary to consider the problems that can arise.

In advising parents of children with disabilities there are fundamental issues that need to be considered as to what the counselling is to achieve and how this should be realised. How do we decide what should be the outcome and is it possible to talk of normal, natural development in a context that is essentially different? Moreover, is it possible to take behaviours that occur naturally and normally and facilitate these in a different situation, such as that created by a child who is deaf? Is it possible, in fact, to facilitate behaviour which is natural and spontaneous in a deliberate way? It is not that there are simple answers to these questions, but it is important that the assumptions underlying our procedures should be discussed and made explicit.

This chapter also considers the relationship between research and practice. Researchers do not necessarily see their role as that of solving problems as they occur in the world, and the way they proceed may well be counter-productive when it comes to applying their findings. Often the questions they ask are not ones that can inform practice. It is necessary for practitioners to be aware of the assumptions that are implied by the sort of advice that they give. In order to arrive at any reasonable practices it must be made clear not only how the procedures relate to our understanding of development but what they imply about our notions of how development should be, and what we accept as normal or desirable.

Acknowledgement

I am grateful to Juliet Bishop for her comments on an earlier version of this manuscript.

References

Chomsky, N. (1957) *Syntactic Structures*, The Hague: Mouton
——— (1965) *Aspects of a Theory of Syntax*, Cambridge, Mass.: MIT Press
Collett, R. (1976) 'Parent guidance', *Journal of the Society of Teachers of the Deaf*, 24
Commission of the European Communities (1979) *Childhood Deafness in the European Community*
Conrad, R. (1979) *The Deaf School Child*, London: Harper and Row
Dale, D.M.C. (1967) *Deaf Children at Home and School*, London: University of London Press
Ewing, A. and Ewing, E.C. (1964) *Teaching Deaf Children to Talk*, Manchester: Manchester University Press
Ewing, A. and Ewing, E.C. (1971) *Hearing Impaired Children under Five*, Manchester: Manchester University Press
Glendenning, H.C. (1976) 'Parent guidance', *Journal of the Society of Teachers of the Deaf*, 24
Gregory, S. (1976) *The Deaf Child and His Family*, London: George Allen and Unwin
——— (1983) Language development in deaf children: delayed or deviant. A paper presented at the Child Language Seminar, University of Strathclyde (March, 1983)
Gregory, S. and Mogford, K. (1981) Early language development in deaf children in J. Kyle, B. Woll and M. Deuchar (eds), *Perspectives on British Sign Language and Deafness*, London: Croom Helm
Hull and District Branch – National Deaf Children's Society (undated). A report on the Pre-school Peripatetic Service for Hearing-impaired Children in North Humberside
Krech, D. and Crutchfield, R.S. (1962) *Elements of Psychology*, New York: Alfred A. Knopf
McArthur, K., Tucker, I., Nolan, M. and Fulbeck, C. (1981) *Some of the Problems Encountered by the Parents of Hearing Impaired Children*, London: National Deaf Children's Society
McCormick, B. (1976) *A Parent's Guide*, London: National Deaf Children's Society
Mogford, K. and Gregory, S. (1980) Achieving understanding: a study of communication between mothers and their young deaf children. Paper presented at the British Psychological Society, Developmental Section Annual Conference, Edinburgh (September 1980)
Millar, G.A. (1963) *Language and Communication*, New York: McGraw Hill Book Co. Inc.
Nolan, M. and Tucker, I. (1981) *The Hearing Impaired Child and the Family*, London: Souvenir Press

Ochs, E. and Schieffelin, B.B. (1983) *Acquiring Conversational Competence*, London: Routledge and Kegan Paul

Tucker, I. and Nolan, M. (1984) *Educational Audiology*, London: Croom Helm

Warnock, M. (1978) *Special Educational Needs*, report of the committee of enquiry into the education of handicapped children and young people, Cmnd. No. 7212, London: HMSO

Whitehill, J.B. (1971) *Don't Turn a Deaf Ear*, London: National Deaf Children's Society

Williams, K. (1972) *You CAN Help Your Deaf Baby*, Burton-on-Trent, National College of Teachers of the Deaf

4 WAYS OF INCREASING PARENTAL INVOLVEMENT IN CHILDREN'S DEVELOPMENT AND EDUCATION

Sheila Wolfendale

The plan of this chapter is to identify some common components in parental involvement, briefly chart the growth of key areas and concepts and to demonstrate that in service settings the link between research and practice is intimate and intricate. The chapter begins by examining developments in parental involvement and some theoretical principles underlying examples in education and other settings. The areas of parental involvement in reading, the Portage scheme and assessment have been chosen as particularly appropriate illustrations of collaboration between parents and professionals in which research and development have been synonymous with the application of theoretical principles. Some problems inherent in the definition of terms are addressed and the final section considers the unique inter-relation of research and practice in the provision of services to families.

Starting Points

'By involving the parents, the children may be helped.' (Plowden Report 1967: para 114)

This assertion, simply and shortly expressed, became a clarion call and the Plowden Report itself, as it turned out, was a rallying point for action that flowed from its recommendations. The significance of the Plowden Report lies not only in its impact when published, nor in its continuing influence in education, but uniquely in its timing.

At the time when committee members were gathering evidence for the Report, information was already available about the American Head Start projects. Echoes of the rationale of Head Start could be discerned in the notion of 'positive discrimination' put forward in Chapter Five of Plowden, 'Educational Priority Areas'. The territory, pre-Plowden, of home–school links (Craft, Raynor and Cohen 1980) had been barren; the EPA projects which had included parental involvement and home–school liaison (Halsey 1972; Woodhead 1976; Mortimore and Blackstone 1982) paved the way for subsequent work in what is turning out to be a blossoming area.

73

It had been an integral part of a substantial number of Head Start programmes to involve parents and a number of writers have outlined prerequisites for effective parental participation, and described the form of such family-focused intervention (Bronfenbrenner 1979; Donachy 1979; Shipman 1979).

Other Government reports on education and child services have, like Plowden, contained key recommendations for a *rapprochement* between parents and professionals and for closer working links between family and school (Bullock 1975; Court 1976; Taylor 1977; Warnock 1978). Each of these reports has invoked and relied upon the evidence from many intervention projects that indicate that parental involvement in educational and community-based programmes is beneficial to children's learning and well-being.

Clearly, the bodies who comprised these committees intended that their suggestions should be heeded and translated into policy, thence into practice. Welton (1982: 45) highlights in these words the difficulties of distinguishing between the impact of research, 'good practice' and the influence of government reports:

> The Warnock Committee worked largely within the current trends of professional opinion. Such Government-appointed committees rarely forage far outside the range of accepted professional opinion, but grant the accolade of good *practice* to a favoured emergent trend within existing practice.

As far as can be judged the usefulness of the recommendations pertaining to parental involvement in the five government reports cited here is that for policy-makers and practitioners they collectively provide official backing for action.

The area of parental involvement highlights issues that pertain to the relationship between research and practice in child-focused services. There are examples of modest, homespun schemes, in local schools where teachers and parents have been working together but would not think of communicating their experience to a national audience. Then there are well-documented and well-publicised initiatives which provide the inspiration and models for work elsewhere. How easy is it, then, to pinpoint exactly the genesis and emergence of developments that are later designated as a 'trend'? And who do we describe as the researchers? It will be seen later in the chapter that innovative development work in service settings for children and their families can legitimately be part of the brief of professionals whose training equips them to incorporate a developmental and evaluative role into their duties.

Universals

A theme which has preoccupied this author for some time (Wolfendale 1983) is whether or not it is possible in the interests of 'child psychology in action' to effect a synthesis across areas (Scott and Grimmett 1977). Workers in the child services wearily attest to an oft-observed lack of unity between agencies; of disparate, sometimes duplicated provision and a dearth of prior inter-agency consultation. Parents' groups organised within community settings by social services may co-exist with, but in ignorance of, similar groups in a local school. Another example from my own experience is where a local education network, set up with care and thoughtfulness to identify pre-school children with possible special educational needs, turns out to exclude non-education personnel who have direct access to parents.

Bradley's (1982) statement on the need for co-ordination for services, whilst issued in the context of under fives provision, nevertheless provides a viable framework for adoption in other areas of service delivery on behalf of children and families. After all, we can by now identify enough 'universals' in terms of the rationales, aims and the means of realising the aims to urge co-ordinated policies in parental involvement on the part of statutory and locally operating voluntary services.

Rationales for Parental Involvement Programmes

Bronfenbrenner persuasively articulated the justification for the inclusion, if not equal participation, of parents in intervention programmes (Bronfenbrenner 1976). The grounds are that the citizen's rights to participation in the community should extend to parents and their rights to have knowledge of, access to, and participation in services to their children, particularly education (see the chapter by Cochran, this volume).

This principle extends the idea of compensatory education for the allegedly disadvantaged minority and broadens the conception to be applicable to all children and their families. There is always contradiction inherent in 'positive discrimination'; whilst it can be viewed as a benign and well-intentioned initiative on behalf of the less advantaged in society, it is at the same time separatist, flouts principles of equal opportunities, drives an insidious and invidious wedge between groupings in society, and finally resolves none of the underlying socio-political dilemmas that confront us all.

The premise for universal applicability is the ecological approach espoused by Hobbs (1978), Bronfenbrenner (1979) and Apter (1982). In mapping an ecosystem for each child it is possible to incorporate shifts of activity, growth points, transient or enduring problems, as well as the people who impinge upon the child and the institutions they represent. Bronfenbrenner affirms that parents (and equivalent main adult caregivers) are supremely placed to be the child's prime educators and ecosystem mapping, which owes much to the topological and life space theories of Lewin (in Bronfenbrenner 1979), could be a useful practitioner's aid in planning family-focus and parental involvement programmes (see Cochran, this volume).

Recent research Wells 1983; Tizard and Hughes 1984) has compellingly demonstrated the power of parents to enhance children's development and learning potential, and in fact to create, wittingly or unintentionally, the conditions that best promote these. This point is made by Davie, Hutt, Vincent and Mason (1984) who give ample examples of 'real life' learning experiences in the home. Whilst research has demonstrated that opportunity for learning at home is characterised by the unique tempo and rhythm of parent–child interaction, it remains the preoccupation of practitioners as well as of researchers as to how to ensure 'goodness of fit' between this experience for the child and more formalised and less spontaneous educational settings.

Aims and Means for Parental Involvement Programmes

There is a range of parental involvement programmes from those with unambitious aims, and low-key routinely available means of realising them, to others with large-scale aspirations with correspondingly complex procedures for their translation to practice. Irrespective of scale, aims in common include: *parents* gaining knowledge about contemporary education, participating directly with the curriculum, via 'helping' in school, or by contracting into a home-based reading programme and getting to know teachers; *teachers* getting to know parents and the family contexts of children they teach, gaining support and endorsement from home; *children*'s performance being maintained or even boosted, and the credibility gap (in their eyes) between home and school being reduced. This author (Wolfendale

1983) has outlined a variety of objectives and outcomes for the participants in the exercise (children, parents, teachers) and ventured a taxonomy for the purposes of providing a solid conceptual framework for this fast-developing area.

Initiatives in Parental Involvement

Education

Take-up has been most extensive in education, with an evident increase in parental presence in schools and in the formation of parent–teacher associations in the 1970s (Cyster, Clift and Battle: 1979). The Cyster survey, as well as that of HMI (1978), attests to the contribution of parents (mothers in the main) in school 'chores' as well as some curriculum involvement, such as hearing children read under teachers' direction (Stierer 1984). Involvement in reading is the most popular form of parental involvement and here events have moved swiftly since the late 1970s. The phenomenon of parental involvement in reading is chronicled a little later in this chapter as one of the major examples of a link between research and practice.

Another example, described later, is that of parental involvement in the area of assessment of children with special educational needs. Yet another development, that may grow in significance as its effects become manifest, is that of the presence of parents on governing bodies. Since the 1980 Education Act took effect and mandated the provision of parent governors, many parents are gaining expertise at local government level. They are developing competence in information gathering, representing, lobbying, acquiring knowledge about articles and instruments of governing, preparing and working through agendas and minute-taking. Training for school governing is becoming available to a wider number of people (cf. Open University 1981; George, in press).

Many initiatives are at the 'micro' level and without reference to other schools within the same local education authority. There are now, however, developments at a 'macro' level, where an LEA may commission or be involved in feasibility studies (Hills 1984; Percival 1984) concerning parental involvement in education and the community, or vote the money for implementation of policy as, for example, in the case of Coventry Community Education Development Centre (see also Newham Parents' Centre 1984; Davis 1984). Although a substantial number of initiatives appear to be duplicates of others, they cannot really even be replications. Each locality's situation differs markedly; the priorities differ, the reasons for adoption are unique to the situation, the responsibilities and deployment of personnel vary. Evaluation has been built in to a number of initiatives (Davis 1984) in recognition of the fact that parental involvement may have been convincingly demonstrated in one case, but not proven to be consistently effective in other situations.

Co-operation Between Agencies

There are now a considerable number of examples of inter-agency collaboration between professionals and parents in the broad area referred to as special educational needs. The best developed is 'Portage' (see pp. 84-8) which brings together personnel from statutory and voluntary services into a working 'partnership' with parents.

Work with the under fives is also proving to be productive territory for exploring inter-agency links locally (Aitman and Samuel, forthcoming) and for involving parents. The aims of a current DHSS funded project, based at the National Children's Bureau and entitled 'Services for Families with Young Children', hint at a theory-base and principles for 'good' practice which the project seeks to uncover and disseminate. In particular, aim no. 2 (of 3) expresses the envisaged network of services in which parents would play an equal part: 'to identify and examine a number of initiatives in which a working partnership is achieved between parents and workers in the health, education, social services and voluntary sectors' (Pugh and De'Ath 1984).

In recent years professional 'para-medical' groups have included domiciliary visiting as part of their practice, in combination with parent and child attendance at health centres and units. Physiotherapists, occupational and speech therapists now have substantial experience in supporting parents who are trying out home-based programmes under their guidance. Another development to watch is the increasing number of appointments of home-liaison workers for young children with special educational needs, posts advocated by the Warnock Report to encourage liaison between parents and local authority agencies.

Multi-disciplinary work has long been a feature of child guidance and it could be argued that the widespread adoption of family therapy in clinics in the UK represents a modest move towards the democratisation of therapy. For families can at last be consulted about problems and priorities and be co-signatories to a contract that stipulates treatment goals and time-limits (Walrond-Skinner 1981).

Some developments in social services parallel those mentioned in this section. Social workers, lawyers and others working in child care became concerned during the 1970s that the best interests of children and their families were not being served by prevailing assessment, court and treatment procedures (Taylor, Lacey and Bracken 1979). The Family Rights Group was formed in 1975 and among other aims, it sets out to ensure parental representation and involvement in such legal and administrative proceedings (see references for addresses, p. 97). For further reading on studies and discussion of community-based services see Bender (1976), Craft, Raynor and Cohen (1980) and Pringle (1980).

The main objective of the first part of this chapter has been to provide a 'broad brush' overview of current work in parent–professional co-operation. What follows now is an attempt to demonstrate the association between research and practice in several selected areas, each of which illustrates the unprecedented extent of co-working between professionals as well as with other 'new' co-workers, the parents.

Parental Involvement in Children's Reading

Earlier in this chapter reference was made to parental involvement in reading, to home and school-based programmes. The traditional custom has been for teachers to send books home (the reading primer or other class book) so that the child can read aloud to his/her parents who note down the pages read on a card and return book and card to school. Current practice has its roots in this time-honoured custom, as well as in the intrinsic interest of parents in their children's educational progress and their desire to contribute in some way. This is an extension of joint parent–child activities that can start from birth, telling and listening to stories (Wade 1984), singing and enacting nursery rhymes and folk-tales.

Parental involvement in children's reading is a rapidly growing area and its take-up and parameters are currently being chronicled (Topping and Wolfendale 1985). Irrespective of scope, the bulk of programmes have in common a number of basic principles, of which the central one is the belief that determined co-operation between teachers and parents can prove to be a positive, fruitful exercise on behalf of children. Among other principles that apply to these programmes are:

(i)   their starting points are in contemporary educational practice;

(ii) they remain schools' responsibility and within the control and direction of teachers, even when 'out of school' personnel are involved, such as educational psychologists and advisers;

(iii) they are aimed not only at maintenance or acceleration of reading progress but also at

    (a) 'spin-offs' associated with children's performance, for example, improved links between home and school;

    (b) promotion of the idea that learning, when extended into non-school settings, can be enjoyable to child and adult;

(iv) they can be described as hypothesis-testing exercises, for even the humblest, first-time try-out represents an exploration for staff and parents and their findings constitute 'evidence' one way or another for a scheme's continued viability.

There are a number of reasons why reading has become such a focus for conjoint home-school activity. Reading is used as a prime educational activity *per se*, is seen as the stepping stone to adult literacy and as a main medium for access to the rest of the curriculum. By involvement in reading schemes parents gain some knowledge about the mysteries of teaching and in fact participate in the teaching. Teachers do not abdicate any part of their function; indeed they may well strengthen and enhance their position when parents perceive the complexities of teaching this key area of the curriculum. With the receipt of appropriate training and guidance, parents can become demonstrably versed in a particular method (see below) and available reading material is usually to hand, whether or not supplemented by library loan or additional resources produced for the scheme by the school.

Take-up of Parental Involvement in Reading

Although the above-mentioned book by Topping and Wolfendale claims to provide the first major review of the 'state of the art', it is not possible to produce facts and figures. Through the networks established by people working in this topic-area, it is possible to 'guesstimate' that in most LEAs there is something going on – the range includes low-key parental involvement in schools, local schemes (a number of schools involved in try-out exercises), and local in-service training where the goal is to equip teachers to introduce schemes in their schools.

A substantial number of local projects are explicitly based upon published work, particularly that now regarded as seminal (for example, the Harringay work– Tizard, Schofield and Hewison 1982; the Belfield Project – Jackson, Pond and Hannon 1981; Hackney PACT – Griffiths and Hamilton 1984; the Derbyshire Paired Reading – Miller, Robson and Bushell, in press). Accounts of these and other influential studies are included in the Topping and Wolfendale review.

If one is to use the growing bibliographies (mostly journal articles, local write-ups, manuals, packs, etc.) and citations as a guide (and this can only be a crude indicator of take-up) then we do have confirmation of exponential growth in the area.

Features of Parental Involvement in Reading

Timing and Length. The majority of schemes involve nightly (or several nights a week) reading sessions of 10-15 minutes each. The work may take place with children in the early stages of reading or with those of any age who have reading difficulties. The length of projects vary, the shortest last four to six weeks, with a renewable option, while others may be longitudinal studies of performance and effects over several years (Belfield, PACT, Derbyshire, Kirklees – see Topping and McKnight (1984)).

Methods. These are becoming increasingly sophisticated as people are effecting better matches between the task and the learner. Topping and Wolfendale needed working demarcations for their review but are well aware that methods can be combined and a comparison of methods is in fact the *raison d'être* of some studies.

(i) *Parents listening to children reading.* Hearing children read has long been standard practice and reading specialists place a high premium on its value (Moyle 1968; the Bullock Report 1975; Southgate, Arnold and Johnson 1981) as both a teaching aid and a learning device. The parent listens to the child reading, is asked to praise often yet appropriately, and is instructed to 'deal' with hesitation or error in whatever way the school has suggested. For example, the parent may be 'allowed' to correct, to provide the right word, or just the first syllable; in a phonics-focused approach 'sounding out' and 'building up' techniques may be the instructional method; another approach may include self-correction as a main means of learning. Hearing children read can be applicable to look and say, key words, sentence methods, phonics and language experience models.

(ii) *Behavioural approaches.* These are characterised by an explicit theoretical rationale, and by the degree of specificity in their implementation. They are applicable to hearing children read as well as to the particular formula of paired reading (see below). Topping and Wolfendale (1985) differentiate and describe four behavioural approaches: reinforcement; pause, prompt and praise (Glyn 1980); precision teaching (PAIRS project, White, Solity and Reeve 1984); and direct instruction.

(iii) *Paired Reading.* A small-scale study involving several children (Morgan and Lyon 1979) has been replicated and extended in many settings, two of which are particularly of note. One is the Derbyshire-based work of Miller *et al.* (see above); the other is a five-year Urban Aid funded project based in Kirklees (Topping and McKnight 1984). The take-up of paired reading is extensive and its reported efficacy is considerable.

Paired Reading comprises two phases: in the first, parent and child read aloud together (simultaneous mode) and the child is required to attempt each word. They read in synchrony with the adult adjusting reading pace to fit the child's. When the child makes a mistake, the adult gives the right word and reading aloud together resumes. The second phase is independent reading – when the children feel confident and ready to read alone they are taught to give a signal (knock on a surface, nudge, touch or other non-verbal gesture) and the adult ceases to read. When a child makes an error, the adult corrects as before (modelling and expecting repetition) and the pair resume simultaneous reading until the child signals once more.

Training. Some of the procedures are elaborate, with manuals and video accompanying teacher and parent training. Standard requisites include parental instruction on 'teaching points' (the famous DO's and DON'Ts sheet), the method(s) to be used and an introduction to the daily/weekly recording system. The training forum can be a straight talk, workshop, demonstration or home visit.

Planning Considerations. This author has found it useful when discussing parental involvement in reading with teachers and as a precursor to action to provide an *aide mémoire*, some features of which are reproduced below. The list is not a prescription but is offered as planning guidelines.

Roles: What part will psychologist, teacher(s), parent(s), child agree to play, and what will be the areas of responsibility.

Who For: Initial learners (infant school) or older children with reading difficulties (junior, middle, secondary).

Material: School books; library loan; remedial/resource centre loan; pre-prepared cards and sheets; storage and access.

Type of Programme: Paired reading; child reading; parent reading; language experience approach. What kind of correction and reinforcement will be built in.

Training: For teacher(s) and parents. Workshop, meeting, visits. One or more sessions. Use of video, role play to make points.

Measurement and Recording: Selection criteria; samples; controls and comparisons; pre- and post-assessment measures; monitoring and probing; record keeping for teachers and parents; when and where to see parents.

Time Span: Decide at planning stage length of reading programme. Build in renewable option.

Criteria for Evaluation: Result of pre, post and any other assessment; teachers', parents', childrens' views; follow-up; cost-effectiveness criteria; repeatability and generalisability. If renewed, does the provision become part of school's home–school policy?

Results and Outcomes. The overwhelming majority of project write-ups report gains over time, in terms of significantly improved reading ages, other measures of reading attainment and associated benefits. Is this the conclusive 'proof' one yearns for in educational research? Can we say that parental involvement in reading 'works', that hypothesis testing gives affirmative evidence? Perhaps the effectiveness is nothing more than the fact that there is more exposure of the participating children to reading?

Even if this is the case, we do need to have more information about the nature of the intervention. Interpretation of the results has to go beyond bluntly measured outcomes to examine the conditions that bring about success. Now, after the first euphoric waves have passed, we can begin to look soberly at the efficacy of different methods and at the quality of the parental teaching.

One remarkable feature of parental involvement in the teaching of reading is that it is creating and sustaining its own momentum; that although the link between research and practice is demonstrable, the chain reaction of events defies simplistic association. The link is not one of pure research preceding practical applications but of research *on* practical applications; research and practice thus become two interrelated aspects of the same scheme. It is not surprising, therefore, that both formal (publication; in-service teacher training) as well as informal (word of mouth, personal contact) means of communicating are playing a part in spreading the word about new ideas and innovative practical schemes.

Research evidence (Young and Tyre 1983) is providing other practitioners within education with information regarding the requisites and conditions for successful outcomes (see the planning *aide mémoire* above for instance). A number of the studies retain as many features of experimental design as is feasible and appropriate for the circumstances – these impart some rigour into an aspect of educational provision that is usually lacking objective evaluation. Even the routine teaching of reading is not usually subject to such scrutiny! Thus, some measure of accountability is guaranteed as the analysis of the findings will determine whether or not the exercise will be repeated. Whether we have finally discovered the formula, which allows the fullest expression of parents as educators such that their presence becomes a guaranteed part of educational provision, remains to be seen.

Portage as a Service for Families

Portage, like parental involvement in reading, is already a success story in terms of its rapid take-up since its introduction to the UK in the mid-1970s and in its demonstrable effectiveness. It is described as a 'home teaching service' and brings together parents of young children with handicaps and early-appearing special educational needs with professionals in child development from a number of disciplines.

The Origins of Portage

What Portage is and how it is used has been well-documented in books and articles (Pugh 1981). It originated in Portage, Wisconsin, USA (hence the name). A local scheme, aimed to develop, implement and demonstrate a model programme serving young handicapped children in a rural area, it received funding in 1969 from the American government under one of the Education of the Handicapped Acts. In 1972 the Portage model was selected to be one of eight exemplary pre-school programmes for handicapped children in the United States, and in 1975 it received from the US Office of Education the accolade of being recommended for national dissemination and replication. By 1977 60 Portage services were reported to be operating in America. Portage was introduced to the UK during the 1970s, the first two services (in Hampshire and in South Glamorgan) having research and evaluative components as integral features.

Adoption of Portage as part of service delivery has taken place in all parts of the UK and has involved parents, children and professionals who have never before worked together. It is spreading into schools and is now regarded as being appropriate for various age-groups.

The Principles and Practice of Portage

The core of the model is the daily teaching activity with the child, carried out by the parents in their own home. Once a week they receive a visit from the Home Visitor (who can be a teacher, psychologist, health visitor, speech therapist or fellow parent) who has received instruction in the behavioural principles underlying the model.

During the visit progress is reviewed, targets achieved are demonstrated and new targets, which are modelled by the home visitor with the child, are set for the coming week. During the week the parent practises and records the outcome of the daily teaching trials on a daily activity chart. The Portage equipment (available from the National Foundation for Educational Research) consists of a detailed developmental check-list, a comprehensive set of activity cards, activity charts, manuals and back-up reading materials (Revill and Blunden 1980; Frohman, Weber and Wollenburg, 1983).

An adequate initial training normally lasts two or three days and consists of theory (behavioural principles), rationale (principles applied to Portage); and application to practice with plenty of try-out or simulation exercises, covering task analysis, teaching targets, prompting, correcting, reinforcing and managing behaviour.

In terms of organisation the Portage model is conceived of as a pyramid (see below) but without the hierarchy usually associated with such concepts.

Figure 4.1: The Portage Structure

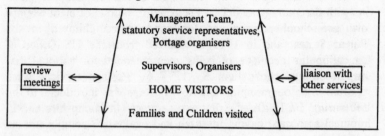

Home visitors report to supervisors (experienced home visitors) who offer support and guidance. Supervisors and organisers report to the management team, members of which are in a position to make recommendations for funding, prepare reports for their committees and provide a liaison role with other sectors of the community. Thus accountability is built in at each stage.

Using Portage

There are thought to be well in excess of 100 Portage services and schemes in existence, mostly aimed at pre-school, but increasingly at older age-groups.

In the UK, funding comes from a variety of sources; it may come from regular local authority service budgets, it may be joint (local authority services) or specially funded (for example, by a voluntary agency). There are an increasing number of Portage organiser posts which are newly created and specially funded. One measure of the significance of Portage is the formation during 1983 of a National Portage Association set up to foster and steer the development of services and to provide a clearing-house for the dissemination of good practice. The popularity of the model has also been amply exhibited by the growth in attendance by parents and professional workers at the Annual Portage Conference (four to date).

Portage has demonstrated beyond any doubt that no one profession in the child-focused disciplines has a monopoly on knowledge of child development and on the skills that are appropriate for problem-solving, for intervening and 'treating'. The behavioural framework can be embraced by workers whose training might not have included such principles and by parents whose prior experience would seem at first sight quite alien and remote from the rigour of applied behavioural analysis.

Evaluation

As with parental involvement in reading, Portage is successful (in its own terms) and each reported success generates the introduction of Portage in other parts of the country. Evidence of the effectiveness of the particular theory–practice match – the hallmark of Portage – is met at various levels.

Individual Child Level. Children make discernible progress, they progress through the developmental check-list and they attain skills. Using pre- and post-baseline measures, progress can be plotted minutely, and success is inbuilt and guaranteed; if targets are not achieved they are revised and the conditions and instructions are reappraised. The deficit model is not invoked; expected, aspired-for performance is finely calculated and participants work hard to avoid errors of judgement in target- and goal-setting.

To assess progress, via the number of new behaviours (skills) attained over a given period of time, is an important index, but not the sole one. Other indices of consumer satisfaction (see below) are as important. External criteria have some value as long as they are not regarded as being definitive and other developmental schedules, or assessment instruments, may represent objective, normative checks upon the significance of *rate* of progress achieved. However, Portage is a finely tuned instrument in its execution and only a comparable means of assessment could provide a viable index of, and check upon, performance; unfortunately, none exists in a widely available form (Gaussen 1984). Another possibility is to compare 'Portage children' with 'non-Portage children'. However, this approach might be considered unethical if the exercise required specially selected groups of children, and it would also face considerable problems in controlling extraneous variables.

Participant Level. A number of evaluation studies (Bendall, Smith and Kushlick 1984) looked at expressed satisfaction and dissatisfaction on the part of parents and other Portage workers. While the majority expressed satisfaction on a number of counts, it is important to remember that the study invited comparisons between Portage and service provision prior to the introduction of Portage.

Policy Level. At planning and decision-making levels the operation of Portage has provided proof that it is a cost-effective means of providing services, that it does not (and is not intended to) supplant existing services for young children. In fact, it supplements these services, and may be seen to enhance them, in terms of maximising professional skills, and reducing the overlap and duplication that is at times inevitable. During 1984 Portage received endorsement from the Department of Science and the Secretary of State for Education.

Evaluation studies (Bendall *et al.* 1984) which examine aspects of Portage to do with take-up, maintenance, time spent on task, involvement of both parents, and professional involvement are emerging with pointers for improving the level of service offered. For example, the place of parents in what is referred to as a partnership (see discussion below) may actually turn out not to be a truly egalitarian relationship; the parent–parent network is not as developed nor as powerful as the professional one.

The theoretical credentials of Portage are impeccable, its origins rooted in the action-research mould of Head Start and the highly credible work of behaviourally oriented psychologists. As for its destinations, articles in Portage Conference proceedings (Cameron 1982; Dessent 1984; Daly, Addington, Kerfoot and Sigston 1985) attest to the versatility of the model and its derivations. Regarding its future, there are a number of areas to be explored, for example, the longer-term translation of newly-found parental skills into later child-rearing and behaviour management of Portage children. These are but speculative examples to demonstrate the potential of Portage in linking research and practice in the long term.

Parental Involvement in Assessment

The third and last example of parental involvement in action with professionals from different disciplines, and one which represents 'development' work, is another from the area of special needs and clinical practice. The reader will recognise a relationship between Portage and parallel work in other areas, certainly in terms of their shared premises: that parents are experts *vis-à-vis* their own children and their skills complement professional skills; they can be highly effective teachers of their children and have the right to be fully involved in decision-making.

There has been considerable derivation and application from the pioneering work of Gesell and his colleagues, during and after the

1930s, into establishing norms of development. Developmental assessment has become a prime tool in the clinician's 'kitbag', though its value as applied to young children has its limitations (Gaussen 1984). However, it is currently proving to be a clinically and diagnostically valuable vehicle when used in conjuction with parents' own skills of observing their children at home and their competence in assessing development (cf. the Portage developmental check-list already mentioned).

Existing schedules have been adapted for conjoint use by parents and other people working with young children. Examples include the PIP charts (Jeffree and McConkey 1978) developed at the Hester Adrian Research Centre, University of Manchester, and the 'All about Me' developmental guide, currently being piloted by this author (Wolfendale 1984b). Cunningham and Sloper (1984) conducted a study into the relationship between maternal ratings of first word vocabulary and Reynell language scores. After exploring the nature of discrepancy, as well as concordance between parental and professional assessment, they concluded: 'we would suggest that parents of handicapped children can make reliable assessment of their children's attainment' (p. 166). Meltzer, Levine, Hanson, Wasserman, Schneider and Sullivan (1983) explored the multiprofessional dimensions of an approach in which contributions to children's developmental assessment were made by parents and others and commented that 'such investigations, it is hoped, will demonstrate zones of commonality among these observers in conjunction with their unique contributions' (p. 211).

Parental profiling (Wolfendale 1984a) explores the parental contribution to assessment in an enterprise in which parents and professionals work together to define a perceived problem, the parents compile a 'child-at-home' profile which complements clinical assessment and plans can then be made for appropriate joint intervention.

Parental Contribution to the 1981 Education Act: Assessment and Statementing Procedures

The Warnock Report cited Portage as an example of contemporary good practice and called for professionals to develop closer and more effective working relationships with parents. The 1981 Education Act has embodied much of Warnock 'thinking' and extends and makes explicit parents' rights in special education, referral procedures, decision-making and assessment.

A DES-based working party, of which this author is a member, has been working on the production of guidelines which will enable parents to present their 'views' on their child, the 'problem', and the best ways of meeting their child's special educational needs. The guidelines, which it is hoped professionals will find useful in assisting them to assist parents to make their rightful contribution, were piloted in 1984 (contact this author for further information).

These initiatives and others based on research (Newson and Hipgrave 1982; Mittler and McConachie 1983) are paving the way towards a more effective match between those engaged in a clinical dialogue. Inherited traditions and recent innovations in child development research are now combining forces with the collective and accumulating stock of parental insights and wisdom.

Definitions and Terminologies

In this chapter, work in hand has been described until now without defining the nature of parental involvement. In principle, parental involvement encompasses a continuum from the most incidental and fleeting participation in school activities to the fullest expression of partnership. In practice, if such activity were plotted on a graph, one would see a sustained rise over time (the last 10-15 years) in activity frequency and an evident 'central tendency' of moderate involvement.

In Britain, the idea of partnership with parents is certainly controversial. Many practitioners (teachers, for example) regard the idea as being impractical and undesirable. The role demarcations must not be blurred, democracy and full voting rights for all parents were never, can never, be part of education. Yet hallowed tradition is being eroded by the advent of parents into curriculum practice (via parental involvement in reading, parents as 'para-professionals' in the classroom) and parental representation on school governing bodies.

These are examples of parental involvement (which can be measured in degrees) but not of partnership. There have been recent attempts to define parent–professional partnership based on practice. Two such definitions are given below, the latter one being couched in terms of partner characteristics:

1. Partnership involved a full sharing of knowledge, skills and experience. A commitment to partnership rests on the assumption that children will learn and develop better if parents and professionals are working together on a basis of equality than if

either is working in isolation. (Mittler and McConachie 1983: 10)
2. The distinction is made (Wolfendale 1983: 15) between the characteristics of parents viewed as 'clients' and those of parents perceived as 'partners' in an enterprise. These latter include:
   – parents are active and central in decision-making and its implementation;
   – parents are perceived as having equal strengths and equivalent expertise;
   – parents are able to contribute to, as well as receive, services;
   – parents share responsibility; thus they and professionals are mutually accountable.

Perhaps the existing checks and balances that maintain the structure in mainstream education will ensure that 'true' partnership with parents can never come about. There is not enough evidence that parents would welcome an invitation to share responsibility to the full (but compare this situation with the Canadian province of Alberta, where parental involvement is mandated, school boards have to demonstrate their policy in order to receive federal funds, and parents are expected to share in decision-making).

We do, however, have sufficient evidence from parental involvement in reading programmes that parents respond enthusiastically to participating in educational processes. Perhaps we need to press on with researching the nuts and bolts of participation before we can prescribe the philosophy.

It was noted earlier in this chapter that Portage is the most advanced exponent of a working partnership between parents and professionals that we have in the UK at present – in terms of a compact and coherently organised service delivery model with clear lines of communication and some in-built accountability. But the professionals are still demonstrably the 'senior partner' in the enterprise and parents are far from being co-instigators.

For partnership to be a realistic aspiration would require a radical shift in power base, vested interest and designated areas of responsibility, along the lines of the Regional Intervention Program (RIP) described as a 'parent implemented coordinated data-based, cost-effective early intervention service for high-risk children in Tennessee' (Hester 1977: 261). Evaluation at all levels is built in to RIP and Hester observes (p. 266) that 'citizen participation, in particular citizen power, in program policy and management is important in warding off inequitable treatment'.

Bridging Research and Practice in Parental Involvement

'Practice', in this chapter, has been used synonymously with 'service delivery' in part to demonstrate how principles have been translated into action, at 'macro' (provision of services in schools, districts, communities) and 'micro' ('on the ground' services, agency resources of personnel and schemes, clinical settings) levels. Practice can then encompass the clinical duet between 'client' and clinician as well as multiprofessional–parent networks.

As can be seen from the examplars outlined in this chapter, as well as a myriad of other examples from applied psychology, many practitioners are also innovators and quasi-researchers. They do not demarcate between research that originates from a 'real' problem to be solved, a social phenomenon to explore, and the problems and phenomena that are already rooted in their daily practice. For many applied psychologists and specialists in child development, their prior training has already equipped them to research as part of their brief; they would see themselves as being equipped to translate and apply the findings of academic research and theory-building to the settings in which they work.

The last 20 years have witnessed a mammoth increase in social science personnel and a keen desire on their part to demonstrate their relevance, to marry humanitarian aspirations with scientific rigour. The purity of such ideals is bedevilled by pitfalls that are endemic within society's existing structures — certainly in 'sophisticated' Western worlds. Power is vested firmly within ruling cliques in the institutions referred to in this chapter and they will not lightly share this with clients and consumers (Barton and Moody 1981; Gleidman and Roth 1981; Tomlinson 1982; Potts 1983).

These realities affect the methodology of hypothesis-testing exercises intended to explore the parameters and ramifications of involving parents in their children's development and education. Ethical considerations also influence methodological niceties; easier said than done to introduce control groups into intervention programmes that are in fact 'for real' and are not regarded by practitioners who care for children on a daily basis (teachers, nursery nurses) as experiments. There is plenty of first-hand anecdotal (but none the less vital) evidence that these practitioners endorse a certain amount of initiative by others on their behalf but proceed cautiously in the wholesale adoption of innovative practice. The area of parental involvement from pre-school to the adolescent years bears out these observations.

Likewise, looking at it 'top-down', committee members and policy-makers often show ambivalence to the recommendations made by the 'change-agents' whom they employ. Applied psychologists experience an inherent tension in their work – they are employed to problem-solve, but this involves some pioneering of methods which pre-empt and anticipate problems, as well as resolve them. Pioneering necessitates researching, mapping and marking terrain. The findings and the proposed solutions are not always comfortable for people whose job it is to be concerned with the administration and maintenance of systems.

But the prognosis is not gloomy if we are prepared to redefine and reappraise the concept of research in applied settings and reassess the role of the researcher. Apart from specific exercises, such as work for a PhD or a specially funded and finite research project, much research work aims, as was stated earlier, to be relevant to practice. Hence there is a dynamism built into the researcher's role especially when that individual stays around to apply the findings, replicate or extend or modify the study. The part that educational psychologists play in instigating, supporting, monitoring and evaluating parental involvement in reading programmes is an instance of the researcher-cum-participant model. Although it can be argued that some objectivity is lost by having participant research, in which the investigator also has a role, equally too much valuable data may be lost by bringing in cold, external researchers who are not attuned to the nuances of a system (a school, a unit, a service like Portage), personality interplay, role conflict and the like. (See McConkey this volume for a discussion of service based research.)

The rationale here is that when dealing with phenomena and problems pertaining to children and their families we need researchers who have knowledge of, and can identify with, the issues under scrutiny – clinicians with experience of working with parents and children on new-style conjoint assessment procedures as described above illustrate this particular point. And society needs evaluators who have knowledge of the systems to ensure, to paraphrase Hester (above), 'equitable treatment'. Thus, research takes place in direct co-operation with the practice that it seeks to serve: 'the research is intervening in the practice and has a say in changing it' (Elliott and Whitehead 1980: 10).

Concluding Comments

It may not be too fanciful to suppose on the basis of existing evidence that the methods of enquiry and analysis of the behavioural sciences have had an impact upon society, especially those provisions that serve the needs of children. Although there exists the particular tension between the findings of research and their eventual effects upon practice, nevertheless the influence upon policy-making is discernible (Zigler, Kagan and Klugman 1983). The constraints are economic as much as they are political and each and both may be used as reasons for inaction, even when research findings *per se* are endorsed by all levels of the hierarchy. (See Galloway, this volume, for a discussion of the effects of research on policy development and policy implementation.)

The realities of the situation need not depress those working as researcher–practitioners. It is tentatively suggested that the most profound influence that research and evaluation may have had upon service delivery is to halt the growth of *ad hoc*, piecemeal services that spring up, unco-ordinated and ill-thought-out in relation to parallel provision. Service growth has evolved in response to immediate need, with no real rationale beyond a certain face validity. Statutory services now have departments of planning, of research and evaluation, they have links with each other, via joint committees and joint funding. The present government, for its own ideological reasons, has encouraged a higher local profile for voluntary associations and, at the community interface, they and the statutory services are working in conjunction.

The area of parental and community involvement is a particularly vital one at present in illustrating how research can be indivisible from practice. The adoption of policy (based on the research–practice interplay) can be evaluated and the loftiest aspirations of research can be translated into viable ideas to be 'handed over' to those who have the constant care of children in nurseries, schools, centres and at home.

References

Aitman, J.B. and Samuel, J.C. (forthcoming) Psychologists in the community, *Early Child Development and care*

Apter, S. (1982) *Troubled Children, Troubled Systems*, Oxford: Pergamon Press

Barton, L. and Moody, S. (1981) The value of parents to the ESN(S) school: an examination in L. Barton and S. Tomlinson (eds), *Special Education: Policy, Practices and Social Issues*, London: Harper and Row

Bendall, S., Smith, J. and Kushlick, A. (1984) *A National Study of Portage-type Home Teaching Services*, Vols. I, II, III, Report No. 162, January, from Health Care Evaluation Research Team, Highfield, Southampton University

Bender, M. (1976) *Community Psychology*, London: Essential Psychology

Bradley, M. (1982) *The Coordination of Services for Children under Five*, Windsor: NFER-Nelson

Bronfenbrenner, U. (1976) Is early intervention effective? Facts and principles of early intervention: a summary in A.D.B. Clarke and A. Clarke (eds), *Early Experience, Myth and Evidence*, Somerset: Open Books

—— (1979) *The Ecology of Human Development*, Cambridge, Mass.: Harvard University Press

Bullock, A. (1975) *A Language for Life*, Report of The Committee of Inquiry, London: HMSO

Cameron, R.J. (ed.) (1982) *Working Together: Portage in the U.K.*, Windsor: NFER-Nelson

Court, D. (1976) *Fit for the Future*, Report of The Committee on Child Health Services, London: HMSO

Craft, M., Raynor, J. and Cohen, L. (1980) *Linking Home and School*, 3rd edn, London: Harper and Row

Cunningham, C. and Sloper, P. (1984) The relationship between maternal ratings of first word vocabulary and Reynell language scores, *British Journal of Educational Psychology*, 54, 16–167

Cyster, R., Clift, P.S. and Battle, S. (1979) *Parental Involvement in Primary Schools*, Windsor, NFER-Nelson

Daly, B., Addington, J., Kerfoot, S. and Sigston, A. (in press) *Portage: The Importance of Parents*, Windsor: NFER-Nelson

Davie, C.E., Hutt, S.J., Vincent, E. and Mason, M. (1984) *The Young Child at Home*, Windsor: NFER-Nelson

Davis, J. (1984) *Evaluation Reports, Liverpool Parent Support Programme*, School of Education, University of Liverpool

Dessent, T. (1984) *What is Important about Portage?* Windsor: NFER-Nelson

Donachy, W. (1979) Parent participation in preschool education, section III in M.M. Clark, and W. Cheyne (eds), *Studies in preschool education*, Sevenoaks: Hodder and Stoughton

Elliott, J. and Whitehead, D. (1980) *The Theory and Practice of Educational Action Research, Classroom Action Research Project*, (CARN) Bulletin No. 4, Cambridge Institute of Education, Shaftsbury Road, Cambridge

Frohman, A., Weber, S. and Wollenburg, K. (1983) *The Portage Home Teaching Handbook*, Windsor: NFER-Nelson

Gaussen, T. (1984) The educational psychologist and under twos – some problems and possibilities in infant assessment, *Journal of the Association of Educational Psychologists*, 6(4), 18–25

George, A. (in press) *Resource-based learning for School Governors*, London: Croom Helm

Gleidman, J. and Roth, W. (1981) *Parents and professionals in W. Swann (ed.), The Practice of Special Education*, Oxford: Basil Blackwell and Open University Press

Glynn, T. (1980) Parent child interaction in remedial reading at home in M.M. Clarke and T. Glynn (eds), *Reading and Writing for Children with Difficulties*, Education Review Occasional Papers, No. 8, University of Birmingham

Griffiths, A. and Hamilton, D. (1984) *Parent, Teacher, Child*, London: Methuen

Halsey, A.H. (1972) *Educational Priority: EPA, problems and policies*, Vol. 1, London: HMSO

Hester, P. (1977) Evaluation and accountability in a parent-implemented early intervention service, *Community Mental Health Journal*, 13(3), 261-7

Fills, R. (1984) *Parental Participation in the Education of Young Children*, project reports, University of Lancaster: Centre for Educational Research and Development

Hobbs, N. (1978) Families, schools and communities: an ecosystem for children, *Teachers College Record, 79, (4),* 756–66

HMI Survey (1978) *Primary Education in England*, London: HMSO

Jackson, A., Pond, B. and Hannon, P. (1981) *The Belfield Reading Project*, Rochdale: Belfield Community Council

Jeffree, D. and McConkey, R. (1978) *Parental Involvement Project, Developmental Charts*, London: Hodder and Stoughton

Meltzer, L., Levine, M., Hanson, M., Wasserman, R., Schneider, D. and Sullivan, M. (1983) Developmental attainment in preschool children: analysis of concordance between parents and professionals, *Journal of Special Education, 17(2),* 203–13

Miller, A., Robson, D. and Bushell, R. (in press) Parental participation in paired reading: a controlled study and an examination of the role and the technique in home–school collaboration, *Journal of Child Psychology and Psychiatry*

Mittler, P. and McConachie, H. (1983) *Parents, Professionals and Mentally Handicapped People*, London: Croom Helm

Morgan, R. and Lyon, E. (1979) Paired reading: a preliminary report on a technique for parental tuition of reading-retarded children, *Journal of Child Psychology and Psychiatry, 20(2),* 151–60

Mortimore, J. and Blackstone, T. (1982) *Disadvantage and Education*, London: Heinemann

Moyle, D. (1968) *The Teaching of Reading*, London: Ward Lock Educational

Newham Parents' Centre (1984) *Nexus, 50, 51,* 747 Barking Road, London E. 13

Newson, E. and Hipgrave, T. (1982) *Getting Through to Your Handicapped Child*, Cambridge: Cambridge University Press

Open University (1981) *Governing Schools*, P970, Milton Keynes: Open University Press

Percival, W. (1984) PACE: project on parents and the community as educators, *Dialogue in Education, 10–11,* Autumn

Plowden, B. (1967) Children and Their Primary Schools, London: HMSO

Potts, P. (1983) What difference would integration make to the professionals? in T. Booth and P. Potts (eds), *Integrating Special Education*, Oxford: Basil Blackwell

Pringle, M. (1980) *A Fairer Future for Children*, London: MacMillan

Pugh, G. (1981) *Parents as Partners*, London: National Children's Bureau, 8 Wakley Street, London

Pugh, G. and De'Ath, E. (1984) *Services for Families with Young Children Project*, National Children's Bureau, 8 Wakley Street, London

Revill, S. and Blunden, R. (1980) *A Manual for Implementing Portage Home Training Service for Developmentally Handicapped Preschool Children*, Windsor: NFER-Nelson

Scott, M. and Grimmet, S. (1977) *Current Issues in Child Development*, Washington, DC: National Association for the Education of Young Children

Shipman, V. (1979) *Maintaining and Enhancing Early Intervention Gains*, Princeton, New Jersey: Educational Testing Service

Southgate, V., Arnold, H. and Johnson, S. (1981) *Extending Beginning Reading*, London: Heinemann Educational Books

Stierer, B. (1984)*Parental Help With Reading in Schools Project*, Unpublished research report, Institute of Education, University of London

Taylor, L., Lacey, R. and Bracken, D. (1979) *In Whose Best Interest?*, London: The Cobden Trust and The National Association for Mental Health

Taylor, T. (1977) *A New Partnership for Our Schools*, London: HMSO

Tizard, J., Schofield, W. and Hewison, J. (1982) Collaboration between teachers and parents in assisting children's reading, *British Journal of Educational Psychology*, 52, 1–15

Tizard, B. and Hughes, M. (1984) *Young Children Learning*, London: Fontana

Tomlinson, S. (1982) *A Sociology of Special Education*, London: Routledge and Kegan Paul

Topping, K. and McKnight, G. (1984) Paired reading and parent-power, *Special Education: Forward Trends, 11(3)*, 12–15

Topping, K. and Wolfendale, S. (1985) *Parental Involvement in Children's Reading*, London: Croom Helm/Nichols Publishing Co., New York

Wade, B. (1984) Story at home and school, *Educational Publication No. 10*, University of Birmingham

Walrond-Skinner, S. (1981) *Developments in Family Therapy*, London: Routledge and Kegan Paul

Warnock, M. (1978) *Special Educational Needs*, London: HMSO

Wells, G. (1983) Talking with children: the complementary roles of parents and teachers in M. Donaldson, R. Grieve and C. Pratt (eds), *Early Childhood Development and Education*, Oxford: Basil Blackwell

Welton, J. (1982) Will the 1981 Act make a difference? in J. Welton, K. Wedell and G. Vorhaus (eds), *The 1981 Education Act and Its Implications*, Bedford Way Papers, 12, Institute of Education, Heinemann Educational Books

White, P.G., Solity, J. and Reeve, C.J. (1984) Teaching parents to teach reading, *Special Education: Forward Trends, 11(1)*, 11–13

Wolfendale, S. (1983) *Parental Participation in Children's Development and Education*, New York: Gordon and Breach Science Publishers

——— (1984a) Parental profiles – my child at home, *Assessment, 1(2)*, Down's Children Association

——— (1984b) All about me, Unpublished developmental guide and notes, available from Child Study Unit, Psychology Department, North East London Polytechnic, The Green, Stratford, London

Woodhead, M. (1976) *Intervening in Disadvantage*, Windsor: NFER-Nelson

Young, P. and Tyre, C. (1983) *Dyslexia or Illiteracy: Realising the Right to Read*, Milton Keynes: Open University Press

Zigler, E., Kagan, S. and Klugman, E. (1983) *Children, Families and Government: Perspectives in American Social Policy*, Cambridge: Cambridge University Press

Addresses of Voluntary Organisations Referred to in This Chapter

Coventry Community Education Development Centre, Briton Road, Coventry, CV2 4LF

Family Rights Group, 6 Manor Gardens, Holloway Road, London N7 6LA

Family Service Units, 207 Old Marylebone Road, London NW1 5QP

PART TWO: SCHOOLS

Legislation has established the school as a central context within which child development occurs. Schools are additionally distinguished in so far as they are explicitly concerned with encouraging and exploiting developmental changes among pupils. To this end, those who care for and teach children in schools receive special training, including aspects of child development, the better to equip them for their professional responsibilities. For all these reasons, schools have attracted the attention of psychologists and they continue to provide one of the focal points of attempts to combine research and practice.

In the opening chapter of this section, Les Smith provides a detailed conceptual analysis of the relationship between research findings and any implications which might be drawn from such findings in relation to classroom practice. He argues that in the past, attempts to use research as a guide to improved practice have floundered upon a confusion regarding the role of empirically derived knowledge.

In Chapter 6 Kathy Sylva attempts to answer the question: Which theories of child development have influenced the evolution of the pre-school curriculum? As a result she comes to the unexpected conclusion that Piagetian theory has had relatively little impact. From an analysis on recent developments in research and practice in relation to the pre-school she argues that, before theories of child development can be considered as appropriate to pre-school practice, they must be modified and elaborated in the light of feedback from classroom experience.

Turning to the role of child development research in special schools, John Harris examines the way in wh'ch theories about the acquisition of language and the development of thinking have been used as bases for making recommendations for improved teaching. Like Kathy Sylva, he argues that the interests and objectives of those who were concerned with theory building were different from those concerned with making practical suggestions for better teaching in schools, and for this reason the recommendations derived directly from research-based theories are unlikely to be effective in the classroom. On a more optimistic note, Mark Masidlover describes the way in which the design and development of the Derbyshire Language Scheme have created conditions in which recommendations for intervention can be modified, elaborated and updated in the light of new evidence from research and following feedback from classroom practice.

The final chapter in this section is by David Galloway who

considers the limitations which are imposed on implementing research findings by external forces such as government policy and financial constraints. If psychologists take their role of instigators of social change seriously, then, Galloway argues, it is necessary to consider carefully what they might realistically achieve within existing constraints, and what factors actively prevent research findings from having positive effects on policy development and policy implementation.

5 FROM PSYCHOLOGY TO INSTRUCTION

Leslie Smith

> It is quite certain that a knowledge of psychology does not *suffice* for one who is to be a good educator. But if it does not suffice, it is none the less necessary. (E. Claparède 1913: 7)

Introduction

Psychological, and educational, research on learning is primarily research on *how children do learn*. Such research is empirical in that observational or experimental evidence is produced to confirm or refute some hypothesis about how learning takes place. A confirmed hypothesis is a true proposition, describing some aspect of the learning-process. A theory of learning provides, systematically and objectively, *learning-propositions*.

Teaching and instructing are human activities focused upon *how to learn*. Some children learn efficiently and some do not. Teachers typically try to ensure that children's learning is efficient. Whilst teachers have an interest in how children learn, they also have an interest in how to improve children's learning. A theory of instruction provides comprehensive *learning-principles*. A learning-proposition is either true or false, unlike a learning-principle which is neither true nor false. Here is an example of a learning-proposition:

(A) Children who learn in formal classrooms gain higher scores in tests of basic skills than do children who learn in informal classrooms. (Bennett 1976)

This proposition is derived from the extensive study of children's learning in primary school classrooms undertaken by Neville Bennett. In support of this proposition, Bennett documents the nature of the empirical evidence upon which that proposition rests. I have no wish to challenge this evidence, although the assessment of the empirical aspects of Bennett's study has generated debate (cf. Gray and Satterley 1978). Rather, my interest is in what follows from (A). Suppose that you accept learning-proposition (A): does it follow that you ought to teach basic skills in a formal manner? The plain answer is: not at all. Since the remainder of this discussion is an elaboration of why this negative response is justified, it is enough to notice right now that (A) is quite different from:

> (A1)   Children should learn basic skills in formal classrooms rather than in informal classrooms.[1]

For the difference between (A) and (A1) is the difference between a learning-proposition and a learning-principle. (A) is true when confirmed by the available evidence and false when disconfirmed by that evidence. (A1) is neither true nor false, for (A1) is a recommendation about what ought to occur rather than a description of what does occur. In short, a learning-principle, such as (A1), is normative.

My argument is that no descriptive learning-propositions ever imply a normative learning-principle. This argument is certainly not new since it was initially put forward some 200 years ago by the philosopher, David Hume (1739). Hume's Rule states that what is or is not the case never settles what ought or ought not to be the case; that descriptive evidence never entails an evaluative conclusion; that values never arise from facts. Interestingly, Hume's Rule is widely accepted by philosophers (Peters 1966; Hudson 1983). And the argument has a clear relevance to the 'application' of psychological research — for example, on the intelligence of black and white children. Suppose that you accept that the mean IQ of a white American child is higher than the mean IQ of a black American child (Jensen 1969). You might not, of course, accept this evidence (cf. Bodmer 1970). But even if you do accept it, no conclusion about what you ought to do follows from this acceptance. One conclusion that you might draw is that black children in America should be allocated extra learning-resources; another conclusion that you might draw is that white children in America should be allocated extra learning-resources; alternatively, you might draw the conclusion that you should do nothing so as to maintain the *status quo*. There are at least three different responses here. Each arises, in some sense, from the psychological evidence. Yet, clearly, each is different from the others. The psychological evidence never 'tells you what to do'; people draw conclusions from the psychological evidence presented to them. And people arrive at different evaluations of the same descriptive evidence – as Hume's Rule suggests.

So my argument is not new. It is, however, opportune – if only because Hume's Rule is not always respected in psychological discussions. My discussion is a reminder that normative learning-principles are not implied by descriptive learning-propositions. Recommendations about how to learn are recommendations made by people and even if people make use of psychological research on learning, the latter never determines what those recommendations actually are. The discussion is in two parts. Firstly, the position adopted by instructional psychologists is reviewed and subjected to criticism. It is argued that instructional psychologists commit themselves to three objectionable views: a preoccupation with prescription; a disregard for the distinction between learning-propositions and learning-principles; and oversight about the status of psychological research on learning. Each objection is documented and discussed with suitable illustration. Secondly, the question of whether there can be a theory of instruction is considered. It is suggested that the main argument of the first section is applicable here as well. It is evident that there is little consensus, at present, about what an acceptable theory of instruction would be like. Permissive learning-principles provide the best fit with the current descriptive base.

Instructional Psychology

Instructional psychology is taken by a host of distinguished sponsors to be a science whose central aim is to provide instructional recommendations on the basis of empirical evidence that arises from psychological, and educational, research. A theory of instruction is descriptive in that it uses the theories and methods of psychology to describe how learning occurs. Such a theory is also normative in making recommendations about how to improve learning, about how learning is optimalised.

A metatheory of instructional psychology is a theory about those features which are central to a theory of instructional psychology. Indeed, two such features have just been identified: a theory of instructional psychology is, firstly, descriptive and, secondly, normative. Since it is this second feature which preoccupies the discussion ahead, it is useful at this point to notice the importance of the first feature.

A theory of instruction is descriptive; that is, it rests upon the available empirical evidence for confirmation of its learning-propositions. Here is why this feature is a necessary feature. Consider

(B1)   In learning to read, novice readers should read a passage
silently. (Welton 1909)

(B1) is a learning-principle, suggesting how initial learning should
take place. Personally, the recommendation strikes me as silly. How
can a child, who cannot read, read a passage silently! Personally, I
would disregard (B1), relying instead upon some alternative
recommendation. Evidently, Welton and I are in disagreement about
what novice readers should do. Welton suggests one method that
novice readers should use; and I disagree. Since Welton has no
empirical evidence in favour of his stance – and since I have none for
mine – there the matter rests. In the absence of empirical evidence,
there is no way in which the difference of opinion between Welton and
myself can be settled. Thus empirical evidence is relevant and
essential to the making of an educational recommendation. The
availability of evidence in favour of a learning-proposition removes
any dispute over a corresponding recommendation from the level of
mere difference between unsupported opinions. For if Welton was
able to produce evidence that, in fact, novice readers do learn to read –
more quickly, more efficiently – if they read a passage in silence, that I
regarded a corresponding recommendation as silly is beside the point.
History provides ample testimony to human fallibility as to what is
and is not a 'silly' point of view. In the presence of empirical evidence,
'flat-earthers' have to beware!

I am accepting, then, that a learning-proposition presents a
necessary condition of a corresponding learning-principle. It is
reasonable to disregard a learning-principle, if no evidence is
provided in its favour. Of course, if a learning-principle happens to
represent your own viewpoint, you might well be disposed to accept
that principle, whether or not there is any evidence in its favour.
Some are willing to accept, for example,

(C1)   Mathematics in the computer age must comprehend and
supplement the computer, not merely imitate it. (Steen 1984)

The same may not be true of you, however. Since Steen, like Welton,
offers an educational recommendation in the absence of empirical
evidence in favour of a corresponding learning-proposition, such as

(C)   In the computer age, children learn mathematics more
quickly when they comprehend and supplement the computer
rather than when they imitate the computer

it would be reasonable to ignore Steen's point of view. What is clear is that metatheorists of instructional psychology are agreed that psychological, or educational, evidence about how learning does occur is *necessary* for the issuing of learning-principles (cf. Bruner 1966; Glaser and Resnick 1972; Gagne and Dick 1983).

But is it also *sufficient*? Just because there is a learning-proposition supported by the available empirical evidence, does a corresponding learning-principle have to be accepted as well? This question is crucial for it appears that metatheorists of instructional psychology, accepting that a theory of instruction has a descriptive component, also stress the normative character of such a theory. Some of the metatheorists contend that a theory of instruction is both normative and prescriptive.

A theory of instruciton is *prescriptive* in the sense that it sets forth rules concerning the most effective way of achieving knowledge or skills ... A theory of instruction is a *normative* theory. It sets up criteria and states the conditions for meeting them. (Bruner 1966: 40 – author's emphasis)

A theory of instruction is a *normative* theory [leading to] a *prescription* for optimizing learning. (Glaser and Resnick 1972: 208 – my emphasis)

A linking science [such as instructional psychology] is essentially a science of design. It is a prescriptive, *normative* science. (Glaser 1976: 304 – my emphasis)

[Instructional psychology involves] a *normative, prescriptive,* theoretical approach. (Glaser 1982: 302 – my emphasis)

Other metatheorists opt merely for the claim that such a theory is simply prescriptive. Resnick (1981: 693) offers suggestions about how 'to make instructional psychology a more *prescriptive* science', whilst Gagne and Dick (1983: 264) state that 'instructional theories are *prescriptive* in the sense that they attempt to identify conditions of instruciton which will optimize learning, retention and learning-transfer'. In both of the latter positions, a theory of instruction is taken to be prescriptive: it identifies the best way in which to promote learning.

In short, all of these metatheorists accept that empirical evidence is necessary for a theory of instruction. They all accept that a theory of instruction is also prescriptive, though some of these theorists admit that such a theory is normative as well. They offer, however, no further elucidation as to how, given a range of learning-propositions, a corresponding learning-principle is to be derived. It seems, that is, that they regard the provision of empirical evidence as sufficient for the issuing of a learning-principle corresponding to the learning-propositions which they have evidence for. And this is to say that the latter is both necessary and sufficient for the former. I will now present three objections to this position.

Prescription, Permission, Proscription

The first objection is that prescription is one (but not the only) type of normative principle. In consequence, the metatheorists distort their construal of instruction which is allocated but one distinctive form. Permissive and proscriptive principles are normative and so prescriptive principles constitute only one type of normative principle.

A learning-principle is normative and so may have a character which is:

Prescriptive: you should learn . . .
           you must learn . . .
           you ought to learn . . .
           learning is optimal when . . .

Permissive: you may learn . . .
           you may not learn . . .

Proscriptive: you should not learn . . .
           you ought not to learn . . .
           you must not learn . . .

A learning-principle provides guidance about how to learn and such guidance can be given in any of these ways. It is a mistake to suppose that Man (human being) and man (male sex) are equivalent; it is a mistake also to suppose that *normative* and *prescriptive* are equivalent since the latter is simply one type of norm.

Certainly, prescriptions are one type of norm; certainly (A1) is a prescriptive principle associated with a corresponding learning-proposition – (A). But there are permissive principles as well, for example:

(D1) A learning-hierarchy may be used in the planning of sequences of instruction. (Gagne 1977: 279)

In Gagne's theory, prerequisite learning has an important place since new learning rests upon previous, including prerequisite, learning which is hierarchically ordered in a step-by-step way. Learning to subtract double digits is 'higher' up a subtraction hierarchy than the subtraction of single digits. Gagne, however, is aware that learning-hierarchies have been devised, if at all, only for certain tasks – such as simple subtraction – and so a teacher cannot rely upon the availability of relevant learning-hierarchies when planning a lesson. None the less, Gagne believes that he has established a learning-hierarchy for some tasks, even if not for all, and it is for this reason that he formulates (D1). In planning lessons, there are occasions when Gagne's recommendation is appropriate as well as occasions when it is not. A permissive principle is, therefore, a suitable principle to commend in this case.

Permissive principles are also suitable when there are several equally valid strategies applicable for some problem. Resnick and Ford (1981: 75–6) document the fact that young children learn to add single digits by use of distinct strategies. Given the problem '3 + 4 = ?', one strategy which children use is to identify the first number (3); to identify the second number (4); and to add the second number to the first. A different strategy is to identify the larger number (4); to identify the other number (3); and to add the second to the first. The two strategies are different; they are both used by young children; and they are both effective ways of adding two numbers. The permissive principle

(E1) When adding single digits, children may add the smaller number to the larger number

is a suitable principle in just such a case, where there are equally effective ways of approaching a problem.

A proscriptive principle (ought not) is not a negative, permissive principle (may not). The (positive) permissive principle (E1) is compatible with its negative counterpart

(E2) When adding single digits, children may not add the smaller number to the larger number.

Quite obviously, children may, or may not, use a given strategy when adding single digits: both (E1) and (E2) are reminders that this is so. Confronted by a child who adds the second number to the first, such principles have a role since they show that a teacher can be tolerant of individual differences of this sort. By contrast, a proscriptive principle is one which excludes such toleration. In the presence of (C1), children should not learn the 'mechanics' of mathematics – for example, how to add and subtract numbers. This injunction prohibits learning of this sort. It is, of course, incompatible with the prescription that

(C2) Mathematics in the computer age must comprehend, supplement and imitate the computer.

It does, then, make a difference as to which normative principle is actually put forward.

In short, metatheorists of instructional psychology show an undue preoccupation with one type of normative principle to the exclusion of other legitimate types. This objection can be stated in a stronger and weaker form. In its stronger form, the objection is that a genus (normative) is conflated with one of its species (prescriptive). Certainly some of the claims made by Glaser are open to this charge. In its weaker form, the objection is that insufficient attention is given to non-prescriptive normative principles with a consequential distortion of the range of positions actually available. Evidently all of the sponsors referred to in this section are open to this charge. In both cases, these metatheorists have incompletely, or even inaccurately, outlined the features possessed by a theory of instruction.

Propositions and Principles

The second objection is that the metatheorists pay insufficient attention to the distinction between a learning-proposition and a learning-principle. Certainly, there is recognition that there is a distinction here. Bruner (1966: 40) states that a learning-principle should be 'congruent' with some learning-propositions, thus acknowledging that there is a distinction. Glaser and Resnick (1972: 208) note that each is 'clearly distinguished' from the other. Gagne and Dick (1983: 289) point out that the attempts to promote instructional effectiveness reviewed by them, all draw upon the existing descriptive base. In short, the metatheorists accept that there is independence between propositions and principles of learning. And this is to say that any of the three kinds of learning-principle described above can be drawn from any learning-proposition!

There is a good reason why this should be so. To place a learning-principle on a secure foundation, information of two sorts is required. Firstly, information is required about how children do learn; that is, learning-propositions are required. Secondly, information is required about the evaluation made of the variables referred to in those learning-propositions. Suppose I tell you that children learn Esperanto more quickly if they use method X; you might retort 'So what'. After all, you might have an interest neither in children, nor Esperanto, nor learning-methods. So your evaluation of the variables referred to in my learning-proposition is important. In general, the conclusion drawn from a learning-principle rests upon premisses of two sorts:

Premiss 1:   learning-propositions descriptive of learning pro-
             cesses or instructional methods;
Premiss 2:   normative principles formulating a set of values
             relevant to the processes or methods referred to in
             premiss 1;
Conclusion: normative principles which prescribe, permit or
             proscribe attention to the processes or methods
             referred to in premiss 1.

Since this schematic outline might seem over-restrictive, here is an example of its straightforward application.

The theory of mastery learning is expounded with customary clarity by Benjamin Bloom. Briefly, Bloom contends that in conventional schooling, time is a constant and so children are allocated the same amount of time in which to learn. It is, therefore, no surprise to find that there are individual differences in the amount of learning that takes place in different children. Under mastery learning conditions, 'amount of learning' is a constant with the consequence that what varies is the amount of time required by different children to attain mastery, that is, to 'learn the same amount'. Certainly, Bloom (1976: 161-201) provides empirical evidence which shows that children who learn under mastery learning conditions do learn more than children who do not. That is, Bloom does provide evidence corresponding to premiss 1. Indeed, the bulk of Bloom's book is devoted to the discussion of the theoretical constructs underpinning the theory and the learning-propositions associated with it. Tellingly, Bloom also provides information corresponding to premiss 2:

behind the theory and its development are some *values* which
must be evident to every careful reader of this book. These values
are implicit in our long search for a theory of school learning . . .
These values may sound like platitudes. (Bloom 1976: 205 –
my emphasis)

Educational values are presupposed by researchers as well as by
teachers. Bloom asserts that his values are platitudes. They are
apparently values which Bloom supposes to be shared by everyone;
well, almost everyone. In particular, Bloom accepts the normative
principle that higher achievement is an improvement over lower
achievement (Bloom 1976: 205). That is, schooling is *better* if it
results in children's gaining higher scores on tests of skills in
mathematics, English and other school subjects. This is, clearly, a
value and it is equally clearly a cognitive value. From this standpoint,
schooling has a cognitive rationale: schooling is better if there is more
learning (higher cognitive achievement) and worse if there is less
learning (lower cognitive achievement).

But not everybody does accept this value! There are at least two
main ways in which the lack of consensus is manifest. Firstly, the
cognitive value accepted by Bloom is ambiguous since it can be
construed differently by different individuals. Secondly, the cognitive
value accepted by Bloom is ambiguous since it, too, can be construed
differently by different individuals. Here are examples of each.

The first type of ambiguity (cognitive) arises because there are
different aspects of cognition, not all of which are taken to be equally
important. When Bloom states that 'better learning' is preferable to
'poor learning' (Bloom 1976: 205), he is well aware that there are
different types of learning since his taxonomy is an attempt to classify
hierarchically that very diversity. Does Bloom (1976) have in mind
Knowledge – whose taxonomic order is low – or Evaluation – whose
taxonomic order is high? It is not clear, even though Bloom (1956)
himself is quite clear that each is different. The same question can be
restated in terms of the model of complex learning put forward by
Rummelhart and Norman (1978). The latter distinguish between
three modes of learning: accretion (factual learning), re-structuring
(insight) and tuning (practice). Clearly, accretion results in learning-
quantity, unlike re-structuring which results in learning-quality.
Different teachers might well have different interpretations as to what
'better learning' is. Is it accretion? Is it re-structuring? Is it both?
These questions are important, if only because recent research, which

makes some reference to the Rummelhart and Norman model, shows that re-structuring is conspicuously absent from the British primary classroom (Bennett, Desforges, Cockburn and Wilkinson 1984). Is the learning in such classrooms 'better' or 'poor', when accretion is present but re-structuring is absent?

Another example of ambiguity (cognitive) arises in attempts to accelerate cognitive development. If cognitive development is accelerated, the child acquires earlier in life a competence that can be put to more use just because that competence is acquired earlier than would otherwise have been the case. One example of this viewpoint is provided in the training given to pre-schoolers on tasks of formal thinking appropriate to adolescents (Engelmann 1971). What is at issue here is not the question of whether the training was successful (cf. Kamii and Derman 1971) but rather the desirability of its success. Piaget expresses the rival position in the claim: 'the real problem is knowing whether it is advantageous to accelerate development . . . Pedagogically, I think it is better for a child to find and invent his own solutions.' (Piaget 1972: 19) The reason given for this latter stance is that children might develop further when allowed to construct their own solutions. What is at issue is whether speed of learning is important or whether extent of learning is important. There is an exclusive choice to be made in that a commitment to one of these positions excludes a commitment to the other. It is, therefore, problematic whether 'better learning' has taken place in a classroom where 'speed of learning' is important or in a classroom where 'extent of learning' is important.

The second type of ambiguity (value) arises because there are different types of normative (evaluative) principle. So even if there is agreement with respect to a specific cognitive feature (quantity of learning, early learning, say) there can still be disagreement about the degree of importance assigned to that feature. The same learning-proposition can be used in support of different learning-principles. Indeed, empirical research on the goals (values) that teachers actually have (Ashton, Kineen, Davies and Holley 1976; Bennett 1976) is testimony to this very diversity. Re-consider

(A1) Children should learn basic skills in formal classrooms rather than in informal classrooms,

which is a prescriptive learning-principle. Certainly, some teachers would be prepared to accept (A1), especially since it has suitable empirical support in learning-proposition (A). But not all teachers would accept (A1), and this for a variety of reasons. Firstly, it is conceivable that a teacher might reject (A1) in favour of

(A2) Children should not learn basic skills.

Such a position would, no doubt, appear dubious to some – anyone, for example, who accepted (A1). But the point is: not everyone does accept (A1)! Perhaps other goals are given importance (social, moral, physical, aesthetic, affective goals, for example) in a deliberate de-emphasis of the cognitive element in education. Secondly, it is probable that many teachers would accept

(A3) Children may learn basic skills in formal classrooms rather than in informal classrooms.

Such a stance would be adopted by any teacher who accepted multiple goals not all of which could be simultaneously attained. Thus a teacher who pursued, jointly, the acquisition of competence in basic skills with the acquisition of high-level competence (problem solving, creativity) or of affective skills (curiosity, attitude to school, independence) would find support for that stance in the learning-proposition offered by P.L. Peterson. In an extensive literature review, Peterson (1979) found that direct instruction results in higher scores when the learning of basic skills is at issue, but that in direct instruction (informal teaching) results in higher scores when high-level understanding or when socio-affective skills are at issue. Clearly, no teacher can teach formally and informally at the same time – yet a teacher can, at the same time, accept diverse goals whose pursuit would preferentially require the adoption of incompatible teaching-styles. One obvious way to interpret this position is to reject (A1) since its (universal) acceptance excludes the effective pursuit of all of a teacher's goals; and to accept (A3) which neither excludes the adoption of a formal teaching-style nor yet makes that adoption mandatory. For (A3) allows a teacher to give selective preference to each of several goals, thus attaining a greater consistency with the totality of learning-propositions that are available. In particular (A3), unlike (A1), is compatible with

(A4) Children may not learn basic skills in formal classrooms rather than in informal classrooms.

This negative, permissive principle has a legitimate role to play where the attainment of multiple goals requires the adoption of incompatible approaches. Both (A3) and (A4) are testimony to the complexity of classroom learning, where the pursuit of a single goal enjoying absolute priority over all other goals is the exception.

In short, for any learning-proposition, such as (A), there are at least three reasonable learning-principles that can be inferred from that proposition. Such learning-principles reflect the different types of normative principle available to people. A learning-proposition never implies a specific learning-principle. People infer learning-principles from learning-propositions on the basis of their own evaluations. This is not to say that learning-propositions are irrelevant. Indeed, the acceptance of learning-principles (A1)-(A3) depended in each case upon a prior acceptance of learning-proposition (A). This is to say that a learning-proposition, which is taken to be necessary for some learning-principle, is not thereby sufficient just because different evaluations of that learning-proposition are possible and rational. When the metatheorists seek to ground prescriptive learning-principles upon a sound descriptive base of learning-propositions, they show an evident disregard for the complexity of classroom learning.

Learning-theories

There is an extensive literature on learning-theory, which is comprehensively reviewed with special attention to its psychological (Bower and Hilgard 1981) and to its instructional (Gagne and Dick 1983) forms. One simple conclusion is apparent to any reader: there is no consensus as to what is 'the' theory of learning. A second conclusion is also manifest in that psychological research on learning is typically experimental research. In experimental research, investigation focuses upon the extent of change in one (dependent) variable when some other (independent) variable is manipulated. How, then, is a prescriptive learning-principle to be extracted from research of this sort? The third objection is simply that the metatheorists make ambitious claims for instructional psychology which are not supportable by reference to current psychological research.

Here is an example taken from current research on the learning-theory associated with tasks of formal thinking, as described by Inhelder and Piaget (1958) who propose 15 tasks illustrative of formal thinking together with a psychological model. Inhelder and Piaget contend that successful performance on their tasks is shown, typically, in adolescence. Their structural model is described by reference to propositional logic. This work has attracted critical attention. Engelmann (1971) contends that even infant school-children display correct performance on one of the tasks (Floating Bodies), provided that they receive suitable linguistic training. Thus Engelmann disputes the age-claims made by Inhelder and Piaget. He also offers a rival interpretation since his model is a consequence of an attachment to a behaviourist theory of learning. Siegler (1983) also rejects the age-claims in question since successful performance on one of the tasks (Balance Task) is forthcoming if junior schoolchildren are encouraged to represent the problem in the correct manner. Siegler's adoption of an information-processing model results in his modification of both the age-claims and the model-claims of Inhelder and Piaget. Case's (1978) research provides another criticism, namely in the assertion that junior school children can successfully perform on tasks of formal thinking (Flexible Rods Task). Whilst Case does recognise the importance of representation, he also refers to the functional basis of his own theoretical claims. Finally, Halford (1982) has offered a reinterpretation of Genevan finding. Halford confirms the age-claims put forward by Inhelder and Piaget; he also accepts a structural model; but the logical description of his own model utilises category theory and is, in consequence, different from the Genevan model. There is, in short, little agreement – even when the same family of tasks is under investigation – as to age of successful performance (infant – junior – secondary schoolchildren); as to type of model (structural – behaviouristic – cognitive – functional); or even as to the logical description which should be given to a structural model (propositional logic – category theory). Since a theory is identified through its associated empirical claims, together with the constructs used in explanation of those claims, it is clear that there are *theories* of formal thinking. We do not have *the* theory of formal thinking. It would, then, be premature to base a prescriptive learning-principle upon a learning-proposition associated with one of these theories. Such a principle would formulate what should take place for improvement in learning to occur. Yet any such prescription would be doubly weak. It would be weak, firstly, because its associated learning-proposition would be dependent upon one out of a range of competing theories. It would be weak, secondly, because that associated theory might turn out to be false. A more prudent response is warranted in such a case, one which some psychologists actually accept. Siegler has this to say about his approach which stresses the role of encoding:

> encoding that is less than optimal *may* constrain the ability to learn. (Siegler 1983: 73 – my emphasis)

By contrast, the stronger, prescriptive claim is made by Case:

> successful instruction *must* somehow accomplish the following objectives: (a) it *must* demonstrate to the student that his or her current strategy can be improved on; and (b) it *must* minimise the load on working memory. (Case 1978: 446 – my emphasis)

From the perspective adopted here, Case's position is too strong not because his approach is rejected but rather because the current proliferation of theories of learning provides a cautionary reminder that permissive principles stretch the available descriptive base.

This same conclusion is reinforced when attention is given to the reliance placed upon experimental research. Suppose an experiment yields successful results; suppose that those findings are replicated in subsequent research. Suppose, in short, that we have good evidence that manipulation of one or more variables is reliably linked to change in some other variable. Such research warrants a learning-proposition such as

(F)   Changes in Independent Variable (as specified in learning theory so-and-so) lead to changes in Dependent Variable.

For example, the Independent Variable may be linguistic training (Engelmann), encoding (Siegler) or minimisation of load on working memory (Case), whilst the Dependent Variable would be performance on a task of formal thinking. What can be validly inferred from (F) alone is that the Independent Variable is sufficient for the Dependent Variable: change the former and you change the latter. What cannot be validly inferred from (F) alone is that a change in the latter is always due to linguistic training; nor that a change in the latter is necessarily due to encoding; nor that a change in the latter will, in every instance, be due to minimisation of load on working memory. A change in the latter may be due to any one of these because, it is assumed, there is evidence that each of these is reliably linked with changes in the Dependent Variable. But an inference from a change in the latter to the identification of any *one* of the former is clearly invalid since there are several distinct alternatives. Thus a learning-proposition arising from experimental research of this sort is inadequate as a base for a prescriptive learning-principle. This is because the learning-proposition provides information about what does happen in the presence of an Independent Variable; it is silent about the range of events which can elicit the Dependent Variable. So when learning (indicated by the Dependent Variable) is at issue, a permissive learning-principle is warranted:

> (F1) Learning (identified through Dependent Variable) may be improved through manipulation of Independent Variable (as specified in learning-theory so-and-so).

A permissive principle is suitable when the descriptive base for a learning-proposition is experimental in the sense specified, that is, when change in one variable is taken to be sufficient for change in another.

It will be noticed that the second reason is stronger than the first reason. The first reason, that is, that there is theory-proliferation, is a historical matter which could be resolved with the advent of the Learning Theory by analogy with the Theory of Relativity or the Theory of Evolution. By contrast, the second reason, that is, that experimental research yields sufficient conditions, is a pervasive feature of any theory based upon experimental research, including any future Theory of Learning. In consequence, there are grounds for doubting whether psychological research on learning ever could generate learning-propositions that were adequate for prescriptive principles of learning.

Theory of Instruction

There are two central claims arising from the argument of the previous section. The first claim is that the presence of some learning-proposition, supported by psychological or educational research on learning, is necessary for a corresponding learning-principle. It is a consequence of this claim that a learning-principle, which lacks empirical support for a corresponding learning-proposition, commands no rational support. This is not to say that any such learning-principle is false – no learning-principle at all can be false, since only a learning-proposition can be true or false. Rather, it is to say that any such principle has autobiographical interest: it is one which *you* support and it is not one for which there *is* support. The second claim is that a learning-principle does not have to be prescriptive, since the complexity of classroom learning makes the adoption of permissive and proscriptive principles a reasonable alternative. This is not to say that no learning-principle should ever be put forward. A self-denying ordinance of that sort is not warranted. Indeed, it probably arises from the mistaken belief that a learning-principle can have the same sort of support as a learning-proposition. But such a belief is mistaken by its failure to recognise the subjective element inherent in any – including prescriptive – learning-principles. A learning-principle is one to which *you* give assent and it is *not* one to which there is assent.

In short, there is only partial escape from subjectivity. Acceptance of a learning-proposition on the basis of appropriate evidence removes one type of subjectivity, namely unsupported belief about how learning occurs. But acceptance of a learning-principle retains another type of subjectivity, namely a preferred value as to how to improve learning. The question which now arises is whether there can be a theory of instruction.

Instructional psychologists often see their task as being that of formulating a theory of instruction – or a technology of instruction – which has a secure basis in psychological theory. Whereas much previous psychological research was research on the learning by animals of simple skills in laboratory settings, future research in psychology is preferentially research on the learning by children of complex skills in naturalistic settings. Classroom learning is a case in point. Evidently one result of the adoption of past approaches in psychology has been the growth of 'deintellectualised practice' (Glaser 1976): even proficient teachers are unable to relate their teaching skills to any theoretically-based research on learning. The same pervasive feature is documented in European research where the isolation of practitioners' and theoreticians' knowledge of learning is noted with regret (Plowden 1967: 518; Olson 1984). Instructional psychologists accept two aims; to improve the psychological base and to identify the instructional principles which are secured by that base.

The goal of placing teaching practice in an intellectual context is, of course, worthwhile. The problem that arises is the problem of how that goal is to be achieved and whether there is any likelihood of its attainment in the near future. Reasonable doubt about such attainment can be justified and here are two reasons for maintaining a sceptical response: the first reason is due to a learning-proposition being necessary for a relevant learning-principle and the second reason is due to the former not being sufficient for the latter.

A theory of learning is not a theory of instruction. A theory of learning describes how children learn. Possession of such a theory provides knowledge relevant to a decision about how to teach a child. But any such theory of learning does not 'tell' its possessor how to teach, if only because different methods of learning are compatible with the same theory of learning. Of course, if a theory of learning is comprehensive, the learning which actually takes place by the use of any given teaching method will be described by that theory of learning. Even so, teachers alone can decide how to teach. A cartographical analogy (Toulmin 1953: 121-3) may clarify the difference. A pure theory in science differs from an applied theory in much the way that a map differs from an itinerary. A map (pure theory) is not an itinerary but is neutral with respect to all possible itineraries that can be devised in relation to a given territory. A map of the London Underground accurately describes the order of the stations on the Underground, together with their interrelations. If the map is accurate, there is a one-to-one relationship between any feature on the map and an equivalent feature in the territory mapped (in this case, the Underground). But an itinerary is not a map since it is a selection of one preferred feature in the territory (as a starting-point), of some other feature (as a destination) and of some route between them. An accurate map will show any itinerary, which *you* care to select. But however accurate the map, if you do not choose the itinerary, that map will not show it for you. The selection of an itinerary is the expression of human involvement in the world. By virtue of involvement in the world, humans have the ability to change the world. They do not have to remain impotent voyeurs of autonomously occurring events. Thus even if we had a map of learning, no learning-principle would be shown upon it, for a learning-principle (itinerary) is not a learning-proposition (map).

The improvement of learning requires several decisions to be made. One decision that is currently required is the selection of a learning-proposition and, in turn, a theory of learning. Yet there is an embarrassingly wide choice, as the discussion of the previous section confirmed. Which theory of learning? A second decision that is currently required is the selection of a theory of instruction, for there are several on offer (Gagne and Dick 1983). In turn, a decision is required about which learning-condition to place a learner in; which cognitive process to foster; which learning-method to use; which learning-outcome to seek. So four more major decisions are required here. And, indeed, that very choice is made more difficult since a decision might be made to foster several cognitive processes in conjunction with several learning-methods leading to several learning outcomes. A comprehensive theory of instruction might be expected to be one which would guide such a choice, and to do so on the basis of relevant learning-propositions. No such theory of instruction is currently available.

In short, one reason for scepticism is that a theory of instruction is analogous to a theory of how to see the London Underground. There are many different ways in which to do either. But whilst there is agreement about the map of the London Underground, there is no such agreement about the Theory of Learning. So whilst any of the multiple ways of seeing the London Underground can be planned and guided by that map, complex decisions about improving learning are currently taken in the presence of many theories of learning no one of which is accepted as the Theory of Learning.

There is an air of defeatism about this conclusion, which misses the point at issue. There are theories of learning and there are theories of instruction – so there is some progress towards the goal of integrating practitioners' and theoreticians' knowledge of learning. And progress is progress, even if it is partial. Yes, of course; but this leads to the second reason for scepticism. A theory of instruction would have to establish not merely which combinations of conditions, processes, methods and outcome are (in)compatible with which. Such a theory would also have to establish which learning-principles, based upon such combinations, are prescriptive, or permissive, or proscriptive, in character. Normative principles do differ with respect to character and so a comprehensive theory of instruction would have to identify the specific character associated with each principle. And this undertaking is not settled merely because there is available an acceptable theory of learning. For a theory of learning simply records what is the case; it does not determine what is best or worst about the cases so recorded.

There is a subjective element in any learning-principle, since the principle expresses the values, commitments, preferences, desires of the person who accepts that principle. As Jerome Bruner puts it:

> a theory of instruction, in short, is concerned with how *what one wishes to teach* can best be taught, with improving rather than describing learning. (Bruner 1966: 40 – my emphasis)

In order to improve learning, a person will accept a learning-principle which expresses what that person believes should (prescriptive), may (permissive) or should not (proscriptive) take place. In consequence, a theory of instruction is confronted by human diversity: teachers do not all want to teach with the same ends in mind. Firstly, teachers differ with respect to the presence vs. absence of some educational end. Secondly, teachers differ with respect to the relative priority given to different educational ends, all of which are accepted: two different teachers may assign different relative positions to the same ends. Thirdly, educational goals may be assigned a differing relative importance within the value-system of a teacher: political, moral and social goals are accepted by teachers with a differential importance accorded to educational goals within that value-system. In the presence of manifest diversity of this sort, how can a theory of instruction establish the normative character of any learning-principle?

A robust reply now arises. If the two sceptical reasons are accepted, there is one conclusion to draw. The conclusion is not just that there could not be a theory of instruction, one which integrated and systematised a range of learning-principles. It would seem that no learning-principle should be proposed on the basis of research. And such a conclusion is self-refuting because it is obvious that there are such principles, principles which command substantial even if not universal support. That is, an instructional psychologist would be minimally content if individual learning-principles could be established, leaving for the future the task of combining them in one theory of instruction.

Such a reply offers a fine compromise. It rejects the defeatism which declares that there never will be an increase in understanding of how children learn, still less about how to improve children's learning. It is also a rejection of the optimistic position that we have – or will have shortly – a complete theory of learning and instruction. Specifically, the compromise accepts as a reasonable challenge the task of trying to interrelate the skills of the proficient teacher (knowledge-how) with those of the researcher (knowledge-that) to mutual advantage. In what way, then, may this be done?

One way in which such interrelation might occur is for a learning-principle to be assigned a *permissive* normative character in the absence of definitive grounds to the contrary. It was shown in the previous section that the metatheorists of instructional psychology have tended to distinguish the descriptive from the prescriptive, whereas their primary consideration is the contrasting of the descriptive and the normative. It is evident that not all instructional psychologists have proceeded in this way. Indeed, such a cautious position is resolutely stated by Donald Norman in a comment upon course-design in problem-solving:

> I do not believe we yet know enough to make strong statements about what ought to be or ought not to be included in a course. (Norman 1980)

Since prescriptive principles have been over-emphasised by the metatheorists, the modest position advanced by Norman is important if only to redress the balance. Yet even Norman, in denying that prescriptive and proscriptive principles are, at present, appropriate does not actually assert that permissive principles have a valid role to play.

Here are three advantages in favour of the formulation of permissive learning-principles. The first advantage is that it is accepted in this discussion that any learning-principle – including a permissive-principle – is one that has empirical support arising from a corresponding learning-proposition. A permissive principle, formulating what may occur, is not here construed as a *carte blanche* to teach according to whim. In its present construal, a permissive-principle is one which rests upon reliable evidence that learning does occur in a specified way. The point of the principle is that it establishes *one* way to improve learning, namely, the way specified. The second advantage is that a permissive principle does not exclude there being alternative permissive principles which lead to learning-improvement in quite different ways. A permissive principle is one which does not exclude there being alternative, and equally valid ways of improving learning. In the presence of a proliferation of learning-theories and human diversity about educational goals, this advantage is important. A permissive principle does not require that there is one way in which to learn nor that there is one way in which to improve learning. A third advantage of a permissive principle is that it has heuristic appeal: we are invited to find out whether there are alternative ways in which to learn as well as to find out whether there are alternative ways in which to improve learning. The formulation of a permissive principle is an invitation to leave open, for future practice or future theory to decide, whether there are alternatives available at all.

Conclusion

One conclusion to draw from this discussion is that it is, in fact, quite easy to formulate a learning-principle: simply ignore how children actually learn and then lay down what others ought to do on the basis of your own preferences. You are welcome to issue learning-principles in this way – do remember, however, that others might well be disinclined to accept any such principle.

A second conclusion is that securing empirical evidence in favour of some learning-proposition – as well as evidence against rival propositions – is an important rational step to take. A deliberate silence has been maintained in this discussion about the relative merits of different ways in which such evidence could be gained. The same silence extends over the delicate question as to which learning-propositions are defensible. Yet anyone who does plan to 'move from psychology to instruction' is being invited to opt for one starting-point in psychology in the certain knowledge that the same starting-point will be rejected by some counterpart. So be it. There is a choice, however, and the fact that any choice will not be universally accepted is not a reason for refusing to choose at all. A learning-proposition which has been submitted to suitable empirical scrutiny is preferable to the total absence of such a proposition.

A third conclusion is that no learning-proposition ever prescribes, permits or proscribes what you are to do. The selection of a suitable learning-proposition is one rational step to take – but it is not the only step. Of course, no one would suppose otherwise when a learning-proposition is formulated in the manner of (A) and a learning-principle in the manner of (A1). Their difference is quite apparent. That difference becomes opaque when claims are made, for a learning-proposition, that 'better' or 'more effective' or 'superior' or 'more efficient' learning occurs in this case as opposed to that case. Any such expression embodies a superb conflation of descriptive and normative elements. In a learning-proposition, learning is 'better' when it is shown in higher scores on a test, in a larger number of children who attain a stated level of attainment or in performance that is quicker than alternatives. In a learning-principle, learning is 'better' when it is enjoined, allowed or excluded. To mask this difference, in a claim about 'better' learning, is not to obliterate it!

A fourth conclusion is that a strong learning-principle, and especially prescriptive principles which enjoy popularity, presuppose agreement both about the specific type of cognition and about its relative priority in a scale of values, whether educational or otherwise. Such a strong learning-principle is vulnerable, if only because the requisite consensus may well be lacking. Despite the official statements made by those who have a genuine concern to serve the interests of both theory and practice, there is an alternative to the heroic course, consisting in the identification of a permissive learning-principle which arises from a secure empirical base.

The final conclusion to draw is that permissive learning-principles are a legitimate type of learning-principle, showing the best fit with the present empirical base.[2]

Notes

1. Learning-propositions are referred to alphabetically. Learning-principles are referred to alphabetically and numerically. This convention is used for ease of reference and so as to highlight whether a proposition or a principle is in question.
2. This chapter is a revised version of a paper which was presented at the British Educational Research Association (1984) Conference, held at the University of Lancaster.

References

Ashton, P., Kineen, P., Davies, F. and Holley, B.J. (1976) *The Aims of Primary Education: a study of teachers' opinions*, London: Macmillan

Bennett, N. (1976) *Teaching Styles and Pupil Progress*, London: Open Books

Bennett, N., Desforges, C., Cockburn, A. and Wilkinson, B. (1984) *The Quality of Pupil Learning Experiences*, London: Erlbaum

Bloom, B.S. (1956) *Taxonomy of Educational Objectives: Handbook I. Cognitive Domain*, London: Longmans, Green

——— (1976) *Human Characteristics and School Learning*, New York: McGraw-Hill

Bodmer, W.F. (1970) Intelligence and race, *Scientific American, 223*, 19–29

Bower, G.H. and Hilgard, E.J. (1981) *Theories of Learning*, 5th edn, Engelwood Cliffs, NJ: Prentice Hall

Bruner, J. (1966) *Toward a Theory of Instruction*, Cambridge, Mass.: Harvard University Press

Case, R. (1978) Implications of developmental psychology for the design of effective instruction in A.M. Lesgold, J.W. Pellegrino, S.D. Fokkema and R. Glaser (eds), *Cognitive Psychology and Instruction*, New York, Plenum Press

Claparède, E. (1913) *Experimental Pedagogy and the Psychology of the Child*, London: Arnold

Engelmann, S.E. (1971) Does the Piagetian approach imply instruction? in D.R. Green, M.C. Ford and G.B. Flamer (eds), *Measurement and Piaget*, New York: McGraw-Hill

Gagne, R.M. (1977) *The Conditions of Learning*, 3rd edn, London: Holt-Saunders

Gagne, R.M. and Dick, W. (1983) Instructional psychology, *Annual Review of Psychology, 34*, 261–95

Glaser, R. (1976) Cognitive psychology and instructional design, *Cognition and Instruction*, Hillsdale, NJ: Erlbaum

(1982) Instructional psychology: past, present and future, *American Psychologist*, *37*, 292–305

and Resnick, L.B. (1972) Instructional psychology, *Annual Review of Psychology*, *23*, 207–76

Gray, J. and Satterley, D. (1978) Time to learn?, *Educational Research*, *20*, 137–42

Halford, G.S. (1982) *The Development of Thought*, Hillsdale, NJ: Erlbaum

Hudson, W.D. (1983) *Modern Moral Philosophy*, 2nd edn, London: Macmillan

Hume, D. (1739) *Treatise of Human Nature*, Oxford: Oxford University Press, 1888

Inhelder, B. and Piaget, J. (1958) *The Growth of Logical Thinking*, London: Routledge & Kegan Paul

Jensen, A.R. (1969) How much can we boost IQ and scholastic achievement? *Harvard Educational Review*, *39*, 1–123

Kamii, C. and Derman, L. (1971) Comments on Engelmann's paper in D.R. Green, M.C. Ford and G.B. Flamer (eds), *Measurement and Piaget*, New York: McGraw-Hill

Norman, D. (1980) Cognitive engineering and education in D.T. Tuma and F. Reif (eds), *Problem Solving and Education*, Hillsdale, NJ: Lawrence Erlbaum Associates

Olson, J.K. (1984) What makes teachers tick? Considering the routines of teaching in R. Halkes and J.K. Olson (eds), *Teacher Thinking*, Amsterdam: Swets & Zeitlinger

Peters, R.S. (1966) *Ethics and Education*, London: George Allen & Unwin

Peterson, P.L. (1979) Direct instruction re-considered in P.L. Peterson and H.J. Walberg (eds), *Research on Teaching*, Berkeley: McCutchan

Piaget, J. (1972) Interview with Piaget, *Times Educational Supplement*, 18 February 1972

Plowden Report (1967) *Children and Their Primary Schools*, London: HMSO

Resnick, L.B. (1981) Instructional psychology, *Annual Review of Psychology*, *32*, 659–704

Resnick, L.B. and Ford, D. (1981) *The Psychology of Mathematics for Instruction*, Hillsdale, NJ: Erlbaum

Rummelhart, D.E. and Norman, D. (1978) Accretion, tuning and re-structuring: three modes of learning in J.W. Cotton and R.L. Klatzky (eds), *Semantic Factors in Cognition*, Hillsdale, NJ: Erlbaum

Siegler, R.S. (1983) Five generalizations about cognitive development, *American Psychologist*, *38*, 263–77

Steen, L.A. (1984) 1 + 1 = 0: new math for a new age, *Science*, pp. 225

Toulmin, S. (1953) *The Philosophy of Science*, London: Hutchinson

Welton, J. (1909) *Principles and Methods of Teaching*, 2nd edn, London: University Tutorial Press

6 DEVELOPMENTAL PSYCHOLOGY AND THE PRE-SCHOOL CURRICULUM

Kathy Sylva

Developmental psychologists have long assumed that pre-school teachers are an eager audience for their research findings. Unlike infant teachers, pre-school staff are freed from the pressure to instruct in literacy and numeracy and can choose to pursue the 'developmental ideal' instead. In other words, the aim for each child is to nurture physical, social, emotional and intellectual potential. But which objectives are reasonable for, say, a three year old? And what is the best way to foster normal development?

In answering these questions many textbooks give prominence to the work of Jean Piaget. From decades of research in Geneva Piaget has constructed a useful timetable for the development of cognitive abilities. His contribution has not ended here because Piagetian theory aims to explain development and not just chart its course. It provides an implicit guide to practice through stressing the child as an active learner, an ever-alert explorer of categories, quantities and relations. This notion of active learning underpins traditional pre-school practice in Britain and elsewhere. But can we trace the emphasis on exploration and play directly to Piaget? It will be argued that the answer is *no*.

The Influence of Susan Isaacs

The British nursery tradition has its deepest roots in the work of Froebel, followed by the Macmillans. More recent, and more important, has been the influence of Susan Isaacs, an extraordinary educator and psychologist who wrote about progressive nursery practice with startling insight into the ways children think and feel. She is best known for her role between 1924 and 1927 as Principal and one of the founders of the Malting House School. Evelyn Lawrence, a member of the staff there, tells about the origins of the school's innovative practice. 'In many discussions before the school began they (Susan Isaacs, her husband Nathan, together with Geoffrey and Margaret Pyke, from whom came the earliest ideas about the school) tried to put aside the accustomed ways of envisaging education and to think the thing through from the start, though naturally their thinking was greatly influenced by that of earlier pioneers.' (Gardner 1969) Although Isaacs knew the early work of Piaget and had respect for it, the philosophy of the Malting House School stemmed more from the educational philosophers rather than the brilliant young psychologist just beginning work in Geneva. Susan Isaacs herself claimed to be most influenced by Dewey and Froebel.

Despite her interest in the work of Piaget, Isaacs disagreed with him on many points, especially his dismissal of logical abilities in children as young as three or four. This disagreement stemmed, firstly, from Isaacs' sensitivity to the contribution of motivation to children's thinking and, secondly, to what might be called children's 'local knowledge in local situations'. She believed that young children are capable of reasoning in a logical and realistic way when personally involved and working or playing with familiar objects. Although she agreed with Piaget that children are often surprisingly illogical, she believed this was most likely to occur in situations when questions were asked of them by adults or where they were set experimental tasks not of their own choosing. Isaacs' painstaking records of the behaviour of the children at the Malting House School demonstrated just how much Piaget underestimated the abilities of pre-school children. 'These (observations) as a whole, I suggest, cut right across any notion of hard and fast mental 'structures'. . . They show, rather, a continuous advance in scope and clarity of noetic synthesis and in the ability to handle experience in more and more complex forms.' (Isaacs 1930: 92) She goes on to criticise Piaget's methods of investigation:

The clinical method, no matter how skilful the user, provides only a limited and stereotyped situation, the character of which necessarily puts the child at an intellectual disadvantage. He is sure to show himself at lower levels than in the more varied and co-operative situations of active daily life in school or home. With children as well as with animals, the psychologist has to offer real problems, those that are significant and attractive to the children or animals themselves. And he has to find ways of measuring and including the typical *best* performance of his subjects if he is to make any pronouncement as to the limits of ability, or to aim at a representative picture of any given age. (Ibid.: 95)

For Isaacs, children show the greatest intellectual maturity when involved in exploration or in spontaneous play. Activities such as these release children's intellectual powers and imaginations. Like Donaldson (1978) and Bryant (1974) several decades later, Isaacs thought that children are capable of various 'levels' in their thinking; they may solve a problem using reversibility on one day, then seemingly forget it on another. Isaacs (1930: 89) tells with glee about Dan, a five-year-old child who intrigued Piaget when the psychologist visited the Malting House School. Although Dan had won Piaget's interest with his realistic account of how a tricycle worked, on another occasion he showed glaring gaps in his causal reasoning.

> The kettle was on the stove boiling, a jet of steam coming out of the spout. Dan (5; 9) and Priscilla (7; 7) waved their hands at it, and Dan spat at the kettle. When Mrs. I. asked him, 'Please don't spit', he replied, 'But I wanted to stop that coming out!'

Isaacs' *Intellectual Growth in Young Children* is filled with rich examples of children reasoning in both logical and illogical ways, depending on the task at hand and the emotions involved at the moment.

Why did the work of Susan Isaacs exercise so profound an influence on nursery work in Britain and, to a lesser extent, abroad? In the years after she left the Malting House School, Isaacs published four of her best known books (including *Intellectual Growth in Young Children* in 1930 and *Social Development of Young Children* in 1933). During this period she supervised students in advanced psychology at University College, lectured at the Morley College for Adult Education, and began her work at the London Psycho-Analytic Society. It was also during this period that she made a weekly contribution to *The Nursery World* where, calling herself Ursula Wise, she answered the questions of both parents and nurses with great knowledge and insight. Her books, especially the two describing the work at the Malting House School, met immediate success and changed contemporary practice. Isaacs' books, articles and lectures made the nursery come alive. Dorothy Gardner cites the comment of an infant teacher: 'she interpreted Dewey better than he interpreted himself'. Most likely Susan Isaacs would have considered this high praise.

Her influence might not have been so great had she not taken the post in 1933 as the Head of the newly formed Department of Child Development at the University of London. Sir Percy Nunn wrote to the Board of Education specifying the two objectives of the new Department. First 'to supply the demands of the more progressive training colleges with experienced people "equipped scientifically" to become lecturers in infant school education' and secondly 'to create a centre for research in the field of child development and infant pedagogy' (Gardner 1969: 88). During her six-year stint as the Head, Isaacs gave lectures, supervised students, continued her writing, travelled abroad, and served on the editorial boards of the *British Journal of Psychology*, the *British Journal of Medical Psychology*, and the *British Journal of Educational Psychology*. All this while working intensively at the London Clinic of Psycho-Analysis. These many roles, and the great visibility they provided, created a wide and enthusiastic audience for her innovative and imaginative recommendations about nursery work.

It has been argued that the contribution of Susan Isaacs was original, based on the writings of Froebel and Dewey but including also her insights into the emotions of young children. She relied very little on cognitive psychological theories. Further, her immense influence came about not only because of her teaching experience at the Malting House School, which was well described in her books, but more importantly because of her work as Head of the Department of Child Development at the Institute of Education. During these years at the Institute she worked tirelessly as a committee member, journal editor and visitor to teacher training colleges in Britain and abroad. It wasn't enough that Isaacs developed innovative practice; this had to be described to others and communicative channels opened up as 'converts' took up her ideas, experienced problems and triumphs, and developed them further.

Piaget's Legacy

Many of those who have followed in the footsteps of Isaacs have used Piaget's theory as the scientific underpinning of progressive nursery practice. So, although Piaget did not *inspire* traditional nursery practice, more recent books on nurseries cite his work as its scientific justification. Are teachers and teacher educators justified in claiming support from Piaget for their modern nursery methods? In other words, what advice does Piaget have for the nursery educator? On close reading it becomes clear that Piaget thought adults could do little by way of 'intervention' or 'planned nurturance' because no environment, no matter how rich, could push the child beyond his genetic timetable. Piaget was disdainful about what he called the 'American question': the query concerning techniques to nudge children along a little faster than their 'natural' pace might dictate.

In a recent issue of the *Oxford Review of Education* Peter Bryant (1984) explores the contribution of Piaget to education. He claims to be surprised that Piaget has exerted such a strong influence on teaching: 'One of the most obvious and at the same time surprising things about Piaget's work is the great interest in it shown by people concerned with education.' He gives two reasons for wondering at their enthusiasm. First, Bryant tells us that Piaget himself was not much interested in the educational process, preferring instead to focus on the spontaneous and natural development of the child.

Bryant goes on, however, to cite a second, more disturbing reason why Piaget was not interested in education. Genevan researchers gave little importance to the work of teachers. Bryant continues 'one way or another' the work of a teacher 'is based on the idea that someone, who has knowledge and skills, can transmit them to others who have less of them or do not have them at all. Yet in Piaget's view this sort of activity had virtually nothing to do with children's intellectual development.' (Ibid.: 251) So, although Piaget's work provides a detailed timetable of intellectual development, it will not lead us to a coherent theory of practice – except for allowing children freedom to explore. There are no guidelines about materials to facilitate development nor indeed on helpful interactions between adults and children. Isaacs, by way of contrast, puts forward a deliberate pedagogy, one based on play, a topic to which Piaget gives short shrift. (See Sylva 1985; and Sutton-Smith 1966 for Piaget's rather dismissive views on play.)

The immense influence of Susan Isaacs on pre-school practice has been described and it has been suggested that she relied very little on the work of Piaget, preferring to look for inspiration to the writings of Dewey and in her own creative teaching at the Malting House School. Peter Bryant has suggested that this was a wise choice because Piaget himself thought little of the teacher's role. Moreover, Piaget was unduly pessimistic about pre-school children's abilities, especially their capacities to think in logical, non-egocentric ways. Isaacs thought differently and Bryant's research has proved her right.

The High/Scope Pre-school Curriculum

Despite Piaget's pessimisms, there have been numerous attempts to create pre-school programmes based directly on his work. One contemporary American curriculum has quite deliberately taken the Genevan research as the starting point for setting objectives as well as methods. It is called the High/Scope Cognitively Oriented Curriculum and the developers (Hohmann, Banet and Weikhart 1979: xiv) proclaim their debt to Piaget:

> ... it was immediately clear to us that Piaget's theories were concerned with the very same issues of cognitive development that were coming up in our own (pre-school) staff discussions . . . The next step was to establish a seminar for the staff in Piagetian theory so that we could see whether the theory could be translated into operational principles for the curriculum . . . The staff then began the slow, difficult, but ultimately rewarding process of organizing the classroom program around Piagetian developmental theory and learning to work within and around the limits of the theory.

Weikart and his colleagues describe how their curriculum gradually evolved in the classroom. At first the nursery staff attempted '*teaching* specific Piagetian tasks related to developmental stages. . .' Gradually the staff gave up on formal teaching of seriation, classification and the like and took on a less domineering role. 'In the next phase of curriculum development . . . the role of the child as "constructor" of knowledge became paramount.' (p. xv) Now children were allowed freedom to take the initiative, instead of acting as recipients of adult-planned activities. In other words, although the Piagetian notion of developmental sequence was adopted from the very beginning, the initiative was in the hands of adults in the early years of the programme. Gradually children were encouraged to share the initiative. In describing the 'new' form of the Cognitively Oriented Curriculum, Weikart and his colleagues state:

> The (new) purpose was to explore the dimensions of the child's thinking instead of asking 'test' questions for a predetermined list of goals. The conversations became real. . . The new focus was on helping children use the pre-school and home environment for *their own activities and goals*. The teacher fits his or her developmental knowledge to the purposes of the child. In a sense the program became less overtly Piagetian by becoming more committed to the fundamental theme of Piaget. (p. xv)

The subsequent versions of the High/Scope curriculum stress active learning. Is it therefore similar to the Isaacs tradition? The answer must be no. Although both Isaacs and High/Scope emphasise the strengths of each child viewed from the perspective of his or her developmental level, the adults in a High/Scope programme take an active role as orchestrators of children's activities. Although children are encouraged to make choices, their freedom is constrained by the limits of a highly structured day.

During each High/Scope session staff help children to make deliberate plans for their work or play. Staff also help children to carry out their plans, and then discuss the outcomes in small groups. The aim of the programme is to instil cognitive skills (for example, concentration, problem solving, and novel ways of doing things) as well as awareness of one's own skill. Instead of allowing free rein, the adult guides play and helps the child reflect on it. Although an important component of the High/Scope curriculum is called 'work-time', an observer on the scene would certainly describe the children's activity as play and the adult's role as facilitator and partner, rather than tyrant.

Those who designed the High/Scope curriculum were at first concerned with disadvantaged children. They feared that more traditional nursery programmes, devoted wholly to free play, would not be successful with disadvantaged children, many of whom rarely played in a sustained and rich way. It was thought that disadvantaged children needed help in maintaining concentration and accomplishing their own goals. A sensitive adult partner could help children formulate plans, describe what they did, then explore any difficulties encountered.

Evaluation and Interpretation

The effects of the High/Scope curriculum appear to be long lasting.[1] Weikart and his colleagues evaluated the effectiveness of their curriculum by randomly assigning children to either pre-school or 'home' groups, then administering objective tests before the programme began, and following up with more tests during the school years. Moreover, they monitored the attitudes of both 'programme' and 'control' (home) children who did not attend pre-school. More than a decade later they tracked down the pre-school 'graduates' and the matched controls at ages 15, 18 and 20 to see how the children were faring in life and to ask them how they viewed their own talents and potential. In all, Weikart had information on two groups of children between the ages of 3 and 20 years: his own pre-school graduates and their controls (Weikart, Epstein, Schweinhart and Bond 1978). Below are summarised the major findings concerning the long-term effects of High/Scope pre-school (Breedlove and Schweinhart 1982). These findings are statistically significant at or beyond the $p < .05$ level.

Educational Achievement. Children who attended pre-school were more likely to complete their schooling than those who did not. Furthermore, the children with pre-school experience tended to spend fewer years in 'special education' schools or classes, than children who had not been to pre-school.

Employment. Children with pre-school experience were more likely to be employed when they became young adults. They tended to support themselves completely by their own (or spouse's) earnings, whereas those without pre-school experience were less likely to be self-supporting.

Delinquency. Children with pre-school experience were less likely to be arrested by the age of 19 than those who had not attended pre-school.

Teenage Pregnancies. Girls with pre-school experience were less likely to be teenage mothers and more likely to have jobs than girls who had not attended pre-school.

The financial costs and benefits of pre-school. By calculating what it costs to place a child in expensive special education, to put him on the dole, or indeed to keep him in detention centre, Weikart has been able to estimate the cost efficiency of his pre-school programmes. They cost the taxpayer money, to be sure, but they saved him money in the long run. Weikart estimates that (in current US prices and adjusted for inflation) for each $US1,000 invested in pre-school education, there is a return of $US4,130 to the taxpayer.

The long-term effects of the High/Scope curriculum have been examined in some detail because they constitute one of the most thorough investigations into the effects of a particular curriculum. The results are impressive, but they may leave the reader wondering *which elements* of the programme contributed to the long-term gains. Was it the emphasis on 'Piagetian skills' such as classification? Or was it the 'active learning' encouraged in the plan-do-review sequence?

There are clues to be found in the interviews with both children and parents. Pre-school graduates (when in secondary school) rated themselves as higher in ability than those who had not attended pre-school. Further, they spent more time at home in preparation. When pre-school graduates talked to interviewers about job aspirations, many said they would like to work in a bank or be a secretary, jobs very different from those of their parents, who, if they worked at all, were in the lowest paid jobs.

Not only did the pre-school graduates view themselves more positively than did the control children, the parents of the two groups made different comments about their children; the parents of children who had attended pre-school were more likely to say that their child 'had done as well in school as (parent) would have liked' or that their child is 'willing to talk about what s/he is doing in school'.

The interviews, conducted with both children and parents, present a striking portrait of individuals who believe in their own capacities. Weikart thinks that the parents and teachers observed the mastery skills inculcated by the pre-school and then reflected back to the child his newly-found competence. A virtuous cycle was established in which the social environment changed, as well as the child, helping him to maintain his skills and confidence through the school years. It is impossible to pinpoint which specific component, or combination of components, in the High/Scope programme put the virtuous cycle into operation. What is known, however, is that guided play – rather than free play – was central to the pre-school experiences of the children, who appeared more committed to school and functioned better as young adults.

The Role of Adults in the Pre-school

The adult's role in guiding play now requires further consideration. Guided play rests on the premiss that children will develop skills and confidence if they make things, solve problems, and figure out the world by their own active efforts. So far, such an emphasis on active learning is not new and was encountered in the work of Susan Isaacs. What is different about High/Scope is the role of the adult – and here those responsible for designing the programme had to look beyond the theories of Piaget to psychologists concerned with the contribution to child development of parents, teachers and siblings: Sara Smilansky[2] and Jerome Bruner.

Bruner views the developing child not as a lone biological organism but as a member of a social network which is rooted firmly in a culture. From the very first weeks of life, Bruner stresses the importance of partnerships in play. The first partnership is between mother and infant but play dyads continue into adult life as, for example, spouses who passionately share a hobby, or tennis partners who play together year in, year out. In his recent work Bruner (1983) argues that language is acquired in the context of social games between child, mother, father, brothers and sisters. Further, Bruner points out that the pre-school child does not lose the need to play with others who are more mature. These partners serve several roles, including elaborator of play and appreciative audiences.

Now we come close to the distinction between guided play, so central to High/Scope and other structured programmes, and the free play of more traditional practice. In guided play the adult takes responsibility for planning a stimulating environment, then helps the child to choose and reflect upon his own activities. Note that the adults encourage, demonstrate and assist; they do not impose choices or dominate actions. The adult performs what Bruner has called 'scaffolding'. Pre-school staff encourage when problems arise, suggest when children run out of steam, and, when it's over, reflect back the child's achievements. This makes *social* the child's play and transforms overt actions into internal thought (see Bruner 1973). The child acquires language for expressing his plans and putting them into temporal context that includes 'before', 'during' and 'after'. Thus, in guided play, the adult helps the child plan, consider alternatives, and review what took place. The external actions of play become internal 'progammes' which are capable of guiding further actions in the future. Guiding children's play is a much more active role than that of supporting it. It's proponents believe that 'just messing about' will not guarantee that children acquire confidence in their ability to carry out plans (be it with beads, paint, or hammer and nails) and communicate them to others. Further, 'just messing about' will not necessarily provide feedback from the social world, a mirror to reflect the child's own mastery. The High/Scope programme, and it's just one of several structured curricula, emphasises the cycle of *plan, do, review*. In this cycle the active child needs a partner-cum-assistant-cum-conspirator-cum-audience. The partner may be parent or teacher.

It may be helpful to return to Isaacs' books to make clear the contrast between the structured and the free approach to pre-school practice. Isaacs (1930: 23) says:

In a school for little children there is ample occasion for meeting the actual movements of the children's minds towards 'finding out' about the world around them. Our theoretical aims in this could be stated from either of the two opposite ends of the problem: (1) To find suitable ways of giving satisfaction to scientific curiosity among all the other educative impulses of children: and (2) To discover the beginnings of the scientific spirit and scientific method in the thought of young children with a view to making sure of their amplest development . . . I have already made it clear that the general methods of the school aimed at encouraging the children's own active efforts in as many directions as possible . . . The chief stimulus was the environment itself.

At the Malting House children were free to explore, to wander, and to fantasise at will. Aside from the midday meal, children did exactly as they wished. Adults were there to follow their lead, to discuss their play and to deal with questions. This is quite different from the High/Scope classroom with its fixed order of plan-do-review, small-group time, tidy-up time, and integration of planning for the 'key experiences'[3] of children. Although the most obvious contrast is the more planned nature of the High/Scope day, there is another, more profound, difference to be seen. The Isaacs child appears to be a young scientist, asking 'why' questions and intent on making discoveries. The High/Scope child does this too, of course, but above all the High/Scope child is a doer, a person who plans and completes things. One is tempted to say that the High/Scope child is not so much a pure scientist as a budding engineer, planning, executing and using feedback! The High/Scope child is Brunel as well as Einstein.

Focus on Active Learning

In sum, both the inheritors of the Isaacs tradition and the pioneers of the new High/Scope programme take as the cornerstone of their practice *active learning*. The former owes more to the active learning emphasis of Dewey than to Piaget; the latter boasts of its allegiance to Piaget, yet has devised a daily and weekly regime in which adults timetable the day, plan specific activities and expect children to participate, and encourage children to verbalise their intentions and outcomes. It is likely that Piaget would agree with the objectives of the High/Scope programme but be doubtful about its methods. The programme seems to assign greater importance to language as an instrument of thought in the tradition of Bruner, Olver and Greenfield (1966) and Vygotsky (1962). It seems likely that Piaget would disagree on the role of language and of the way in which in the High/ Scope approach adults *share* the initiative with the child, rather than following the child's leads.

To sum up the story so far, the High/Scope curriculum, ostensibly based on Piaget, seems to have drifted quite a bit off course. It may be in keeping with the spirit of Piaget's work but it is really the outcome of innovative staff thinking and creative practice on the classroom floor. Although those who designed the High/Scope programme took Piaget as their starting-point, they turned to other psychologists and to their own insights. In the end, they used solid classroom trials to invent means of *ensuring active learning*, rather than hoping it would spontaneously occur.

Piaget, the most important developmental psychologist of our century, has turned out to have little direct influence on the pre-school curriculum. His theory contributed little to the traditional British practice and had to be extensively modified in the American programme, which pays greatest homage to his work. It now seems that developmental theory is either useless in guiding practice, or beneficial only as a starting-point for innovations in the classroom. Must this always be the case?

Involving Practitioners in Research

The last section of this chapter concerns an effort on the part of developmental psychologists to conduct research of direct relevance to practitioners; research useful in day-to-day nursery planning. The Oxford Pre-school Research Group began in the mid-1970s when Jerome Bruner, then Watts Professor of Psychology at Oxford, decided that researchers and practitioners might profitably collaborate in designing and conducting research on pre-school practice. The team began by listing the reasons why practitioners in the past had a deaf ear to research results. Wood and Harris (1977) came up with three reasons why pre-school practitioners might shy away from research findings (the following is abbreviated and paraphrased).

Statistical Thinking. Researchers think in terms of samples, means, ranges and 'significance'. To scientists, these terms have an inescapable quality about them, whereas practitioners think about

individual children, unique persons who may well be different from
the norm; often this uniqueness seems more crucial to the task at hand
than all manner of norms.

Differences in Goal Structures. Practitioners have a multitude of
goals; they deal with the whole child and every day see how the many
facets of development intertwine. Researchers, by way of contrast,
focus an analytic searchlight on one, or perhaps two, aspects of
development. They think they need to do this so that the variable of
interest can be isolated and manipulated; they do so, unfortunately, at
the risk of losing credibility with practitioners. Their goal is to analyse
into parts, not to nurture wholes.

Distinction Between Conducting Research and Using It. Practitioners who conduct research are invariably enthusiastic about it,
whereas consumers of other people's findings are prone to quibble
and carp. Why? Wood and Harris (1977: 12) suggest one reason: 'It
seems that many of us need a personal investment in the creation of an
instrument or technique if we are to receive its products enthusiastically or to take them as a basis for action.'

The Oxford Pre-school Research Group bore in mind the list drawn
up by Wood and Harris when designing their study into the
concentration and complexity of play in local nurseries and
playgroups. They formed a team of researchers and practitioners to
design the study; they decided to work in 'the field' of nurseries and
playgroups rather than in the laboratory; and they vowed to share the
results at every stage, so they could be debated and interpreted by
practitioners and researchers alike. The course of this collaborative
research, which was only partially successful, is described in an
appendix in Bruner's book *Under Five in Britain* (1980). What
concerns us here is that an assumption was made that pre-school
practice could not be based on the findings of developmental
psychology because (1) most of these had emanated from the
laboratory, (2) until recently theories of cognitive development have
ignored the social context of learning, and (3) Piagetian theory was
too pessimistic about children's capacities and would lead to a
curriculum which undersold children's skills.

To counter these drawbacks, the new research project aimed to
conduct observational studies which would document the factors
in the pre-school associated with 'intellectual challenge', that

is, the stretching kind of play in which children solve problems, transform objects and actions, and make constructive use of feedback from their efforts.

The results of these studies are reported in *Childwatching at Playgroup and Nursery School*, Sylva, Roy and Painter (1980) and may be summarised briefly:

(1) In the presence of adults, children's play is more likely to be rich and sustained than when they are on their own.
(2) Children's play is usually more complex when they engage in structured activities, rather than purely expressive ones.
(3) Child-peer language is usually more complex during expressive play than structured play.
(4) When not in the presence of an adult, children are more likely to play in complex, imaginative ways when they are in a child–child pair rather than alone or in larger groups.

This is not the place to discuss the findings in full but rather to explore the effects on British pre-school practice of the Oxford findings. In the main, the reaction of practitioners was cautious. Some innovative teachers took up the results and changed their provision to include more structured materials, for example, construction toys, puzzles, etc. Others attempted to encourage more peer pairs with a view towards increasing complex play. On the other hand, many practitioners did not know of the Oxford group or thought little of its research. Unlike Susan Isaacs, the Oxford Research Group did not contribute to teacher education, did not regularly come into contact with the HMI, and rarely presented papers at educational conferences. Although, in a sense, they did produce 'relevant' research with the potential of improving nursery practice, it was disseminated in a haphazard way and made ripples instead of waves. Unfortunately, the group did not have the Head of the Institute of Education's Department of Child Development on their team! The moral here is that producing relevant and 'collaborative' research findings is only half the story; they must be fed into the educational establishment via personal contact and regular, professional colleagueship. (See chapters by Desforges and McConkey, this volume.)

Before concluding, let's turn to the major findings of the Oxford group concerning the factors that encourage problem-solving, complex play and imaginative activity. Are they compatible with Piagetian theory? The answer is no. The findings about the facilitating influence of teachers could not have been predicted by Piagetian or 'cognitive' developmental theory because this line of research has traditionally taken place in a laboratory. The Oxford group found that some play activities fostered complex thinking more than others – that all play was not equally challenging to the young mind. No doubt this would not surprise Piaget, but researchers in the cognitive/ developmental tradition have not systematically compared different categories of play. Lastly the finding concerning the intellectual richness associated with playing in pairs, instead of in groups, would not be predicted by Piagetian theory which tends to ignore the effect of different social groupings on children's thought.

Conclusion

It is now time to summarise the relationship between developmental psychology and the pre-school curriculum. As one of the most influential workers Susan Isaacs derived pre-school practice from Dewey and her own experiences as a teacher; she ignored (what was to become) the monumental theory of Jean Piaget. Further, her influence was great because of her active role in teacher training and a variety of professional organisations. She exerted a *personal* influence, not just a literary one. The American High/Scope curriculum, while giving applause to Piagetian theory, was changed quite a bit in the classroom; in fact new theorists, such as Bruner and Smilansky, were necessary to supplement Piaget's work. The High/Scope history shows the influence of developmental psychology to be germinal, but not total. Lastly, the work of the Oxford Pre-school Research Group, while representing a genuine collaboration of researchers and practitioners, had only marginal impact because it was not firmly fixed in the educational networks. For developmental psychology to serve a useful role in guiding pre-school curriculum it will have to follow a truly collaborative research regime of both field and laboratory studies, while at the same time forging links with the professional institutions of education. Only then can it make a direct and lasting impact on what happens in ordinary pre-schools.

Notes

1. Some of the material in this chapter has been described in Sylva (1984).
2. Weikart and his colleagues acknowledge their debt to Smilansky, especially the

help she provided on a visit to Ypsilanti in 1964. See Hohmann, Banet and Weihart (1979).

3. These key experiences bear such Piagetian-sounding names as classification, seriation, number concepts, spatial relations and time.

References

Breedlove, C. and Schweinhart, L.J. (1982) The cost-effectiveness of high quality early childhood programs, A report for the 1982 Southern Governors' Conference, South Carolina

Bruner, J.S. (1973) Language as an instrument of thought in A. Davies (ed.), *Problems of Language and Learning*, London: Heinemann

— (1980) *Under Five in Britain*, London: Grant McIntyre

— (1983) *Child's Talk*, New York: Norton

—, Olver, R.R. and Greenfield, P.M. (1966) *Studies in Cognitive Growth*, New York: Wiley

Bryant, P.E. (1974) *Perception and Understanding in Young Children*, London: Methuen

— (1984) Piaget, teachers and psychologists, *Oxford Review of Education*, *10(3)*, 251–60

Donaldson, M. (1978) *Children's Minds*, London: Fontana

Gardner, D.E.M. (1969) *Susan Isaacs*, London: Methuen

Hohmann, M., Banet, B. and Weikart, D.P. (1979) *Young Children in Action: A Manual for Preschool Educators*, Ypsilanti, Michigan: High/Scope Educational Research Foundation

Isaacs, S. (1930) *Intellectual Growth in Young Children*, London: Routledge & Kegan Paul

— (1933) *Social Development in Young Children*, London: Routledge & Kegan Paul

Sutton-Smith, B. (1966) Piaget on play: a critique, *Psychological Review*, *73(1)*, 104–10

Sylva, K., Roy, C. and Painter, M. (1980) *Childwatching at Playgroup and Nursery School*, London: McIntyre

— (1984) A hard-headed look at the fruits of play, *Early Child Development and Care*, *15*, 171–84

— (1985) Play in *Personality, Development and Learning*, the Open University

Vygotsky, L.S. (1962) *Thought and Language*, Harvard: MIT Press

Weikart, D.P., Epstein, A.S., Schweinhart, L. and Bond, J.T. (1978) *The Ypsilanti Preschool Curriculum Demonstration Project: Preschool Years and Longitudinal Results*, Ypsilanti, Michigan: High/Scope Educational Research Foundation

Wood, D. and Harris, M. (1977) The Oxford Pre-School Research Group: An Experiment in Psychological Intervention, *Prospects* (Unesco) (mimeo)

THE CONTRIBUTION OF DEVELOPMENTAL
PSYCHOLOGY TO THE EDUCATION OF MENTALLY
HANDICAPPED CHILDREN IN SPECIAL SCHOOLS

John Harris

Introduction

This chapter examines the role of developmental theories with respect
to teaching practices in special schools for mentally handicapped
children. Since mentally handicapped children experience delayed or
deviant development compared to normal children, and as one of the
goals of educational intervention with mentally handicapped children
is the establishment of normal patterns of development, it is often
assumed that the formulation of theories of normal development will
have important implications for teaching. In this chapter I will
question this assumption and argue that theories of normal development have failed to provide a useful platform for intervention
strategies in special schools.

Part of the problem concerns contemporary views about the nature
of psychological theories. Far from being objective descriptions
which have broad generalisability, it is suggested that theories in
social sciences are relative to the specific problems which they
address, and to the historical, social and epistemological conditions
which prevailed at the time they were being developed (see, for
example, Ingleby 1974; Henriques, Holloway, Urwin, Venn and
Walkerdine 1984). From this perspective, the applicability of any
theory will depend upon the problems addressed by the practitioner
being the same problems as those addressed by those who constructed
the theory. Furthermore, successful application will depend upon the
extent to which those who seek to apply a theory, or its technological
products (for example, tests, assessment instruments, teaching
schemes), work with a clear knowledge of the aims of the theory
builder, the kinds of questions which were being addressed and the
range of assumptions which initially made the theory intelligible.
However, it is clear that during the transition from theory building
about normal child development, to theory application in institutions
such as special schools, the emphasis shifts from one of understanding
and explaining to one of a concern with action and intervention. It will

be argued that teachers are concerned with fundamentally different problems to the traditional developmental theorists and that they do not therefore share the same philosophical and psychological presuppositions. (For a discussion of this problem in relation to the pre-school curriculum see Sylva, this volume.)

Sinha (1981), in discussing the work of the Bristol Teacher Research Group, suggested that in view of different professional and practical interests, teachers and psychologists needed to set aside established and entrenched views about the nature and aims of research and negotiate a set of shared meanings which could serve as the basis of collaborative research. This could then lead to greater participation by practitioners in the process of defining the goals and procedures of psychological research in the context of special education.

In contrast to Sinha's call for research which *begins* as a collaborative enterprise, there are still numerous examples of psychologists and educationalists adopting a traditional view of the research practice dichotomy, and seeking to take 'successful' theories from the field of developmental psychology and determine suitable strategies for application within educational settings. For example, if one adopts a relatively restricted set of criteria for evaluation, it can be argued that psychologists have met with considerable success in generating developmental theories about the growth of logical thinking and about language acquisition. In both these areas, strong claims have been made with respect to the relevance of the theories to the education of mentally handicapped children. And yet 'good' theories have not provoked significant changes in practice. This chapter discusses this failure in terms of the nature and limitations of contemporary developmental theories and the model of dissemination by which research has been packaged for practice.

The chapter begins with a review of the 'theory to educational practice' literature in relation to theories concerned with language acquisition and the development of logical thinking. In each case the evidence is considered in relation to three areas of educational practice, namely, pupil assessment, the curriculum and methods of instruction. This is followed by a discussion of the extent to which child development theories can provide a template for teaching normal developmental sequences and the neglected role of psychological processes, both in relation to research and educational practice. Thirdly, the chapter considers the role which research traditionally plays in the generation of curriculum innovations and the mechanism by which such innovations are made available to practitioners. It is suggested that this process plays an essential part in maintaining a system whereby research concerned with theoretical questions about normal development can continue to form the basis for the generation of practical innovations for the education of mentally handicapped children. The chapter closes with some comments regarding the future direction of research if teaching in special schools is to be based upon a firm and appropriate theoretical foundation.

Piaget's Theory and Special Education

Piaget has provided developmental psychologists with what continues to be their single most important account of cognitive development, and it is for this reason that this section is specifically concerned with the impact of Piagetian theory on special education. However, before considering the uses which psychologists and educators have advocated for Piagetian theory in special schools, it is necessary to consider a more fundamental issue for those who would seek to apply the theory; on what basis can Piaget's theory about normal development be extended to the development of mentally handicapped individuals? Interestingly, the evidence sought and the justification for extending Piaget's theory to special education is concerned with the generalisability of Piaget's developmental stages to other populations, as if this could in itself constitute a rationale for using Piaget's theory as a basis for instruction. In a recent review, Weisz, Yeates and Zigler (1982: 240) examined the evidence in relation to two specific hypotheses. First, the *similar sequence hypothesis* is a predication that retarded and non-retarded individuals will negotiate the four stages in the order which Piaget described with respect to normally developing children, with only the rate of progress and the final level achieved differentiating the mentally handicapped population from normal (that is, non-handicapped) individuals. On the basis of 28 cross-sectional and three longitudinal studies the authors concluded that 'the hypothesis seems to be generally supported in studies of retarded individuals regardless of etiology, with the possible exception of individuals suffering from pronounced EEG abnormalities'.

According to Weisz *et al.*, the *similar structure hypothesis* predicts that familial retarded persons will function at a similar level, in relation to Piagetian tasks, as non-retarded individuals matched for general level of intellectual development. All the studies reviewed in relation to this hypothesis suffered from the limitation imposed by the use of Mental Age (MA) as an index of mental development (Baumeister 1967; Ryan 1973; Brooks and Baumeister 1977) and the results supported the similar structure hypothesis only in relation to 'non-organically-impaired' children. Since it is organically-impaired children who are most likely to have very low IQ and MA scores which do not accurately reflect their abilities in less constrained settings, one is left with the dilemma of whether to question the relevance of Piagetian theory to such mentally handicapped children, as it is inconsistent with psychometrically derived estimates of their intellectual status, or alternatively, to reject the psychometric evidence as being inconsistent with their performance on tasks designed to assess cognitive structures. Irrespective of this ambiguous evidence in relation to the similar structure hypothesis, the strong evidence of a normal sequence of development has been regarded by a number of researchers as representing a prima-facie case for using Piaget's theory as a basis for introducing teaching innovations in special schools (Wolinsky 1962; Woodward 1962; Reid 1978).

Piagetian Theory as a Basis for Assessment in Special Schools

Since cognitive structures are seen by Piaget as the principal determinants of a child's capacity for intelligent action (although performance constraints may prevent children from functioning at the limits of their competence, (Piaget 1970; Piaget and Inhelder 1969), a number of psychologists have regarded Piagetian theory and the associated methodology as offering educationally relevant forms of cognitive assessment in relation to pedagogic decisions about what and how a child should be taught (Woodward 1970; Klein and Safford 1977; Reid 1978; Fincham 1982). Some writers have apparently regarded Piagetian theory as a panacea to all problems of educational assessment with mentally handicapped individuals:

> potentially, the development of scales of operational schemes can be one of the most stimulating and fruitful breakthroughs in the diagnosis of learning dysfunction. It can give to teachers an analysis of dysfunction similar to that which the laboratory analysis of biological dysfunction gives to the physician. (Wolinsky 1962: 254).

In the light of such enthusiasm it is worth considering why assessments based upon Piagetian theory have not been more widely adopted in special schools during the intervening period of 20 years. For the teacher, information derived from pupil assessment may have a variety of functions including placement of a child in a class or teaching group, assessment of a child's progress or regress over time, the setting up of teaching objectives, the identification of appropriate teaching methods, and the evaluation of teaching approaches in relation to baseline performances. Furthermore, to be acceptable in the classroom, assessment procedures must be time–cost effective; the teacher must believe that the time expended in making the assessment will provide an adequate return in terms of relevant information. Against these criteria, Piagetian-based assessments have a number of disadvantages. Firstly, to yield information which has construct validity in terms of the theory, asssessment requires not only skills and a detailed knowledge of the theory beyond that possessed by most teachers but also the flexibility to spend a considerable amount of time with each pupil (Tamburrini 1982). Furthermore, as Fincham (1982) points out, Piaget's method cannot be reduced to a normative psychometric scale without seriously distorting the original theoretical position regarding the individual subject's construction of knowledge. The concept of stage is derived from the child's interaction with a problem and not from the problem itself (Selman 1975). Secondly, it is not clear what significance the delineation of structural competencies has in relation to pedagogical decisions as described above, particularly when viewed against other performance variables which might seem more important in the context of special education (for example, attention span, social responsiveness and capacity to communicate). Additional problems concern the validity of diagnostic procedures, even under ideal research conditions (Smedslund 1969; Smedslund 1977; Brown and Desforges 1977), and the extent to which mental structures are predictive of problem-solving across settings (Smedslund 1977; Donaldson 1978). Piagetian theory views the child as a biological entity and development as an individual process of construction. For teachers, by virtue of their professional role, and increasingly for developmental psychologists, development is viewed as a social enterprise in which knowledge and the capacity for intelligent thought is derived from close involvement with others; assessment procedures which relegate the human capacity for social interaction to the status of an extraneous performance variable may deliberately overlook some of the major cognitive influences of schooling (Donaldson 1978; Vygotsky 1978; Walkerdine 1982).

Piagetian Theory as a Basis for the Special School Curriculum

The rationale for adopting Piagetian stages as a basis for school assessment has been that an understanding of a child's level of functioning can help the teacher to decide what skills and concepts the child is likely to be able to learn. However, if cognitive structures constrain learning by preventing a child from assimilating ideas in advance of his current level of functioning, and yet make it relatively easy for children to understand and learn material presented at or below their current stage of development, it might make more sense for teachers in special schools to concentrate on encouraging development of cognitive structures *per se* (Reid 1978). For example, Woodward (1962: 17) argued that 'the educational task with children who have not the concepts of number and space to be able to learn elementary calculations etc. is that of providing them with appropriate manipulative and other experiences that will foster the development of those concepts'. More recently, DeVries (1978) has criticised the emphasis of stage transitions as an educational objective in pre-school for three reasons. First, she argues that because the broad theory of cognitive development is illustrated by Piaget with respect to relatively narrow scientific concepts, there is a danger that a stage emphasis will result in an educational focus on scientific knowledge at the expense of more general aspects of cognitive development. Secondly, DeVries suggests that the focus on structural levels or stages tends to overshadow the constructivist *process* of development which, she claims, ought to be the central theme of attempts to explore the educational applications of Piaget's theory. Thirdly, transition through the stages overlooks the importance of co-ordinations of mental structures within stages, that is, the occurrence of structures d'ensemble (Piaget 1970).

Woodward's position was that if a Piagetian framework could be utilised to assess children, then teachers could attempt to provide 'the experiences that are appropriate to the point the child has reached in this sequence, so that development of the next step may thereby be encouraged' (Woodward 1962: 25). As Woodward acknowledged, within the Piagetian framework experience can only ever be partly determined by the teacher, since the psychological significance of what is presented depends upon the activity of the child. However, numerous attempts have been made to provide a more precise description of the environmental conditions which are maximally effective in promoting cognitive development among both normal and mentally handicapped children. The absence of consistent results in these training studies with respect to mentally handicapped children (Klein and Safford 1977) may be attributed, at least in part, to the considerable methodological problems involved in demonstrating that particular experiences result in specific structural changes (Brown and Desforges 1979). In the majority of training studies, intervention procedures have involved attempting to improve children's performance on one or more of the traditional Piagetian tasks. Similarly, educators who have adopted a stage transition emphasis for the school curriculum (for example, Furth and Wachs 1975) have based teaching activities on the various problems initially designed by Piaget to assess cognitive status (DeVries 1978). This approach may be criticised on a number of grounds. The tasks were originally designed as aids to assessment and performance on the task ought not to be equated with the development of cognitive structures; nor is there any evidence that task-related activity in itself is sufficient to promote the development of general structures (Selman 1975). Secondly, the teaching of specific tasks is only likely to achieve changes in isolated operations, as compared with the development of integrated and co-ordinated operations which characterise the structure operationale d'ensemble (DeVries 1978). Thirdly, such teaching assumes that in order to proceed in terms of structural levels or stages, the child must succeed on all the stages of the different tasks. But whereas the theory claims that there is a constant universal sequence for developmental stages, Piaget made no such claim in respect of performance on specific tasks. Consequently, 'to organise an educational programme on the basis of sequences found for the tasks is therefore to reduce the sequence of development to sequences which are research artefacts' (DeVries 1978: 78).

Wickens (1974: 189) has argued that the implementation of Piagetian teaching practices in schools implies a transition from a closed system of education, in which the teacher prescribes the content of what is to be learned by the pupil and administers rewards and punishments in accordance with the extent to which pupils meet performance expectations, to an open system in which 'the teacher's function is to create an environment in which the learner is interested in exploring and studying about what is relevant to his interests'. Such a transition to a developmentally orientated curriculum would entail a number of fundamental revisions regarding the role of the teacher, the philosophy of the school and the criteria by which schools are rendered accountable (Kohlberg and Mayer 1972). The alternative involves the modification of Piagetian theory so that educational applications are consistent with a closed system. Notwithstanding DeVries' criticisms concerning attempts to teach structure through training on specific tasks, some developmental psychologists (for example, Shearer and Shearer 1972, 1976; Kiernan 1981) have gone one step further and suggested that behavioural repertoires of skills which define success in relation to specific Piagetian tasks are, in themselves, characteristic of developmental progress. Such a behavioural analysis can then be used to justify the dislocation of developmentally sequenced teaching goals from the processes of development by which they are normally attained. According to this argument, since the development of normal children is characterised by the attainment of certain skills which appear to have functional significance, then developmental progress can be achieved if those skills can be taught to mentally handicapped children. However, any notion of developmental continuities may be explicitly rejected (Kiernan 1981) and the selection and sequencing of task related skills reduced to adult intuition regarding the skills a child is likely to need to cope effectively with common experiences. Such an approach isolates the task from the theory and undermines any claims for a theoretical or a developmental rationale with respect to the content of a teaching curriculum.

Piagetian Theory and Teaching Strategies

For the educationalist working within a Piagetian framework, a fundamental problem revolves around Piaget's insistence on the central role of equilibration and the extent to which mentalism pervades his account of the role of experience in development. Bereft of empirical indices of either equilibration or logico-mathematical experience (Flavell 1971; Brown and Desforges 1979), educationalists have identified three related principles on the basis of which they have attempted to evolve a set of pragmatic recommendations for good teaching practice. These principles are: indirect intervention through the planned management of educational settings; the central role of child activity; and the opportunities afforded by conflict between experience and knowledge structures (Kamii 1974; DeVries 1978; Brainerd 1978). However, since the theory does not generate predictions regarding the effects of specific experiences in relation to structural change (Bryant 1983), teachers are left with general exhortations; for example, to 'help the child construct knowledge by guiding his experience' (Kamii 1974: 212) without any more guidelines for relating intervention to desired changes in the pupil. Indeed, Bryant (1983) has argued that Piaget's explanation of developmental progress is fundamentally flawed, since the notion of conflict is only sufficient to tell a child that either one or both possible solutions or explanations is wrong; it cannot in itself inform the child how to transcend the contradiction with which he is faced. Thus, with regard to teaching methods, Piaget leaves teachers with a difficult choice; they must either accept Piaget on trust and plan an educational environment which will be consistent with these guidance principles (indirect teacher influence, child action and conflict), or look elsewhere for a theory which is more directly relevant to their own needs, aims and educational philosophy.

Theories of Early Language Acquisition and Special Education

Theories of language acquisition have changed dramatically during the last 20 years, both in relation to what it is that children are thought to be learning when they acquire language and in terms of the social and psychological processes which have been implicated. And each change in theoretical perspective has been interpreted in terms of its implications for language intervention with mentally handicapped children in special schools. The familiar question of whether mentally handicapped children develop language abilities which are simply delayed, or whether they constitute a separate population with language which progresses along a different path compared to normal children, is seen as having serious implications for the extent to which the considerable volume of research on normal children is relevant to producing guidelines for language intervention in special schools (for example, Graham and Graham 1971; Yoder and Miller 1972; Ryan 1975; Freedman and Carpenter 1976; Cummins 1977; McLean and Snyder-McLean 1978).

One widely supported view is that the mentally handicapped child makes slow but normal progress (Lenneberg 1967; Ryan 1975; McLean and Snyder-McLean 1978). This is consistent with informal observations that when mentally handicapped children do develop language it is usually a recognisable variant of the language of their normal peers and that mentally handicapped and normally developing children have broadly similar opportunities for language acquisition. Studies which have attempted formal comparisons have tended to confirm the view of slow but otherwise normal development. (Ryan 1975; Rondal 1976; Coggins 1976). However, all comparison studies are limited by the difficulty of finding suitable measures on which to match normal and handicapped children prior to obtaining measures of relative linguistic performance. Comparisons based upon psychometrically derived measures, for example, Mental Age or IQ, are subject to all the criticisms which have been made regarding the inherent bias in such tests, particularly the differential loading on linguistic comprehension and production (Prehm 1966; Baumeister 1967; Ryan 1973, 1975; Brooks and Baumeister 1977). Similarly, attempting to equate children on some general measure of linguistic attainment such as MLU (Ryan 1975) raises questions about whether observed differences ought to be interpreted in terms of the validity of the initial comparison measure or of inherent developmental differences in the dependent language measures (Harris 1983). After making detailed comparisons between the early semantic relations expressed by a group of normally developing children and a group of Down's syndrome children, Harris concluded:

> the evidence suggests that the language of young Down's syndrome children does not conform to a model of slow but otherwise normal development. On the other hand the evidence is not consistent with a picture of linguistic deviance. Instead, it is proposed that it is more accurate to consider the early language of Down's syndrome children as similar to that of normal children, but with variations in the extent to which the different linguistic sub-skills are co-ordinated and synchronised over time. (Ibid.: 163)

The extent to which the *processes* by which mentally handicapped children acquire language are similar to the processes underlying language acquisition in normal children is more complicated. In the first instance, mentally handicapped children are *not*, by definition, in the same position to take advantage of language learning opportunities as normal children. If the diagnosis of mental handicap is taken to imply specific deficits which make learning more difficult (Cromar 1981) then one might seek ways of manipulating the environment to compensate for such deficits. For example, peripheral and irrelevant stimuli might be removed from the learning situation to help a child who has attentional problems and lacks the ability to concentrate, or repetitions of simplified input might be used for children with memory deficits. However, if delay is taken literally to mean that mentally handicapped children take longer to process information, there are additional difficulties, since it is not possible to slow down interpersonal and speech processes as one might slow down a film. Given that the problem of learning language is defined by the nature of the skills to be learned, the existing knowledge which the child brings to the situation and the social and psychological strategies or processes available, it seems unlikely that language acquisition can be mediated by the same processes in both normal and mentally handicapped children.

Theories of Language Development and Assessment in Special Schools

The extension of descriptions of early child language to include structural, semantic and functional characteristics (Lock 1980; Wells 1981) suggests that these are the areas which need to be examined during assessment of children with delayed or deviant language abilities while the increasing emphasis on language as a communicative and social process indicates that as far as is possible assessment should focus on children's abilities within naturalistic settings (McLean and Snyder-McLean 1978; Rees 1978). However, while naturalistic recordings and detailed transcriptions have enabled researchers to generate elaborate descriptions of child language, it is difficult to see how similar detailed descriptions can be produced as part of a normal classroom assessment. A recent survey by Gibbs (1982) found that whereas 91 per cent of teachers in special schools used some kind of formal assessment procedure, other than informal observation and judgement, over half used standardised, all-round assessments in which language was included as a sub-section and nearly a quarter used standardised instruments, such as charts of normal development and developmental tests. The teachers reported that the most frequently used test by speech therapists working in the schools was the Reynell Language Development Scale, while psychologists tended to rely upon the WISC, the Stanford–Binet and the Griffiths Scale. Overall, these data suggest an emphasis on normal development as the yardstick by which to assess developmental changes in mentally handicapped children and a considerable gap between the level of description which research studies have suggested as being appropriate and the kinds of description most commonly derived from instruments used in classroom assessments. An additional problem is that all the assessment instruments in Gibbs's study focused on language as an individual cognitive attainment which could be demonstrated within artificial test settings or on the basis of semi-naturalistic observations. However, contemporary theories of language acquisition suggest that assessment should also be concerned with the ways in which children are engaged in social interactions and the language learning opportunities which arise as a consequence (Seibert and Oller 1981). This would shift the focus of concern away from language products to the social and psychological processes which presumably mediate development, and would include as part of the assessment the role of parents and teachers in facilitating appropriate language learning opportunities.

The third major impact of research on language acquisition by normal children has been the suggestion that certain social and cognitive abilities, established prior to the onset of spoken language, might place constraints on what can be achieved through intervention. This implies that a careful assessment of such prerequisite abilities ought to be part of any psychological assessment for language intervention (Bricker and Bricker 1973; Kahn 1975; McLean and Snyder-Mclean 1978; Mahoney, Crawley and Pullis 1980).

The Content of Language Instruction in Special Schools

Broad descriptions of language acquired by normally developing children have also been incorporated into the recommendations which have been made for language curricula in special schools and the emphasis on early cognitive and social prerequisites of language have been interpreted as additional areas which need to be targeted within intervention programmes (Bricker and Bricker 1973; McLean and Snyder-McLean 1978). There are two ways in which descriptions of natural langue have been used for designing language teaching curricula; the first involves ignoring developmental sequences and taking a description of adult linguistic skill to generate a set of graded learning objectives which are logically ordered and consistent with the teaching methods employed (Kiernan 1984). A second strategy involves using observed developmental sequences as a basis for establishing the order of successive teaching objectives (Mahoney *et al.* 1980). Whereas the first strategy ignores development, the second makes the assumption that the most effective way of encouraging development is to move the mentally handicapped child through the same sequence of behaviourally defined steps or stages which are thought to characterise normal development. However, both these approaches ignore developmental processes either on the grounds that teaching technologies have designed more efficient ways for children to learn (Kiernan 1984) or on the grounds that an understanding of normal developmental processes cannot make a contribution to helping a population which is, by definition, abnormal (Kiernan 1981). As a result a large number of intervention programmes, designed to be used by parents as well as teachers, have adopted developmentally ordered sequences for objectives but have chosen to recommend that these can be achieved through procedures which have little in common with developmental processes (see Harris 1984a for a review).

An additional problem is that developmental sequences are broad generalisations based on studies of either a large number of children or studies of individuals; in either case they fail to take account of individual variation (Nelson 1980). And it is because of the individual variations found in the developmental sequences of both normal and mentally handicapped populations that generalised descriptions of developmental sequences cannot be used to generate predictions about what might be a natural sequence of development for any individual mentally handicapped child. Yet this is precisely the data which is used when researchers make claims about developmentally based forms of intervention (Miller and Yoder 1972; Miller and Yoder 1974; McLean and Snyder-McLean 1978; Leeming, Swann, Coupe and Mittler 1979).

Other assumptions behind the use of developmentally based language sequences are that either language behaviour on its own is an appropriate goal for intervention (thus brushing aside the majority of the child language research which has been conducted since Chomsky's (1959) denunciation of Skinner's 'Verbal Behaviour' or that since behaviour is only a reflection of more abstract cognitive and linguistic competencies, training the behaviour will, *ipso facto*, realise the competencies (Harris 1984b). Both of these assumptions ignore the relationship between language behaviour and underlying linguistic knowledge; between language defined as an intra-individual attainment and language as a developmental and social process.

Methods of Language Teaching in Special Schools

The idea of a language curriculum represented by a sequence of behaviours which mimic the sequence of changing language skills (and by implication language competencies) in normal development has resulted in a number of strategies for eliciting specific linguistic responses. These include questioning strategies (Crystal, Garman and Fletcher 1976; Leeming, Swann, Coupe and Mittler 1979; Robson 1980, 1981), modelling and imitation (MacDonald, Blott, Spiegel, Hartman and Gordon 1974) and various drills (Crystal, Garman and Fletcher 1976). Generally, appropriate responses are reinforced, either with tangible reinforcers or with praise. This and other similar research has given rise to a large number of language teaching programmes both for parents of mentally handicapped children and teachers in special schools. Unfortunately, there are only very limited data available regarding the extent to which such programmes are implemented in homes and schools and how far they are successful in teaching 'normal language' to mentally handicapped children (Harris, 1984a; Howlin 1984). A different line of research has involved examining the inter-personal processes which are thought to underly progress in language acquisition among normal children, as compared to the processes which are implicated in the acquisition of language by mentally handicapped children at similar developmental levels. For example, a study by Jones (1977) indicated certain difficulties for Down's syndrome children in maintaining joint visual reference between themselves and their mothers with respect to a given play object. Brinker (1982) has suggested that the availability of pre-existing conceptual themes or maps, with respect to a play context (for example a dolls' tea party as compared with putting a doll to bed), determines the ease with which young mentally handicapped children acquire new lexical items. In addition, a large number of studies have been conducted to examine the linguistic environment experienced by mentally handicapped children and adults. Unfortunately, many of these studies have been concerned with simply quantifying degrees of variation in the language of a typical population, instead of examining the processes by which mentally handicapped children acquire language in conversational contexts (Kogan, Wimberger and Bobbitt 1969; Marshall, Hegrenes and Goldstein 1973, Buium, Rynders and Turnure 1974).

A small number of intervention studies have indicated ways in which the conversational interactions can be influenced to enhance the mentally handicapped child's opportunities for developmental progress. These range from direct attempts to change the ways in which adults talk to children, by giving specific instructions (Whitehurst, Novak and Zorn 1972; Chesaldine and McConkey

1979), or by modelling what are thought to be appropriate adult 'styles' of conversation (Seitz 1975; Seitz and Marcus 1976), to more subtle attempts to measure changes in adult patterns of interaction following changes in materials, activities or settings (Harris 1984c).

Each of these naturalistic approaches emphasises the unpredictability of specific developmental outcomes, the significance of the child's contribution to developmental processes and the need to encourage sensitive and flexible patterns of response among the relevant adults. Interestingly, these studies do not preclude the use of purely functional criteria being employed to evaluate success, independently of any presumed normal sequence of developmental products. They do suggest that an understanding of the social and psychological processes which mediate language acquisition among normal children may provide the best framework for understanding the processes which are implicated in the acquisition of language by mentally handicapped children, and hence, the best starting-point for school-based intervention. As yet there is little indication that a non-normative process approach to language intervention is being implemented in schools.

Developmental Theories and the Practice of Special Education

From this brief review, it is possible to identify certain features of the process by which psychologists and educationalists have sought to assimilate developmental theories to educational practice. Walkerdine (1984) has suggested such theories are 'inserted' within existing educational practices which, in turn, are related to particular ideological standpoints. Piagetian theory and ideas about language development have been seen as having a greater impact in special schools in relation to assessment and the delineation of teaching goals than in respect of the generation of new teaching methods; whereas the notion of behaviourally defined developmental sequences is compatible with the ideology of instruction and training, the more complex question of developmental processes is not only less clearly articulated in the research literature but it also raises fundamental questions about the ways in which teachers carry out their professional responsibilities and, ultimately, about the very nature of those responsibilities.

Teaching Normal Development

Piaget's theory of cognitive development and socio-psychological accounts of language acquisition depict a *'normal'* sequence produced by *normal* processes. For schools which by definition are concerned with helping abnormal and deviant children, the idea of a natural sequence of stages, which can be held up as representing an ideal state to which teaching efforts should be directed, has proved overwhelming and irresistible. Successive approximations towards 'normal' functioning have become the explicit concern of special schools and, alongside the behaviourist's notion of 'normal adaptation' and the psychometric ideal of a normal IQ, developmental theories have established an alternative conception of what 'normal' might mean (Walkerdine 1984). However, in order for developmental theories to be accepted as relevant within special education, it has been necessary in the first instance to demonstrate that mentally handicapped children are appropriate candidates for 'normalisation'. That is to say that, in adopting developmental theories as a basis for intervention, schools would be promoting and endorsing some underlying set of forces which are as 'natural' and 'normal' for the mentally handicapped child as for the normal child. By adopting theories based on, and initially directed at, normal children, special schools are necessarily acquiescing to a model of delayed but otherwise normal development. Sufficient research has been carried out to show that the changes in mentally handicapped children over time can be fitted into a sequential description of the changes which occur in normal children. But this is still a long way short of demonstrating that the *theories* of normal development are also *theories* of development in the case of mentally handicapped children in special schools. Those theories are only adequate if one accepts as an initial premise the idea that the education of mentally handicapped children is restricted to the pursuit of normal developmental sequences, as characterised by theories of normal development. The prevalence and popularity of such normative theories of mental handicap can be understood in terms of the concept of conditions of possibility (Henriques *et al.* 1984). From this perspective, psychological theories are seen as both a response to specific historical conditions and social practices and, at the same time, by incorporation within social and educational practices, the means by which an established set of views is sustained and legitimated through the acquisition of scientific respectability and objectivity. Piaget's theory and stage descriptions of language acquisition fit with existing social and educational views about the 'normalising' and 'optimising' function which special schools have for the natural developmental tendencies of individual children and they enable schooling agencies to be relatively explicit in terms of how they seek to achieve their goals by formalising a 'developmental curriculum'.

The Role of Developmental Processes

The focus on developmental sequences as a basis for the special school curriculum (for example, see Harris 1984b; Kiernan 1981; Shearer and Shearer 1972, 1976) has resulted in the reinterpretation and systematic distortion of developmental theories in order that they might serve as the basis of formal educational intervention. Behavioural responses, once used as indicators for diagnosing competencies, have subsequently been regarded as ends in themselves, or at least as teaching objectives via which those underlying competencies can be achieved. A consideration of developmental processes within educational contexts raises additional, but less immediately obvious, problems. If the handicapped child is essentially normal in respect of observed or desirable developmental sequences, then the defining psychological characteristic for abnormality must be developmental processes which have somehow failed to initiate or provoke development at the appropriate speed or in the appropriate direction. Once it is accepted that the processes of development have failed, or are at least inadequate, then it may seem appropriate to disregard such 'natural' predispositions and intervene through a process of systematic instruction. Furthermore, since instructional technology is designed to help the teacher achieve arbitrarily defined objectives, it is considered appropriate to target those behaviours which characterise 'normal' development as the object of teaching (Kiernan 1981). Once again this argument rests squarely on the assumption that theories and descriptions of normal development are an appropriate basis for the design of instructional strategies.

An alternative position is that theories of cognitive and language development have reduced the validity of the traditional distinction between content and process in development to that of an arbitrary descriptive (in)convenience. For example, the assessment of a child as being at a particular sensori-motor sub-stage in relation to the object concept may turn out to be as much a statement of socio-psychological processes as it is about any presumed state of abstract mental structures (Sinha 1982). Similarly, a child credited with subject–verb–object (SVO) sentences does not necessarily possess SVO mental structures; rather the assessment is a statement about observed social and inferred psychological processes operating at particular times under certain circumstances. In terms of intervention and teaching strategies it makes just as much sense to focus on the social and psychological processes rather than behaviour in isolation or inferred structures. If processes are considered paramount in terms of naturalistic and developmentally orientated intervention, then the aims of special schools would be simply the facilitation of appropriate developmental processes (for example, Harris 1984b, c). This approach encounters two problems. The first is that the ideology of instruction, the system of organisation and the methods associated with formal education are incompatible with developmental processes as the aim of special education, and considerable changes would be necessary before this could come about (Harris, in press). The second problem is that theories of normal development are contextualised within social practices and common-sense ideologies about normal children which support the validity of those theories within educational settings (Walkerdine 1984).

Mentally handicapped chilren are treated differently to normal children in a wide variety of ways including medical procedures for diagnosis and assessment, through contemporary educational practices, of which segregation is only the most evident, through the complex web of social stigma and self-consciousness among parents and, finally, as a result of their own inability to conform to socially constructed views of what constitutes normality. By implication, theories of normal development are not adequate as theories which describe and explain the inter-personal processes which operate in the development of mentally handicapped children. To invoke such theories as the basis for structuring methods of intervention with mentally handicapped children is inappropriate, since there is no evidence that the social and psychological processes upon which those theories depend operate within the context of special schools. This is essentially the same criticism which has been made of wholesale generalisations of theories of development across cultures (Irvine 1983) and from one sub-cultural setting to another (Brice-Heath 1983).

Normal Development and the Special School Curriculum

Theories of child development have been successfully incorporated within the practices and ideology of ordinary schools because it has been possible to render them compatible with the existing social and educational practices and with contemporary views of individual development as being both predictable and natural (Walkerdine 1984). Walkerdine argues that Piaget's theory has been invoked as support for ideas about spontaneous conceptual development (in so far as it is beyond the direct control of teachers) and that developmental stages have come to be regarded as the principal determinants of a child's readiness for learning school subjects. Development is seen as a 'given' which, accurately assessed, can be used to structure, sequence and 'time' the delivery of the school curriculum and to diagnose where necessary the cause of the failure. But special schools are characterised by the very fact that they *cannot* count on normal rates of developmental progress. Bereft of nature's template for curriculum organisation, they have tackled the problem at source by attempting to create the conditions which will allow mentally handicapped children to develop more normally, more quickly. This has been possible partly because approximations towards normal development are seen as desirable goals in their own right and also because development is seen as a necessary precursor to the teaching of other skills and abilities. Theories of normal development have thus been given considerable emphasis by psychologists and educationalists, but they have been projected into an unchanged organisational structure and an ideology of instruction which originated within schools where development could be taken for granted. The failure of developmental theories in special schools is thus the failure to recognise the relationship which theories bear to the contexts within which they evolve; it derives from the false assumption that theories encapsulate some abstract and absolute facts about human development.

Research into Practice

In the preceding section it has been argued that psychologists are able to utilise theories of normal development as a basis for intervention in special schools, partly because of the ways in which theories are systematically distorted as they are transferred to the domain of special education, and partly because handicapped children are fitted to a pre-existing theory of normal development. A third influential factor is the prevailing model of the nature of the relationship between research and research-based theories and applications to practice. A traditional formulation of this relationship is that psychological research gives rise to objective scientific knowledge in the form of theories and that this is the only appropriate basis for generating innovations in pedagogic practice. The problem then becomes one of translating scientific facts into useful and appropriate normative statements for classroom practice (see Smith, this volume). One way in which this can be achieved is to familiarise students undertaking teacher training with contemporary theories relating to child development (see Desforges, this volume). Alternatively, since development is regarded as one of the principal goals of special education, the prevailing model indicates that the special school curriculum ought to be concerned with the systematic implementation of psychological theories of development, as if those theories can specify development in the same way that a syllabus and a set of teaching methods specifies the curriculum for different subject areas in the ordinary school. This gives rise to a typical sequence which characterises psychological intervention within special schools.

Developmental Theories as Bases for Curriculum Packages

Principles for teaching developmentally relevant skills are derived from theories of child development and other psychological theories and are subsequently translated into procedures and materials for use by teachers in classrooms. After appropriate experimental work, further testing and modification of the materials within classroom contexts, these are packaged and disseminated as independent 'kits', or curriculum units, which can be conveniently slotted into lesson periods within the existing school timetable. A number of important implications arise from this model. First, the teacher and child within the classroom are isolated from the theory upon which the kit was based, and necessarily so, since theories of normal child development are not concerned with teachers and mentally handicapped children or with pedagogic practice; relevance has to be established through the process of theory implementation.

Secondly, since the aim of the translation process is to deliver a theory-based curriculum in the form of materials and procedures, the teacher is treated as an extraneous variable, the effects of which must be controlled and homogenised so as to avoid distortion and bias. Ironically, the theory which the teacher is supposed to be delivering to the children has already been 'laundered' to make it fit in with established ideologies surrounding development and the aims of special education. However, the attempt to create 'teacher proof'

Figure 7.1: A Model of the Process of Translating Child Development Research into Educational Practice in Special Schools

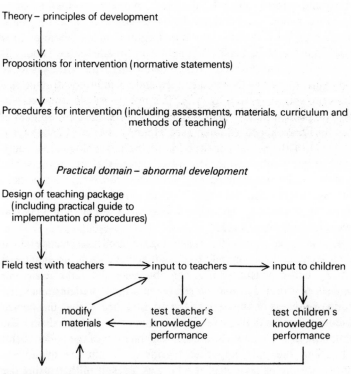

methods and materials further distances the teacher from the domain of theory and inhibits teachers from interpreting or changing the contents of the curriculum package. Once packaged for dissemination, there is little opportunity for the process of implementation within the practical domain to provide feedback either to the teacher or to the psychologist who devised the package. As a result the theories from which recommendations for practice are derived remain dislocated from the domain of application and isolated from the individuals who implement the recommendations, as well as the children who are the objects of those recommendations.

Thirdly, the model inevitably results in teachers being provided with procedures for applying theories which, in themselves, are not theories about handicapped children or the schools in which they are educated. Such procedures represent attempts to create 'normalising' behaviours, within narrowly specified contexts, without acknowledging the wider social and psychological contexts of the home and school. And yet it is within the broad context of the home and the school that the child needs to function more adequately, and it is precisely these environments which determine what it means to be handicapped and how the handicapped child is to be constructed as a social subject; they thus provide the only possible contexts for generating educationally relevant theories about the development of mentally handicapped children (see Henriques *et al.* (1984) for a discussion of the social construction of the psychological subject). Forms of intervention which do not recognise the role of the social world in creating possibilities for children to interpret and understand their experiences can only result in training exercises directed at isolated and arbitrary behaviours devoid of social and personal (psychological) significance.

The reason that a model for translating research into practice which places such emphasis on field trials can achieve such irrelevant and arbitrary end-products is precisely because the field trials are established within a frame of reference which predetermines the criteria of success on the basis of the original theory. Because choice of theory is a reflection of overriding concerns with 'normalising' the functioning of individual children, independently of the wider social world, then the only important variables within the evaluation exercise are the behaviour of teachers as a result of their using the curriculum package, or subsequent changes in the behaviour of pupils. The child is expected to internalise the contents of the curriculum which has been packaged by the pschologist and delivered to the teacher. Subsequently, the child is expected to deploy those curriculum-based skills and abilities in a variety of appropriate settings. (Interestingly, what exactly is meant by appropriate settings is never specified – since a full specification is not possible.) Generalisation is thus seen as a problem of individual learning and a measure of the success of learning. Failure to generalise is regarded as a failure of the child to learn, a failure of the teacher to teach or a failure of the kit to package the theory in an appropriate way; it is seldom seen as representing a challenge to the theory.

This model thus leads to the creation of forms of psychological intervention in special schools which are derived from theories of normal development. They treat the handicapped child as a unitary subject, divorced from the immediate social context of home and school, and in need of specific training to match images of normality encapsulated in theories of child development.

Conclusion

Although this review has taken a critical position with regard to the way in which theories of child development have been implemented within special schools, the review is not anti-theory; indeed, as I have tried to show, one of the main problems is that special education does not have an adequate theory to describe and explain the development of mentally handicapped children. On the other hand, it is suggested that the notion of translating theories of normal development into practice in special schools is ill-conceived and unlikely to be productive. Theories about normal children may be helpful provided that they are not seen as a panacea for all the questions and problems which exist in special education. For example, theories of normal child development make it possible to examine the similarities and differences with respect to normal and mentally handicapped children in much the same way as they highlight differences between children of different ages, different sexes, and children reared in different cultures. However, such a view need not be predicated upon the belief that 'underneath' normal and mentally handicapped children are the same, or indeed, that they ought to be the same. Secondly, theories of normal development can help psychologists to identify appropriate and productive questions with respect to the development of mentally handicapped children – for example: what assumptions underly the study of development in the first place? How can we understand the ideological constraints upon views about what developmental theories are for, and how they operate (for example, Ingleby 1974; Henriques *et al.* 1984). To what extent is development best conceived of as an individual process and what benefits are to be gained from studying it as an inter-individual socially mediated process (Butterworth and Light 1982)?

Thirdly, theories of normal development may be regarded as providing the best starting-point for theorising about mentally handicapped children's development, bearing in mind that the characteristics of handicap and concomitant social sequelae are likely to create so many anomalies that every hypothesis derived from the study of normal children would need to be empirically tested. Rather than specific frameworks and descriptions within which mentally handicapped children can be inserted (and where they do not fit, educated or trained to fit), the study of normal development may provide perspectives and orientations which indicate appropriate avenues for exploration. The review does underline the numerous pitfalls which arise from the pressure for psychologists to intervene in the field of special education and to employ theories of normal child development in order to implement social and educational imperatives for 'normalcy' (Ingleby 1974). Two of the major advantages of a psychological theory explicitly concerned with the development of mentally handicapped children would be that it would create a powerful counterbalance to pressure for 'normalisation' within special schools, and secondly, that it would lead to forms of intervention consistent with the social and psychological processes specifically implicated in the development of mentally handicapped children. The place where we need to begin the search for such a theory of handicapped children's development is not in textbooks which describe the development of normal children but in the schools and hospitals and homes where mentally handicapped children live and grow up.

References

Baumeister, A.A. (1967) Problems in comparative studies of mental retardates and normals, *American Journal of Mental Deficiency*, 71, 869–75

Brainerd, C.T. (1978) *Piaget's Theory of Intelligence*, New York: Prentice Hall

Brice-Heath, S. (1983) *Ways With Words: Language Life and Work in Communities and Classrooms*, Cambridge: Cambridge University Press

Bricker, D. and Bricker, W. (1973) Infant, Toddler and Pre-school Research and Intervention Project Report Year III, Unpublished report, Institute on Mental Retardation and Intellectual Development, George Peabody College for Teachers, Nashville, Tennessee

Brinker, R.P. (1982) Contextual contours and the development of language in M. Beveridge (ed.), *Children Thinking Through Language*, London: Edward Arnold

Brooks, P.H. and Baumeister, A.A. (1977) A plea for consideration of ecological validity in the experimental psychology of mental retardation: a guest editorial, *American Journal of Mental Deficiency*, 81, 407–16

Brown, G. and Desforges, C. (1977) Piagetian psychology and education: time for revision, *British Journal of Educational Psychology*, 47, 7–17

(1979) *Piaget's Theory: A Psychological Critique*, London: Routledge and Kegan Paul

Bryant, P. (1983) Piaget's struggle and the struggle about Piaget in S. Modgil, C. Modgil and G. Brown (eds), *Jean Piaget: An Interdisciplinary Critique*, London: Routledge and Kegan Paul

Buium, N., Rynders, J. and Turnure, J. (1974) Early maternal linguistic environment for normal and Down's syndrome language learning children, *American Journal of Mental Deficiency*, 79, 52–8

Butterworth, G. and Light, P. (1982) *Social Cognition: Studies of the Development of Understanding*, Brighton: Harvester Press

Chesaldine, S. and McConkey, R. (1979) Parental speech to young Down's syndrome children: an intervention study, *American Journal of Mental Deficiency*, 83, 612–20

Chomsky, N. (1959) Review of Skinner's Verbal Behaviour, *Language*, 35, 26–58

Coggins, T.E. (1976) The Classification of Relational Meaning Expressed in Early Two-word utterances of Down's Syndrome Children, Unpublished doctoral dissertation, Graduate School of Wisconsin: Madison

Cromar, R. (1981) Reconceptualising language acquisition and cognitive development in R.L. Schiefelbusch and D.D. Bricker (eds), *Early Language; Acquisition and Intervention*, Baltimore: University Park Press

Crystal, D., Garman, M. and Fletcher, P. (1976) *The Grammatical Analysis of Language Disability*, London: Edward Arnold

Cummins, J. (1977) The linguistic and cognitive development of mentally retarded children: a review of recent research, *Mental Retardation Bulletin*, 5(1), 9–29

DeVries, R. (1978) Early education and Piagetian theory: applications versus implications in J.M. Gallagher and J.A. Easley (eds), *Knowledge and Development: Piaget and Education*, Vol. 2, New York: Plenum Press

Donaldson, M. (1978) *Children's Minds*, Glasgow: Fontana/Collins

Fincham, F. (1982) Piaget's theory and the learning disabled: a critical analysis in S. Modgil and C. Modgil (eds), *Jean Piaget: Concensus and Controversy*, London: Holt Rinehart and Winston

Flavell, J.H. (1971) Stage related properties of cognitive development, *Cognitive Psychology*, 2, 421–53

Freedman, P.P. and Carpenter, R.L. (1976) Semantic relations used by normal and language impaired children at stage 1, *Journal of Speech and Hearing Research*, 19(4), 784–95

Furth, H.G. and Wachs, H. (1975) *Thinking Goes To School: Piaget's Theory in Practice*, Oxford: Oxford University Press

Gibbs, T. (1982) Language assessment of ESN(S) children, *Special Education: Forward Trends*, 9(1), 23–6

Graham, J.T. and Graham, L.W. (1971) Language behaviur of mentally retarded children: syntactic characteristics, *American Journal of Mental Deficiency*, 75, 623–9

Harris, J.C. (1983) What does mean length of utterance mean; evidence from a comparative study of normal and Down's syndrome children, *British Journal of Disorders of Communication*, 18(3), 153–69

(1984a) Early language intervention programmes: an update, *Association of Child Psychology and Psychiatry Newsletter*, 6(2), 2–20

(1984b) Teaching children to develop language: the impossible dream? in D.J. Muller (ed.), *Remediating Children's Language: Behavioural and Naturalistic Approaches*, London: Croom Helm/San Diego, College-Hill Press

(1984c) Encouraging linguistic interactions between severely mentally handicapped children and teachers in special schools, *Special Education: Forward Trends*, 11(2), 17–24

(1985) The limits of psychological intervention in special schools, *Early Child Development and Care* (in press)

Henriques, J., Holloway, W., Urwin, C., Venn, C. and Walkerdine, V. (1984) *Changing the Subject: Psychology, Social Regulation and Subjectivity*, London: Methuen

Howlin, P. (1984) Parents as therapists: a critical review in D.J. Muller (ed.), *Remediating Children's Language: Behavioural and Naturalistic Approaches*, London: Croom Helm/San Diego, College-Hill Press

Ingleby, D. (1974) The psychology of child psychology in M.P.M. Richards (ed.), *The Integration of the Child into a Social World*, London: Cambridge University Press

Irvine, S.H. (1983) Cross-cultural conservation studies at the asymptote: striking out against the curve in S. Modgil, C. Modgil and G. Brown (eds), *Jean Piaget: An Interdisciplinary Critique*, London: Routledge and Kegan Paul

Jones, O.H.M. (1977) Mother–child communication with pre-linguistic Down's syndrome and normal infants in H.R. Schaffer (ed.), *Studies in Mother–infant Interaction*, London: Academic Press

Kahn, J.V. (1975) The relationship of Piaget's sensori-motor period to language acquisition in profoundly retarded children, *American Journal of Mental Deficiency*, 79, 640–3

Kammii, C. (1974) Pedagogical principles derived from Piaget's theory; relevance for educational practice in M. Schwebel and J. Raph (eds), *Piaget in the Classroom*, London: Routledge and Kegan Paul

Kiernan, C. (1981) *Analysis of Programmes for Teaching*, Basingstoke: Globe Educational
— (1984) The behavioural approach to language development, Paper presented to the British Psychological Society Annual Conference

Klein, N.K. and Safford, P.L. (1977) Application of Piaget's theory to the study of thinking of the mentally retarded; a review of research, *Journal of Special Education*, 11, 201–16

Kogan, K.L., Wimberger, H.C. and Bobbitt, R.A. (1969) Analysis of mother–child interactions in young mental retardates, *Child Development*, 40, 799–812

Kohlberg, L. and Mayer, R. (1972) Development as the aim of education, *Harvard Education Review*, 42, 449–98

Leeming, K., Swann, W., Coupe, J. and Mittler, P. (1979) *Teaching Language and Communication to the Mentally Handicapped*, Schools Council Curriculum Bulletin No. 8, London: Evans/Methuen

Lenneberg, E.H. (1967) *Biological Foundations of Language*, New York: Wiley

Lock, A. (1980) Language development – past, present and future, *Bulletin of the British Psychological Society*, 33, 5–8

MacDonald, J.D., Blott, J.P., Spiegel, B., Hartman, M. and Gordon, K. (1974) An experimental parent-assisted treatment program for preschool language-delayed children, *Journal of Speech and Hearing Disorders*, 31, 395–416

McLean, J.E. and Snyder-McLean, L.K. (1978) *A Transactional Approach to Early Language Training*, Columbus Ohio: Charles Merrill

Mahoney, G., Crawley, S. and Pullis, M. (1980) Language intervention: models and issues in B. Keough (ed.), *Advances in Special Education*, Vol. 2, New York: JAI Press

Marshall, N.R., Hegrenes, J.R. and Goldstein, S. (1973) Verbal interactions: mothers and their retarded children versus mothers and their non-retarded children, *American Journal of Mental Deficiency*, 77, 415–19

Miller, J.F. and Yoder, D.E. (1972) A syntax teaching program in J.E. McLean, D.E. Yoder and R.L. Schiefelbusch (eds), *Language Intervention and the Retarded: Developing Strategies*, Baltimore: University Park Press

(1974) An ontogenetic language teaching strategy for retarded children in R.E. Schiefelbusch and L.L. Lloyd (eds), *Language Perspective: Acquisition, Retardation and Intervention*, Baltimore: University Park Press

Nelson, K. (1980) Individual differences in language development: implications for development and language, *Developmental Psychology, 17*, 170–87

Piaget, J. (1970) Piaget's theory in P.H. Mussen (ed.), *Carmichael's Manual of Child Psychology*, 3rd edn, New York: Wiley

Piaget, J. and Inhelder, B. (1969) *The Psychology of the Child*, London: Routledge and Kegan Paul

Prehm, H.J. (1966) Verbal learning research in mental retardation, *American Journal of Mental Deficiency, 71*, 42–7

Rees, N. (1978) Pragmatics of language: applications to normal and disordered development in R.L. Schiefelbusch (ed.), *Bases of Language Intervention*, Baltimore: University Park Press

Reid, D.K. (1978) Genevan theory and the education of exceptional children in J. Gallagher and J.A. Easley (eds), *Knowledge and Development*, Vol. 2, London: Plenum Press

Robson, C. (1980) Project TASS Phase One, Final Report, Unpublished report, Huddersfield Polytechnic

——— (1981) Project TASS, Follow-up Final Report, Unpublished report, Huddersfield Polytechnic

Rondal, J. (1976) Maternal Speech to Normal and Down's Syndrome Children Matched for Mean Length of Utterance, Unpublished research report, No. 98, University of Minnesota

Ryan, J. (1973) When is an apparent deficit a real deficit: language assessment and the subnormal in P. Mittler (ed.), *Psychological Assessment of the Mentally Handicapped*, London: Churchill Livingstone

——— (1975) Mental subnormality and language development in E.H. Lenneberg and E. Lenneberg (eds), *Foundations of Language Development: A Multi-disciplinary Approach*, Vol. 2, London: Academic Press

Seibert, J.M. and Oller, D.K. (1981) Linguistic pragmatics and language intervention strategies, *Journal of Autism and Developmental Disorders, 11(1)*, 75–88

Seitz, S. (1975) Language intervention: changing the language environment of the retarded child in R. Koch and F. De La Cruz (eds), *Down's Syndrome (Mongolism): Research, Prevention and Management*, New York: Bruner/Mazel

Seitz, S. and Marcus, S. (1976) Mother–child interactions: a foundation for language development, *Exceptional Children, 42*, 445–9

Selman, R.L. (1975) Book review of *Thinking Goes to School: Piaget's Theory in Practice, Harvard Educational Review, 45(1)*, 127–34

Shearer, D.E. and Shearer, M.S. (1976) The Portage project: a model of early childhood intervention in T.D. Tjossem (ed.), *Intervention Strategies for High Risk Infants and Young Children*, Baltimore: University Park Press

Shearer, M.S. and Shearer, D.E. (1972) The Portage project: a model for early childhood education, *Exceptional Child, 39*, 210–17

Sinha, C. (1981) The role of psychological research in special education in W. Swann (ed.), *The Practice of Special Education*, London: Blackwell/Open University

——— (1982) Representational development and the structure of action in G. Butterworth and P. Light (eds), *Social Cognition: Studies of the Development of Understanding*, Brighton: Harvester Press

Smedslund, J. (1969) Psychological diagnostics, *Psychological Bulletin, 71(3)*, 237–48

——— (1977) Piaget's psychology in practice, *British Journal of Educational Psychology, 47*, 1–6

Tamburrini, J. (1982) Some educational implications of Piaget's theory in S. Modgil and C. Modgil (eds), *Jean Piaget: Concensus and Controversy*, London: Holt Rinehart and Winston

Vygotsky, L.S. (1978) *Mind in Society: The Development of Higher Mental Processes*, Cambridge, Mass.: Harvard University Press/Chicago University Press

Walkerdine, V. (1982) From context to text: a psychosemiotic approach to abstract thought in M. Beveridge (ed.), *Children Thinking Through Language*, London: Edward Arnold

—— (1984) Developmental psychology and the child centred pedagogy: the insertion of Piaget into early education in J. Henriques, W. Holloway, C. Urwin, C. Venn and V. Walkerdine (eds), *Changing the Subject: Psychology, Social Regulation and Subjectivity*, London: Methuen

Weisz, J.R., Yeates, K.O. and Zigler, E. (1982) Piagetian evidence and the development-difference controversy in E. Zigler and D. Balla (eds), *Mental Retardation: The Development-Difference Controversy*, Hillsdale, NJ: Lawrence Erlbaum Associates

Wells, G. (1981) *Learning Through Interaction: The Study of Language Development*, Cambridge: Cambridge University Press

Whitehurst, G.J., Novak, G. and Zorn, G. (1972) Delayed speech studied in the home, *Developmental Psychology*, 7, 169–77

Wickens, D. (1974) Piagetian theory as a model for open systems of education in M. Schwebel and J. Raph (eds), *Piaget in the Classroom*, London: Routledge and Kegan Paul

Wolinsky, G.F. (1962) Piaget and the psychology of thought: some implications for teaching the retarded, *American Journal of Mental Deficiency*, 67, 250–6

Woodward, W.M. (1962) The application of Piaget's theory to the training of the subnormal, *Journal of Mental Subnormality*, 8, 17–25

—— (1970) The assessment of cognitive processes: Piaget's approach in P. Mittler (ed.), *The Psychological Assessment of Mental and Physical Handicaps*, London: Methuen

Yoder, D.E. and Miller, J.F. (1972) What we may know and what we can do in J.E. McLean, D.E. Yoder and R. Schiefelbusch (eds), *Language Intervention with the Retarded*, Baltimore: University Park Press

8 THE DERBYSHIRE LANGUAGE SCHEME: RESEARCH TO PRACTICE IN REMEDIAL LANGUAGE TEACHING

Mark Masidlover

Introduction

Schools for mentally handicapped children need to consider teaching skills which in most normal children develop without formal tuition. There is a consequent need for knowledge of areas such as language development and self-help skills so as to provide guidelines for the curriculum. The psychologist who advises such schools needs to have similar knowledge as well as being aware of the learning difficulties of the children.

Research on normal development seems indispensable if one is to devise intervention techniques: what skills does a normal child have? How do they develop? What factors facilitate or impede their development? One problem which faces the practitioner is the incomplete picture research provides of development. Some researchers would argue that given our current state of knowledge we can neither adequately characterise the skills or be certain of methods of assessment and remediation. Clark (1982a: 149) in a discussion of language assessment states: 'We need to know more about the process of normal language development before we can construct useful [assessment] tools.' If we cannot identify skills the child has, how can we begin to remediate? The children's needs seem urgent and yet the above is almost a philosophy of inaction. Clark herself (1982b) admits that regarding a phenomenon as too complex is likely to lead to paralysis in the researcher and she then goes on to discuss the simplifications that have been employed in language development research to facilitate action.

Equally, anyone intending to use research findings as a basis for an intervention project is forced to simplify. Conflicting evidence must be ignored and controversies in the literature must be resolved so as to produce a theoretical framework which can guide action. If research is to help shape educational practice, then it may require further simplifications. For example, when a teacher is interacting with a child, there are only so many variables that can be considered whilst teaching is in progress.

The problem in providing simple frameworks to facilitate action is that they may lead to simplified views of reality and act as blinkers restricting vision of pertinent variables and interrelationships. There is an additional problem in research areas where theories change rapidly. How can one develop a strategy based on research when it may be quickly outdated by new findings? The project described in this chapter was concerned with the development of a language intervention strategy for mentally handicapped children — the Derbyshire Language Scheme.

It was felt that any attempt to use research findings as the basis for teaching practice must recognise the provisional nature of theory. Research was seen as a pool of possibly pertinent information, not as a source of instant solutions. The utility of such information was to be based upon the effectiveness of techniques generated by theory; adaptations and reformulations were to be made whenever it was felt that the original framework was inadequate.

Thus research is not considered as some sacrosanct body of knowledge which can provide new and better solutions for educational practice. The limitations of research data (and the deviations from them), in order to meet the needs of the children, were never considered 'problems'. The difficulty was constructing a coherent guiding framework, simple enough to facilitate action, yet flexible enough to allow reformulations. This 'evolutionary approach' it was felt would enable experience with the children and new research to influence the overall perspective. Disseminating such an approach raised difficulties which have not been resolved.

The chapter describes the original strategy, reformulations in the approach, the mode of dissemination and the problems associated with it.

The Organisation of the School-based Project: Designing for Dissemination

Research on child development and education tends to have a slow and sporadic effect on teaching practice. In part this may be due to the separateness of research institutes and educational establishments with researchers making occasional forays into schools to conduct investigations and then publishing the results couched in terminology only understandable to other researchers. (See chapters by Desforges and McConkey, this volume.) In addition to this, the techniques utilised in research studies may be inappropriate for use in schools either because they involve specialised equipment or extensive individual teaching not available in the educational system.

With an eye to these problems the project was based at a school rather than a university. A psychologist and teacher were to work in collaboration on a daily basis. The strategy adopted and techniques used were *not* to involve major changes in school organisation, and equipment was to be generally available to schools. Thus, the project attempted from the outset to ensure that the strategy developed could be used in the existing educational system.

The teacher saw approximately 35 children drawn mainly from nursery, infant and junior classes. Children whose language ability as measured by the Reynell Language Scales exceeded a three-year level were excluded from the project (Reynell 1969). The children who were seen varied widely in ability and included some with additional handicaps, such as hearing impairment, partial sight and hyperactivity. Again, this was based on the premise that the system of teaching should be flexible enough to cater for the range of children found in other schools for mentally handicapped children. Most children were seen two or three times a week either individually or in small groups. The duration and number of sessions varied according to the child's ability. A child with a very short attention span might be seen for two five-minute sessions every day, whilst a more able child might attend two group sessions a week. All the children were to be placed on individual programmes based on their abilities and problems. The school-based project lasted from 1972 to 1978 and over its duration some 50 children participated. On average children were involved in the scheme for four years.

The Original Formulation: Language Remediation with an Emphasis on Social Use and Spontaneity

The skills selected to be the focus of remediation and the techniques used to encourage their development related directly to the ultimate purpose of the remediation. The criterion for successful intervention was that the children used language skills spontaneously in social interaction in everyday settings. They would be expected to initiate conversations as well as respond to other people's language. The teaching was to emphasise this from the outset. Activities were to be used which were intrinsically interesting to the children. A two-way flow of communication was to be cultivated where they could influence the course of events.

This 'communication oriented' approach has become fashionable recently particularly with developments in the field of pragmatics and socio-linguistics (Yoder and Calculaot 1981; McLean and Snyder-McLean 1984; Wilcox 1984). The approach may be widely advocated but is it likely to be effective? The use of shared contexts of interest and an emphasis on child-led interaction was selected because it seemed effective in motivating the children as well as cultivating skills directly relevant to normal communication. There is supportive evidence from pure and applied studies that the approach is likely to produce a higher level of language usage and may influence the rate of language acquisition. For example, in a long-term study of 128 chidren recorded at home without an observer present, Wells (1979a) found a significant positive relationship between the rate of language development at 2½ years and the proportion of speech addressed to the child in the context of shared activities, such as doing the housework together, play with adult participation, etc. Nelson (1973) suggested that acceptance of the child's attempts at communication and avoidance of a dominant correcting role could facilitate language development among normal children.

From studies related to teaching normal pre-school children and deaf children (Hubbell 1977; Wood 1980; Wood and Wood 1983) there is evidence that less control from the adult (that is, fewer questions and commands) leads to an increase in frequency of the child's utterances and their length. Harris (1984) has also demonstrated that in classroom activities with mentally handicapped children less direction from the teacher was associated with a marked increase in spontaneous utterances.

However, it is not 'spontaneity' *per se* that is the sole criterion of successful remediation. The language used by the child must also be appropriate. Beveridge and Brinker (1980:58) discussed a study where it was shown that a high proportion of the spontaneous utterances, produced by mentally handicapped adolescents in school, gave unsolicited information. The authors noted that the 'giving of unsolicited information to people who are probably already in possession of it does not represent the use of language in accordance with the normal rules of adult conversation'. Thus, although spontaneity was to be encouraged, other rules relating to normal conventions of language use had to be conveyed.

There were additional reasons for selecting a strategy which attempted to simulate normal parent-child interactions. The problems of generalisation had been cited in numerous studies (for example,

Garcia and De Haven 1974; Harris 1975). It was felt that in part these problems might be due to the wide discrepancy between a highly structured teacher-dominated interaction and the informal nature of the settings in which the child normally communicated. It was suggested that mentally retarded children have problems in attending to relevant cues (Zeaman and House 1963) and making abstractions from specific activities to similar activities in different surroundings (Irwin 1970). In the language remediation setting one might well be exacerbating the problems by increasing differences between the remediation setting and everyday communication settings. In the project, therefore, a deliberate attempt was made to provide the children with a high proportion of teaching settings which used equipment and patterns of interaction which were similar to those they encountered outside school.

Instant Reformulations: Teacher Domination as a Movable Parameter

The facilitation of spontaneous use of language was to be based on a relationship with the child in which the adult did not dominate the interaction but encouraged the child to communicate. There was an immediate clash with the practical demands of the work. The children were subject to remediation programmes because their language was considered deficient. The purpose of the remediation was to alter their communication skills. If one accepted their imperfect attempts they might not improve but, on the other hand, if they were continuously corrected, the adult might dominate the interaction and actually discourage the children from communicating. Brinker (1982:259) puts the dilemma succinctly by stating that the key question for interventionists revolves around:

(1) The extent to which we actively interpret children's messages so they continue to communicate.
(2) The extent to which we demand messages in forms that approximate those used by the language community.

How do you 'demand messages in a form that approximate those used by the language community' without directing the child and dominating the session?

The approach taken was to select games likely to encourage a normal child to use the structure which was the focus of the session. For instance, a tea party game might be used to encourage 'more plus a noun'. Children would be given a very small amount of food and drink and when they indicated they wanted more the teacher would model the utterance 'you want some more cake' or even 'more cake?' The teacher is aware of the teaching objective, but the child is merely responding to the 'demand characteristics' of a relatively normal setting. There is thus no focusing on language, or even 'correct language', as far as the child is concerned. A good language activity, in the terms of the project, was one in which the language was so natural to the activity that a naïve observer would not be aware of the purpose of the session. Here one can see the process of 'reformulation' gradually shifting the style of intervention away from the original guiding framework. In selecting an 'eliciting context' the teacher dominates the choice of activity. If subtle modelling does not seem to help the children improve in their use of language, then the model may be made more explicit with direct prompts for the children to repeat, thereby increasing the level of teacher domination. The 'guiding framework' still provides a goal in terms of the style of interaction which will be considered as successful intervention. A child who starts by imitating will be encouraged gradually to use that language to initiate action without prompting. In these terms practice is informed by research and not constrained by it.

The Language Curriculum

The Place of Normal Developmental Data

As should be apparent from the preceding discussion, syntax and vocabulary are seen as the means by which a child communicates. 'The primary goal of the intervention becomes facilitation of generalised communicative functions for which syntatic structures and semantic content are only the tools.' (Seibert and Oller 1981)

In order to monitor the communicative functions of the child's language one has to have a framework of expected functions. If some do not appear, then it is useful to know the range of structures a normal child might use for them, as a basis for teaching. The children in the project were developmentally delayed, and it was felt that functions and structures used by young normal children would be appropriate.

For children just beginning to use single words. 'Topic Headings' based on Nelson's study (1973) were used to select vocabulary which would be most obviously functional for a particular child – food, toys, body parts, etc. The approach focused on the child's interests and needs and hence there was no standard vocabulary prescribed. Descriptive studies were used where sufficient details of context were available (Bloom 1970; Leopold 1949) and some functions were included based on a taxonomy of those in adult language (Robinson 1972). These were adjusted as new research studies appeared (Halliday 1975; Bates 1976; Carter 1979). A similar approach was taken on early word combinations, Brown's work (1973) providing the early data. Subsequently this was updated with data from Bloom, Lightbrown and Hood's study (1975).

The check-lists of possible teaching objectives — the 'Progress Records' — listed the structures in approximate developmental order. The child would participate in a communication game and the structures and functions used would be noted in these individual records. The language skills recorded were not necessarily the teaching objectives selected by the teacher. In fact spontaneous use of non-elicited utterances was considered better evidence that these were part of the child's productive system than utterances which had been vaguely encouraged.

At this level the approach was low key — facilitating contexts and general encouragement — with the teacher 'monitoring' the way the child was developing. The programme could, however, take on a more 'directive' approach if the child never appeared to use language for certain functions. Thus, eliciting contexts would be used and the teacher would model the types of utterance wanted. In these circumstances normal developmental data on functions and related structures provided guidelines on the types of utterance to be modelled.

The Limitations of Normal Developmental Data

A knowledge of research on normal development allows for the design of remedial programmes which attempt to bring the abilities of mentally handicapped children more in line with their normal peers, the normal sequence of emergence of skills being used as an approximate guide to the order of difficulty for teaching. Such sequences are generally 'averages' derived from groups of children, whose development when looked at individually never quite follows the average pattern. Recently there has been considerable discussion of individual variation in language development (Nelson 1973; Lieven 1978, 1980) and criticisms of intervention programmes which force children through an 'average' route. Unfortunately, it is difficult to accommodate individual variation once a decision to intervene has been made.

The approach described so far allows for 'pushing the child from behind' by using eliciting contexts and monitoring the child's utterances. Thus, so long as children use forms which convey their intended meanings, these will be encouraged and the children can diverge from a preformulated average route.

It is when the children cannot code their intentions in language that the interventionist might model a language construction, based on normal child development. This may not be the construction that particular child would have used if allowed to develop independently. The questions for the practitioner are 'will the child ever develop this skill independently?' 'Can I afford to wait, and for how long?' The importance of the skill to the child and the delay in its appearance relative to other skills the child has are all borne in mind but if a decision to teach is made, then developmental data can provide the basis for an informed guess regarding suitable objectives. The possibility that the child's development is being distorted may be regarded as the inevitable cost of intervention.

The Teaching of Aspects of Syntax which are not Functional in Child Communication

Certain parts of speech although essential to grammatically correct English none the less convey very little information. For example, if the child omits the definite article and says 'Give me book' instead of 'Give me the book' the teacher may understand exactly what is wanted and certainly the addition of 'the' is unlikely to make very much difference.

In normal development such parts of speech appear when a child is typically using three- to five-word utterances. If one tries to adhere rigidly to normal developmental sequences, then the teaching would have to focus on the use of these words at a time when, from the child's point of view, they may be totally without meaning. The teaching itself would need to change in style. The child says 'Give me book', the teacher ignores a totally adequate message and focuses on 'correct' language. 'Say give me *the* book.' The child may now become more concerned with the 'correctness' of utterances rather than communicating freely. This could substantially impede progress, or at least make the child far less willing to talk.

For these reasons the teaching of certain aspects of grammar was deferred until the children were competent and confident using a large range of basic sentence patterns. This put the programme out of line with 'normal development'. Thus a practitioner is rarely treating 'normal development' as sacrosanct; deviations are made because children do vary, particularly 'abnormal children'.

Research and Practice: Practitioner's Electicism and Researcher's Dogma

Fashions sweep through language remediation as they do through many areas of education. In the 1960s the teaching of aspects of syntax was the focus of many remediation programmes (for example, Miller and Yoder 1972). In the 1970s the social use of language began to be emphasised and by the 1980s the key element in remediation was seen to be the way that children used language in normal social interaction (for example, McLean and Synder–McLean 1984).

Obviously, this is very much in line with the approach taken in the Derbyshire Language Scheme but, in reading research papers and certainly in discussion with researchers, attitudes seem to have become polarised. Thus, some authors seem to be suggesting that, since language is for communicating, syntax is not only secondary but should not be taught, if in doing so one clashes with the style of a communication oriented approach. But practitioners cannot afford to be fanatics and totally ignore certain skill areas just because the current philosophy is 'functional communication is all'. If part of the goal of the remediation is to help the children sound normal, then at some stage the practitioner may decide that non-functional aspects of syntax should be included in the remedial programme, even if this requires departing from the main theme of the remediation. As can be seen in the previous discussion, practitioners temper their judgements by due consideration of other factors such as the child's general level of confidence and competence. Dogmatic adherence to a particular philosophy irrespective of the children's needs is a luxury only possible at a distance from remediation.

Appraising the Results of Intervention

In the introduction to this chapter it was emphasised that the original guiding framework was seen as provisional, adaptations being made when either the techniques which were used seemed ineffective, or the results obtained were judged by use as inadequate. This section describes one such adaptation.

In the early days of the project, a child who had participated in a highly didactic programme requiring responses in full sentences was overheard in conversation with a visitor to the school:

Visitor: 'What's your name?'
Child: 'My name is Elizabeth.'
Visitor: 'How old are you?'
Child: 'I am eight years old.'

The child's responses sounded stilted and abnormal.

She had 'generalised' the rule that full sentence responses were required to a context where the majority of children would have answered in single words. The project's teaching activities were scrutinised in an attempt to ensure that the language response required was 'normal'. If it was judged that a normal child would be likely to answer with a single word, then this was to be accepted. Equally, if it was felt that a full sentence was required, then the 'demand characteristics' of the setting were to be arranged accordingly.

Another example may help to illustrate the point. A game was designed to elicit the past tense. Children draw cards depicting a child carrying out some action, for instance 'brushing teeth', and are required to mime it to the remainder of the group. One of the other children is then asked 'What did he do?' In the circumstances 'brushed his teeth' is acceptable. In order to elicit a full sentence, two children would mime an action consecutively and another child would then be asked to remember who did what. In these circumstances it seems far more likely that a child will use a full sentence 'James brushed his teeth', 'Julie washed her face'.

To an extent the reformulation of activities had to be based on personal experience as the research literature covered limited aspects of language, and the data on 'eliciting contexts' were often minimal. However, those research studies which did describe the contexts of early utterances of a particular form were examined to ascertain if any points raised were pertinent to remediation. For instance, Hood and Bloom (1979) discussed the contexts of young children's early expressions of causality. Children tended to use 'because' in relation to their ongoing activities or imminent intentions and expressed a negative in about 60 per cent of their utterances:

'Could you read this to me because I don't know how.'

The paper was examined for naturally occurring events which could be adapted into teaching activities to elicit and encourage the use of 'because'. In this case the children could be asked to attempt a task which they would wish to do but circumstances could be arranged so that the teacher's help was needed. The request might be to fetch a box of sweets which was on a shelf just out of the child's reach, or perhaps a tin of sweets which was extremely difficult to open might be handed to the child; children might be asked to bring a toy from a cupboard for the next game, only the cupboard would have been left locked. The hope was that the child would request help, or perhaps indicate in some way that the task was too difficult. In these circumstances the teacher could then model the use of 'because' by extending the child's own utterance. 'Can't you reach it? . . . Oh dear, it's because it's too high.' Equally the teacher might simply ask 'Why can't you get it?' and expand 'too high' to '*because* it's too high'.

The problem with this type of activity is that although it makes the teacher sensitive to an appropriate context, it does not allow for repetition of the structure because it would be somewhat unnatural to repeatedly ask children to carry out impossible tasks. This difficulty is not exclusive to the use of 'because'. Many other structures may not occur frequently in child or adult language. In order to create a teaching activity it may be necessary to move away from situations which have high 'ecological validity' simply to allow opportunities for the child to practice the structure.

The developmental data thus served to indicate circumstances which were likely to elicit utterances in normal children and as a crude index of possible difficulty. Research studies are also used to consider the limited range of meanings that a structure may serve for a child. The modal auxiliary 'can', for instance, is used in the early stages to describe the child's own ability or inability and in requests for help, or action, to others: 'Can you lift me up: I can't see' (Fletcher 1979; Wells 1979(b)). Thus activities were intended in the project to elicit 'can' for just these functions, whereas in commercial kits 'can' was taught in relation to the abilities of classes of animals such as 'Dogs can bark', 'Cats can purr'. The latter was not considered a useless skill, but suffered from the same disadvantages as the card material used to teach 'because' – limited relevance to the child's needs, and being somewhat more abstract than the early uses described in the literature.

The Interplay of Theory and Practice: The Development of 'Comprehension Activities'

The last section showed how, even when the guiding framework was extended, an attempt was made to integrate this with known research findings. Thus the new framework is still shaped by the wider research field but the problems of children often force the practitioner to deal with areas where there is a dearth of research. In attempting to develop remedial techniques the practitioner experiments with different approaches, and the results of the process may lead to a total shift in theoretical orientation. In the case of the project, the design of activities to improve the comprehension skills of one group of children had just such an effect.

At the outset, there were some 15 children in the project who did not talk. They were at varying levels of comprehension ability from around 18 months to a three-year level, as measured by the Reynell Scales (Reynell 1969). An attempt was made to develop language activities in which they could participate at their own level of comprehension, without talking. Remediation aimed at expressive language skills or alternative forms of communication were carried out in parallel. In 1972 there seemed to be a limited amount of published research on the development of comprehension skills (Eisenberg and Strauss 1968; Huttenlocher and Weiner 1971; Huttenlocher 1974). The information was used in conjunction with techniques and data derived from clinical and psychometric assessment of young children's comprehension, including the English Picture Vocabulary Test (Brimer and Dunn 1966), the Reynell Scales (Reynell 1969) and the Sentence Comprehension Test (Hobsbaum and Mittler 1971). The range of structures and vocabulary assessed were extended and the assessment techniques were adapted into games. An illustrative example is provided below:

The children are asked to help dress two manikins – flat cut-out representations of a man and a woman – with lay-on clothes. The various items of clothing are laid out in front of them. The clothes are carefully designed so that the owner is obvious. In fact the children would initially be taught who was the owner of the clothes at previous sessions – before the comprehension requests were used. The children would then be asked for 'mummy's shoes', 'daddy's hat', and so on. There was a deliberate element of randomness built in (not so extensive that it contravened 'normal' expectations) and, to be consistently successful, the children needed to listen to the name of the article of clothing and the owner. The game did not use 'comprehension requests' exclusively. The children could have decided to dress one manikin fully and hence the name of the owner would become redundant, that is, the teacher would ask for daddy's clothes only. However, within the activity, at least part of the game utilised requests where the children needed to listen to the full possessive construction to respond correctly to the teacher's request. The use of this and other similar activities exerted a powerful influence over the total approach to remediation which is more apparent in retrospect than it was at the time.

In many language intervention programmes the focus is purely on eliciting expressive language; the assumption is made that the teacher will automatically adjust language input to the child's level of comprehension ability. The comprehension game in the project made no such assumptions. There were direct observations of whether or not the child seemed to understand. Attention was paid to contextual cues, vocabulary and language structure used by the teacher. In time it became easier to recognise difficulties in comprehension and devise methods of circumventing them. The teacher could appraise the child's performance on a large range of tasks over a long time-period. It became possible to ensure that when new material, routines or vocabulary were introduced, the manner of introduction was well within the children's comprehension ability and they could focus on the changes.

It is not only the development of the teacher's awareness of factors influencing comprehension that is considered important but also the shift in emphasis from eliciting expression to ensuring that the child understands. Brown (1977:26), in providing advice on facilitating language learning, states: '. . . seek above all to communicate. To understand and be understood. To keep your (yours and the child's) minds fixed on the same target.' Not only did comprehension activities impose objectives which moved the remediation in the direction of Brown's advice; they also led to the development of routines in which other communication skills could be emphasised for children who could talk. Consider the example of the child who had just dressed the two manikins described earlier. There had been no pressure for speech. Simple language which related to the materials had been used. The teacher now took control of the clothes and helped the child to dress the manikins. Children were encouraged to request the clothes that they required. This procedure, where the children took over the teacher's former role, was termed 'role-reversal'.

The clothes were not necessarily laid out in full view; they could be in a pile in front of the teacher. As the individual items could not be seen, the children needed to state both the name of the owner and the article of clothing in order to obtain a specific item. The game was now a 'referential communication' setting in which the children's language needed to provide relevant information to the listener. It utilised a clear repetitive structure, a simple routine which the child could learn and a reversal in roles which allowed the child to direct the activity. It had much in common with early games with infants, which are felt to have a powerful influence on the development of communication (Ratner and Bruner 1978).

Dissemination: The Packaging of an Evolutionary Approach

It can be seen from the preceding sections that the needs of practice had led to a continuous extension in areas of remediation and related techniques of intervention. From an emphasis on the use of expressive language, the teaching had increased in range to include comprehension skills, referential communication skills and other abilities needed for competence in communication. The 'evolutionary approach' had allowed for reformulation but the original 'simple guiding framework' was no longer quite so simple. The project had intended to create an intervention strategy which was relevant and transferable to practitioners working with mentally handicapped children. Its relevance seemed likely but its transferability questionable. Reformulations had led to a comprehensive but complex system of remediation. The complexity was seen as a major obstacle to its acceptance by other practitioners. There was a need to simplify, yet without sacrificing the essentials of the strategy.

It was decided that certain basic instructional techniques concerned with the encouragement of the children's use of language and the appraisal of comprehension skills would be developed into an assessment battery. The selection of initial teaching objectives would be based on the results of this assessment. Thus 'users' were introduced to the key elements of the scheme in a practical manner. They saw the children's responses in what amounted to a trial-teaching activity. The successes and problem areas delineated during this assessment phase were used to select initial teaching activities described in the Teaching Manuals. The Teaching Manuals, however, were not limited to the 'basic techniques' used in the assessment but dealt with areas such as the design of eliciting contexts, restrictions in meaning and use in early language development, etc. Thus, once users were familiar with the simplified framework, this was extended to become more comprehensive through their use of teaching activities.

The published material described above was only provided on specially designed training workshops, where the evolutionary nature of the strategy could be emphasised. The assessment battery was described as a collection of practical tests of communication skills which could be adapted, both in terms of the activities used or the skills assessed, yet still remain within the basic guiding framework. The audience were involved in problem-solving sessions where they were required to adapt these tests for children whose handicaps prevented the tests being used in their original form. Practitioners were thus being asked from the outset to understand the rationale underlying the assessment, and adapt it to the needs of children. There was no preformulated, standard approach which was to be applied rigidly. Equally, the teaching activities contained in the Teaching Manuals were subjected to similar modifications during the training course.

The practitioner was thus presented with the scheme with a parallel message of the need to adapt and improvise. The fact that the assessment phase restricted itself to a narrow range of skills allowed for a phased implementation. A limited teaching programme could be devised and introduced quickly and then, whilst evaluating the effectiveness of these techniques, other remedial activities could be introduced gradually. The intention was to create a package which was 'user friendly' without sacrificing the comprehensiveness of the approach.

This concern with the presentation of information is not considered peripheral to the problem of linking research to practice. If researchers wish to have an impact on the educational system then they must accept responsibility for translating ideas into practical procedures for implementing change within the existing educational system. It is felt that the strategies necessary to meet this objective must be under their control to minimise the possibility of oversimplification and distortion.

Training Courses: The New Feedback Loop

The training courses were not only a vehicle for dissemination; they also provided feedback on ambiguities in presentation, and practical problems impeding implementation which could be modified by altering the content of the scheme or the training course itself. Just as the project format had attempted to make the remediation appropriate to the children, so the course format allowed for the 'package' to be adapted to the needs of users.

The original project came to a close in 1978 although the scheme continued to be used at the school and other establishments. The scheme was subject to continuous minor modifications from 1978 onwards, based on problems encountered by new 'users'. In 1982 it was realised that there was a substantial amount of information relating to the use of the scheme which was not contained in the printed material. These omissions were leading to methods of use which were in direct conflict with the intention of the designers. The scheme was therefore revised to emphasise certain aspects of the style of teaching and to incorporate new activities developed by other users. It was also decided to incorporate, as far as possible, new research findings which seemed relevant to the remediation.

Thus the scheme has continued to evolve. By this stage the Teaching Manuals particularly could not be said to have been designed by the original project team. New ideas had been added from other 'users'. The format, the philosophy, and the guiding framework were still recognisable but the scheme had become a co-operative enterprise.

The Problems of Disseminating an 'Evolutionary Approach'

The first and most obvious difficulty is that in order to convey information about any strategy one has to 'crystallise' the approach as it stands at a given date. No matter how much emphasis is given on training courses to the necessity for modifying the approach, there can be no guarantee that 'users' will take the effort to do this. Modifications implemented by the designers were possible but became increasingly difficult as the scheme grew in popularity. Apart from the sheer amount of work involved in communicating changes, there is a need to remain within a framework with which the 'user' is familiar. This restricts the modifications which are possible.

There is an additional problem which has been touched upon in the section describing 'packaging'. As pointed out in the introduction, practitioners (like all human beings) can only deal with a limited amount of information at a time. The phased introduction of the scheme was intended to 'parcel' aspects of the strategy so they could be assimilated whilst the adult was working with a child. Unfortunately, there is no guarantee that the practitioner will work through the various levels of use. For a practitioner who wishes for fast results within the teaching session, heavy modelling of target utterances, using simplified settings, may be the preferred approach. The notional 'average' sequence of development becomes the syllabus of target utterances. With behavioural methods currently in fashion, repetition of these structures to a preformulated criterion of success could further push the teaching in the direction of total teacher domination, a loss of any real 'communication', and a total lack of appraisal of whether the child uses the skills spontaneously. Thus the simplifications made to make research data available to inform practice become constraints on the child's development and powerful intervention procedures may be employed which were deliberately avoided in the original project.

It is hard to envisage an easy solution to this problem. One can merely convey what amounts to personal preferences – be cautious about moving away from natural settings and normal interactions. We are not aware of all the skills involved in communication or the variables in the setting which affect its development.

Practice – Centred Research

For all the problems inherent in the approach, it is felt that some of the original objectives were met. The scheme is now widely used in schools for mentally handicapped children in the United Kingdom and hence the original intention of disseminating 'practice influenced by research' has been attained. It has not been advertised and its popularity has grown through recommendations by practitioners; hence it could be considered to be useful and used.

To a large extent it is felt that its success is due to the importance which was attached to normal practice. The central concern of the project was the effects of intervention on a variety of children. There was no attempt to use a single technique and assess its effectiveness across children; the focus was on helping teachers to select techniques which seemed to work for an individual child. Equally, there was no assumption that in attempting to improve 'communication skills' the original focus of remediation would be adequate. In fact, as discussed in this chapter, problems which seemed specific to a small group of children illuminated areas of skill which were relevant to large numbers of children.

The approach was collaborative with the researchers working long term with a teacher, and in the course of that collaboration relative status altered. It was not a case of the elite researcher offering solutions, but of a problem-solving partnership utilising research findings and adapting them to meet specific needs. The approach could best be characterised as an attempt to create effective practice by working directly with children.

The approach is 'practice-centred' and it is felt that it is just such an orientation which is neglected in research on intervention. There seems to be an emphasis on ascertaining general rules on effectiveness of specific techniques, without any parallel work on parameters that may influence their application in real-life settings. Just as in-depth studies of small numbers of children in language development research has generated hypotheses for cross-sectional and experimental studies, so an in-depth recording of practitioners' attempts to intervene successfully could provide similar insights into the process of intervention. Research has been used in this project to inform practice, but the traffic seems too one-way: practice should inform research. It is not difficult to envisage a project similar to the one described in this chapter, but with a stronger research link, so that techniques of teaching, behaviour of the child both within and outside the teaching session, individual characteristics of both teachers and children are recorded and a detailed analysis made of those factors which might influence intervention.

References

Bates, E. (1976) *Language and Context: The Acquisition of Pragmatics*, New York: Academic Press

Beveridge, M. and Brinker, R. (1980) An ecological-developmental approach to communication in retarded children in M.F. Jones (ed.), *Language Disability in Children*, Lancaster: MTP Press

Bloom, L.M. (1970) *Language Development: Form and Function in Emerging Grammars*, Cambridge, Mass: MIT Press

Bloom, L.M., Lightbown, P. and Hood, L. (1975) Structure and variation in child language, *Monographs of the Society for Research in Child Development 40* (serial No. 160)

Brimer, M.A. and Dunn, L.L.M. (1966) *English Picture Vocabulary Test*, 2nd edn, London: NFER

Brinker, R.P. (1982) Contextual contours and the development of language in M. Beveridge (ed.), *Children Thinking Through Language*, London: Edward Arnold

Brown, R. (1973) *A First Language*, London: Allen and Unwin

— (1977) Introduction in C.E. Snow and C.A. Ferguson (eds), *Talking to Children* Cambridge: Cambridge University Press

Carter, A.L. (1979) Prespeech meaning relations: an outline of one infant's sensori-motor morpheme development in P. Fletcher and M. Garman (eds), *Language Acquisition*, Cambridge: Cambridge University Press

Clark, R. (1982a) Assessing language in the home in A. Davies (ed.), *Language and Learning in Home and School* London: Heinemann Educational Books Ltd

— (1982b) Theory and method in child language research: are we assuming too much? in S. Kuczaj (ed.), *Language Development: Syntax and Semantics*, Hillsdale, NJ: Laurence Erlbaum Associates

Fletcher, P. (1979) The development of the verb phrase in P. Fletcher and M. Garman (eds), *Language Aquisition*, Cambridge: Cambridge University Press

Garcia, E. and De Haven, E. (1974) Use of operant techniques in the establishment of and generalisation of language: a review and analysis, *American Journal of Mental Deficiency*, *79*, 169-78

Halliday, M.A.K. (1975) *Learning How to Mean*, London: Edward Arnold

Harris, J. (1984) Encouraging linguistic interactions between severely mentally handicapped children and teachers in special schools, *Special Education: Forward Trends*, *11(2)*, 17-24

Harris, S.L. (1975) Teaching language to non-verbal children – with emphasis on problems of generalisation, *Psychological Bulletin*, *82*, 565-80

Hobsbaum, A. and Mittler, P. (1971) *Sentence Comprehension Test (Experimental Edition)*, Hester Adrian Research Centre: University of Manchester

Hood, Lois, and Bloom Lois (1979) What, when and how about why: a longitudinal study of early expressions of causality *Monographs for the Society for Research in Child Development*, *44(6)*

Hubbell, R.D. (1977) On facilitating spontaneous talking in young children, *Journal of Speech and Hearing Disorders*, *42*, 216

Huttenlocher, J. (1974) The origins of language comprehension in R.L. Solso (ed.), *Theories in Cognitive Psychology*, Loyola Symposium, New York: Wiley

Huttenlocher, J. Eisenberg, K. and Strauss, S. (1968) Comprehension: relation between perceived actor and logical subject, *Journal of Verbal Learning and Verbal Behaviour*, *7*, 527-30

Huttenlocher, J. and Weiner, S.L. (1971) Comprehension of instructions in varying contexts, *Cognitive Psychology*, *2*, 369-85

Irwin, O.C. (1970) Cognitive trends in mentally retarded children in H. Carl-Haywood (ed.), *Socio-Cultural Factors in Mental Retardation*, New York: Appleton Century Crofts

Leopold, W.F. (1949) *Speech Development of a Bilingual Child*, Evanston, Ill.: Northwestern University Press

Lieven, E.V.M. (1978) Conversations between mothers of young children: individual differences and their possible implication for the study of language learning in N. Waterson and C. Snow (eds), *The Development of Communication*, New York: Wiley

— (1980) Different routes to multiple word combinations, *Papers and Reports on Child Language*, *19*, 34-44, Stanford, California: Stanford University

McLean, J. and Snyder-Mclean, L. (1984) Recent development in pragmatics: remedial implications in D.J. Muller (ed.), *Remediating Children's Language*, London: Croom Helm/San Diego, College-Hill Press

Miller, J.F. and Yoder, D.E. (1972) A syntax teaching programme in J.E. McLean, D.E. Yoder and R.L. Schiefelbusch (eds), *Language Intervention with the*

Retarded, Baltimore: University Park Press

Nelson, K. (1973) Structure and strategy in learning to talk, *Monographs of Society for Research in Child Development, 3(149)*

Ratner, N. and Bruner, J. (1978) Games social exchange and the acquisition of language, *Journal of Child Language, 5*, 391-401

Reynell, J. (1969) *Reynell Developmental Language Scales (Experimental Edition)*, London: NFER

Robinson, W.P. (1972) *Language and Social Behaviour* Harmondsworth: Penguin

Seibert, J.M. and Oller, D.K. (1981) Linguistic pragmatics and language intervention strategies, *Journal of Autism and Developmental Disorders, 11(1)*, 75-88

Wells, G. (1979a) Variation in child language in P. Fletcher and M. Garman (eds), *Language Acquisition*, Cambridge: Cambridge University Press

———— (1979b) Learning and using the auxiliary verb in English in V. Lee (ed.), *Language Development* London: Croom Helm

Wilcox, M.J. (1984) Developmental language disorders: preschoolers in A. Holland (ed.), *Language Disorders in Children* Windsor: NFER-Nelson

Wood, D. (1980) A developmental psychologist looks – with teachers – at the education of deaf children, *Educational Analysis, 2(1)*, 61-83

Wood, H. and Wood, D. (1983) Questioning the pre-school child *Education Review, 35(2)*, 149–62

Yoder, D.E. and Calculator, S. (1981) Some perspectives on intervention strategies for persons with developmental disorders, *Journal of Autism and Developmental Disorders, 11(1)*, 107-23

Zeaman, D. and House, B. (1963) The role of attention in retardate discrimination learning in N. Ellis (ed.), *Handbook of Mental Deficiency*, New York: McGraw Hill

9 POLITICAL CONSTRAINTS ON THE USE OF RESEARCH FINDINGS IN SCHOOLS: EXPERIENCE IN ENGLAND AND NEW ZEALAND

David Galloway

Introduction

The utilitarian argument that educational research should contribute to the greatest good of the greatest number is well known and not really controversial, at least in the long term. A clear implication here is that research results should have some influence on practice. Nevertheless, the question is not straightforward. To start with, not all educational research has the explicit aim of influencing professional practice. Much of the more specialist work on perceptual and psychological variables in 'dyslexic' children, for example, may realistically aim to contribute to knowledge about the processes involved in learning to read. Whether it is likely to have any immediate implications for teachers frequently seems much more doubtful. The question, then, concerns the priority that society should place on research that may contribute to knowledge, even though the immediate spin-off in terms of professional practice is unclear. To rephrase the question: What price serendipity?

Another problem centres on the triangular relationship between researchers, the bodies which commission research and the subjects of the research. Both those who commission research, and the human-subjects whom we study, believe that the results should be of value to policy-makers. This is uncontroversial. There is an important distinction, however, between policy development at a political or organisational level, and policy implementation at a professional practice level. Policy development implies a decision to promote one policy in favour of another. Examples are: (i) at national level, a comprehensive system of secondary education in preference to a selective system; (ii) at LEA level, integrated provision for children with moderate learning difficulties, rather than separate special schools; (iii) at school level, mixed ability classes in preference to streaming or banding. In this sense, a policy-maker may be Secretary of State, chairman of the education committee or a head-teacher. I shall argue that research does not assist policy-makers in policy development, and that it probably should not.

Policy implementation is another matter. Here the researcher's task is more limited; namely, to assist policy-makers in implementing existing or proposed policies. One model here, favoured by HMI, is to describe good practice, defined as practice which achieves its stated aims. The researcher may, of course, regard those aims as problematic. Another model is to identify problems in implementing the policy. These may include internal inconsistency in the aims, inadequate funding and poor or inappropriate teaching technique.

It is not clear that the distinction between policy development and policy implementation is always recognised by funding bodies. Comparative studies, for example, imply a choice between alternative policies, particularly when an experimental paradigm is used. There is, not infrequently, a tension between the stated aims of the research, as formulated in the research proposal, and the unstated aims as they exist in the minds of the researcher and of the consumers. The proposal is likely to have been modified in the light of discussions between the researcher and the funding body. Yet these discussions, too, have their hidden agenda, for example: is the establishment of an on-site unit for problem children associated with a reduction in the number of pupils suspended for disruptive behaviour? The hidden agenda, though, may be more practical: these units are cheaper than special schools; what's more the secondary heads want them; are you going to find evidence to support our new policy?

Confusion in the aims of policy oriented research is one reason why the implications of research, as seen by the researcher, are seldom put into practice. The conflicting interests involved are related to these. The notion of Margaret Thatcher and Sir Keith Joseph as impartial, disinterested observers of the educational scene, eager to base national policy on the pearls of wisdom falling from equally impartial, disinterested educational researchers, is entertaining precisely because it is ludicrous. In this chapter I will argue that research is carried out in a social and political context. Both the researchers and the consumers are part of that context. The consumers include funding agencies as well as clients, who may have different, even conflicting, interests. The construction of knowledge cannot be seen as an objective pursuit of truth. Rather it develops from a particular way of looking at society. What causes researchers, policy-makers and professionals to look at society in one way rather than another is a product of their own experience, which will influence their perceptions of the aims and functions of research. Viewed in this light, it would be somewhat surprising if academics, policy-makers and professionals shared the same expectations or had the same priorities.

Experience suggests that the response to research is based less on its content than on how that content fits into the social and political climate of the day. Possibly the two most well-known educational research reports in the 1970s were *Teaching Styles and Pupil Progress* (Bennett 1976) and *Fifteen Thousand Hours* (Rutter, Maughan, Mortimore and Ouston 1979). Bennett's observation, that differences between teachers within a school were greater than differences between teachers in different schools, attracted little attention, compared with his conclusion that more formal teaching styles seemed to assist pupils' progress. In the post-Plowden era, coinciding with growing recognition that schools were continuing to reflect divisions within society, this was a popular message with critics of the education system. Bennett's subsequent re-analysis of his data (Aitkin, Bennett and Hesketh 1981), in which he reached rather different conclusions, was less acceptable to the same critics and aroused relatively little interest either among teachers or among the general public.

The attraction of Rutter's work, too, resulted as much from its academic quality, which has been strenuously debated (for example, Radical Statistics Education Group 1982), as from its conclusions. These were popular for two unrelated reasons. First, it gave teachers a feeling that they, through their own efforts, could improve the quality of schooling, with measurable benefit to their pupils. Second, politicians and administrators were able to argue that the school's buildings and resources were less important influences on pupils' progress than professional variables within schools. At a time of growing recession, there was a three-fold appeal in the conclusions of this research: (a) that home background was not all-determining; (b) that new buildings and expensive resources were not related in any obvious way to pupils' progress; and (c) that the school's climate, implicitly created by teachers, was of critical importance.

This chapter develops the arguments: (a) that educational research is concerned primarily with policy implementation rather than with policy development; (b) that research can realistically try to influence the implementation of policy only if researchers are sensitive to the social and political context in which policy develops. I shall draw on experience in three policy-oriented research programmes. The first was carried out in Sheffield in 1978-9. Funded by the DES, it investigated truancy and disruptive behaviour. The second was funded by the New Zealand Education Department from 1981-2, and reported on provision for disruptive pupils. The third also took place in New Zealand in 1981-2, funded jointly by the New Zealand Educational Institute, the primary teachers' union, and by the Mental Health Association of New Zealand. This project was concerned with stress, health and job-satisfaction in primary teachers.

On-site Units for Disruptive Pupils

One project in the research in Sheffield was a study of seven secondary schools which had established a special group for disruptive and/or disturbing pupils. These on-site units differed from off-site units in two ways: (i) they were based in an existing secondary school; (ii) they only admitted pupils from the host school. In addition to the seven schools with units, we included three secondary schools whose heads had decided, as a matter of policy, not to have any such units. The rationale for this project was threefold. First, on-site units were becoming an increasingly popular form of provision, both within the Sheffield LEA and nationally. They were not, perhaps, being seen as the solution to the problems presented by disruptive pupils, but certainly they were regarded as an essential ingredient. Second, corporal punishment and suspension from school were both becoming topics for political debate, and on-site units were seen, in some quarters, as constructive alternatives to either sanction. Third, the fact that some schools did *not* want an on-site unit suggested the possibility that alternative approaches might be educationally more desirable – and possibly cheaper.

Thus, when we started this part of the research, it seemed that the DES and the LEA wanted information on the effectiveness of these units on specified criteria. I further thought, naïvely, that this information might be of use to the LEA in developing future policy. Were special groups an effective way of dealing with the organisational problems presented by disruptive pupils and/or of meeting the needs of the pupils themselves? Were some schools successful in educating disruptive or potentially disruptive pupils without establishing an on-site unit, and if so how?

The results have been described in detail elsewhere (Galloway, Ball, Blomfield and Seyd 1982). The point here is that, in at least one important sense, the effectiveness of the on-site units was not at issue, at least in Sheffield. The reason was that head-teachers were continuing to seek support for on-site units and the LEA was encouraging such initiatives. In contrast, when a head-teacher sought help for a scheme that would have involved additional support for disruptive pupils, and for their teachers, within the ordinary class, he was advised informally that a proposal for a special group would stand a greater chance of success.

The decision regarding policy development was whether or not to encourage on-site units for disruptive pupils. At an informal level this decision had been taken before the research started, based on considerations over which the research had no influence. Once a bandwagon has started to roll, a mere research project is unlikely to stop it. In the late 1970s, the 'political' attractions for head-teachers and for administrators of special units for disruptive adolescents created a bandwagon which has still not lost its momentum. The research showed that the units had no effect on suspension rates, and none on rates of referral to special schools. There was strong indirect evidence that they were extremely unlikely to offer a viable alternative to corporal punishment. The evidence on whether teachers, as opposed to head-teachers, found the units helpful, for example by removing a disruptive pupil from their classes, was ambiguous; in some schools this seemed to be the case, but not in others.

At an intellectual level the conclusions were interesting, at least to the researchers. Their impact on policy development was negligible. For policy implementation, the research needed to address a quite different set of questions, concerning the policies and resources needed for on-site units to operate effectively, meeting the needs of selected pupils, and helping the school to fulfil its wider goals. The research did, in fact, also tackle these issues. In the absence of systematic study, its impact is a matter for conjecture. Our role was to provide a focus for informed debate by practitioners, with the aim of reviewing and reforming current policy. This is both a more modest and a more realistic aim than influencing the development of policy.

Off-site Units

The continuing popularity among educational administrators of off-site units raises some interesting questions, both for policy-makers and for researchers. By June 1981 the New Zealand Education Department had established seven off-site units for disruptive secondary school pupils. Each catered for pupils from at least eight schools. At a policy development level, it was clear that these units were intended as a constructive response to the pressures which, it was felt, the presence of an unruly minority of pupils placed on teachers. The units had attracted a good deal of media attention. To the extent that those head-teachers in areas not served by a unit were urging the Department of Education to establish one, they seemed to be regarded as highly successful. In the course of preliminary discussions, it became clear that the request for these units was based on the belief, at policy development level, that attendance by disruptive pupils would help teachers in ordinary schools, as well as the pupils removed from ordinary schools.

At one level, this was clearly an unrealistic belief. The number of secondary schools in each unit's catchment area ensured that most schools' 'share' of places would be no more than two or three each year. Indeed, on the basis of equitable distribution of places, some schools could not hope to place more than one child in the unit each year; thus a majority of teachers in each school would not have been teaching the pupils selected for off-site units. Moreover, it was unlikely that all, or even most, of the teachers who *were* teaching them were actually experiencing major problems. This seemed likely in view of the evidence of teachers from whose classes children had been removed to attend Sheffield's on-site units, from extensive clinical information showing that teachers are seldom unanimous in their description of a pupil's behaviour, and from the head-teachers' letters of referral, which tended to emphasise specific instances of misbehaviour, rather that long-term problems affecting a number of teachers. Whatever else off-site units might have achieved, it was clear, before the research started, that they could not have hoped to perform any constructive service to the majority of teachers in the referring schools. This left us with the question of whether off-site units benefited their pupils. Although numerous anecdotal and impressionistic accounts had been published, systematic research was conspicuously lacking. Our own conclusions have been reported elsewhere (Galloway and Barrett 1984). In one sense, though, they were irrelevant to policy development. This point is well illustrated by a realistic, if somewhat cynical, education officer in Britain. He explained to me why his LEA was opening an off-site unit. Having done his arithmetic, he was under no illusions about the number of children each referring school might be able to offload. He agreed that the unit would be of minimal relevance to the overwhelming majority of teachers in referring schools. He argued, though, that it was necessary in order to maintain head-teachers' morale, by demonstrating that 'something was being done'.

In a logical world, one might think that head-teachers would soon realise that an off-site unit was not the answer to their schools' problems. The experiment could then quickly be abandoned. However, there are two reasons why this was never likely to happen. First, a variety of Parkinson's Law states that the number of disturbing children, thought to need special education outside the ordinary school system, continually increases to exceed the available supply of places. The extensive evidence for this is reviewed elsewhere (Galloway 1985). Second, off-site units provide a convenient administrative solution for pupils who have been suspended or expelled from school.

Here the researcher has two options. One is to provide a critique of the *role* of existing off-site units in the secondary education system. This critique may see the units in favourable terms, perhaps acting as a sanctuary for pupils who cannot cope with the demands of an ordinary school. Alternatively, the critique may see them in a less favourable light. This argues that they preserve an unsatisfactory *status quo* by insulating schools from the need to tackle the policies and classroom practices which contribute to disruptive behaviour in the first place. Sending a child to the unit is less demanding, for example, than reviewing and modifying teaching practices or school policy. Yet however valid and perceptive the critique may be, its effect on policy development is likely to be negligible. The researcher's second option is to provide a critique of the units themselves. Here the researcher's task is to consider how an existing policy may be implemented. This involves identifying both the strengths and the limitations in current practice. These may have implications both for classroom practice and for policy-makers. In our own case, the latter included recommendations on the desirable size of future units, staffing levels, staff qualifications and in-service training.

Efforts to put the recommendations into practice, though, are inevitably limited by constraints on policy-makers themselves. We identified professional isolation of teachers in off-site units as an important factor in the severe management problems which had affected at least one unit in the past. We argued that similar problems were likely to occur again, if the teacher's professional isolation could not be reduced. To the best of my knowledge, no one disagreed that this was a sensible, if predictable, recommendation. Unfortunately, cuts in the education budget required cancellation of the annual course for directors of off-site units. Hence, their isolation from each other and from other influences in special education actually increased, in spite of the generally accepted validity of a recommendation to the contrary.

Stress, Health and Satisfaction in Teaching

The limitations of research in policy development are most starkly illustrated in our research on stress, health and satisfaction in primary schoolteachers. This project also illustrates why researchers spend more time on issues relevant to policy development, on which their findings will have little or no influence, than on policy implementation, where they stand at least a chance of a hearing.

Funding bodies do not regard the results of contractual research, and of any other available research, merely as a contribution to knowledge. Inevitably, and rightly, they use the results to promote debate, and hopefully changes, in the areas they consider important. After we had submitted our report, the New Zealand Educational Institute, as the principal sponsor, published a preliminary response. In this the NZEI identified the results they considered most interesting.

1. High levels of stress and low levels of satisfaction were reported by teachers under 30 years old and by teachers who did not hold permanent posts.
2. Comparison with an earlier New Zealand survey indicated an increased prevalence of medical symptoms which are often associated with stress.
3. Teachers expressed considerable dissatisfaction about conditions of employment and about society's attitudes towards teachers. Parent-teacher interviews were seen as an important source of stress by young teachers. In socially disadvantaged areas, both principals and class teachers reported high levels of stress from a variety of sources.
4. The curriculum areas most frequently reported to cause stress were reading and maths. Lack of opportunity for in-service education was a frequently reported source of dissatisfaction.
5. Relations between principal and staff could result in a good deal

of stress for both. Here, too, the conclusion was that in-service training could be of value.

6. Teachers in schools with inadequate buildings and playgrounds tended to report more stress than their colleagues in more favoured schools. Principals of schools with below average financial resources reported more stress than their more fortunate colleagues. There was also a tendency for staff to report more satisfaction and/or less stress when the principal was aged less than 50, and in smaller schools where the principal had full-time classroom responsibility.

It is always interesting, and occasionally revealing, for researchers to hear what the consumers of research regard as the principal findings. This list, though, seemed quite reasonable. For clarification, I would only add that potentially important and statistically significant differences between teachers were associated with four, relatively independent, groups of variables. These were: (i) biographical variables, such as the teacher's age; (ii) a variable that may be related to management style, namely the head-teacher's age; (iii) structural variables such as the school's buildings and whether classrooms were open-plan or conventional; (iv) catchment area variables, such as the number of children coming from homes experiencing some difficulty and the school's ethnic composition (Galloway, Boswell, Panckhurst, Boswell and Green 1985).

The results had obvious implications for policy. These were identified by the principal sponsor under four headings: (i) the need for security of employment for young teachers and teachers with limited tenure; (ii) the need for increased in-service education both for head-teachers and for class teachers; (iii) the need for additional support for teachers in 'high-risk' schools, notably those serving socially disadvantaged areas; (iv) the need for a general upgrading of buildings and resources.

These all required political decisions involving money. They were all known to be intrinsically desirable before the research started. Whatever results had been obtained, everyone would still have believed they were intrinsically desirable. The research, then, may have helped the principal sponsor by supporting, or legitimising, its existing policies. It is doubtful whether the research changed these policies, or even whether it could have done so.

The same principle seemed likely to determine the government's response. Quite legitimately, the principal sponsor used the research to support its existing policies. These policies, though, were *not* based on the research. Nor should we expect politicians and administrators to base policy on research. Like everyone else involved in policy development, they will use research findings, when they are available and when it suits them, to justify existing or proposed policies.

In the economic climate at the time, it was improbable that the research results would be used to justify an increase in the education budget. The more likely response was encapsulated in the comment of a fairly senior civil servant, to whom I was introduced shortly after publication of the first research report: 'David Galloway . . . ah yes. You did that thing on teacher stress, didn't you? The results were a bit of a yawn, weren't they? The most stressful things for primary school principals (are) wet weather and having to make up their minds!'

I should add that I found none of this at all surprising, nor even particularly disappointing. From the outset, it was clearly understood that this research was the first of two stages. Its principal aim was to lay a sound theoretical and empirical foundation for the second stage. This was to involve an intensive study in selected schools, with the broad aim of identifying variables in school management and classroom practice associated with differing levels of stress and of job satisfaction. The first stage of the research did no more than identify particular groups of teachers for the more intensive observational phase of the research. Teachers in open-plan classes, for example, were shown to report less stress than their colleagues in conventional classrooms. At the end of the first stage, we could only speculate on the reasons. To produce information of practical value to teachers in their professional work, we needed to study school and classroom process variables at a deeper level than was possible in the questionnaire surveys of the first stage of the research.

The reasons for the second stage of the research not taking place have been described elsewhere (Galloway 1983). The point at issue here is that the questions which exercise the minds of policy-makers are frequently not the ones which most concern practitioners. Funding agencies, particularly government departments and professional and voluntary organisations, are often controlled by policy-makers. If my argument is correct – that research is generally used to justify existing or proposed policies – then the gap between the implications of research and its impact becomes inevitable.

Discussion

A central theme in this chapter is that research takes place in a political context, and is itself part of that context. An interesting example of this occurred during the research on teacher stress. The principal sponsor, the primary teachers' union, had long been pressing for reduction in class size. The government had been resisting this pressure, arguing that there were higher priorities for the available resources. Each side publicised arguments and evidence to support its case, in an increasingly acrimonious debate.

Technically, it would not have been difficult to extract from the questionnaire responses the relationships between class size and self-reported stress or satisfaction. Both on academic and on political grounds, we decided not to do so. The problem was simply that government policy was only one of the factors affecting class size. Other factors included: (i) falling school roles, with the associated threat of transfer or redundancy for teachers; (ii) the school's location: many rural schools had fewer children per class than urban schools; (iii) internal school organisation: sometimes the most experienced teacher in the school is given the largest class; alternatively, an exceptionally small class may be created to cater for children with special needs.

If we had used class size as a variable on which to compare groups of teachers, we would have obtained one of three possible outcomes: (i) teachers of large classes reporting more stress and/or satisfaction than teachers of small classes; (ii) teachers of large classes reporting less stress and/or satisfaction; (iii) no significant differences between the two groups. None of these outcomes would have been in the least surprising, since the available data would not have enabled us to speculate, even in a semi-informed manner, on what they actually meant. In other words the results would have been meaningless. Yet if they had been provided, the temptation for interested parties to use them out of context would undoubtedly have been enormous.

There is an argument that research results may contribute to policy development through their long-term influence on public and on professional opinion. This model sees research as having an indirect influence on policy development. It provides a focus for debate. Occasionally, it may even define the issues for debate, though this is rare, since funding agencies have a natural inclination to exercise their own control over the agenda by deciding what and who to support. Nevertheless, there is some doubt as to whether research does, in fact, influence policy decision, even indirectly and over a long period of time.

The debate on secondary school reorganisation illustrates this point. Certainly, the wealth of sociological research in the 1950s and 1960s demonstrated tensions in the tripartite system established by the 1944 Education Act and, more specifically, in the eleven-plus selection process. That research did not, and could not, demonstrate that another system would be preferable. Since secondary school reorganisation, further research has demonstrated tensions in the curriculum and management of comprehensive schools. Again, this research has not, and possibly cannot, demonstrate that a return to a selective system would benefit a majority of pupils. The parents who opposed comprehensive reorganisation in the 1960s and 1970s did so for precisely the same reasons as the parents who argued in favour of it, and as the parents who successfully opposed their Education Committees' proposals to return to a selective system in 1983-4; they feared that their children would receive a second-class education. The conflicting interests could each cite research to support their views. Indeed, since the question was essentially ideological rather than cognitive, it was inevitable that they should do so. Research findings do not and cannot exist in a vacuum. They require interpretation. This interpretation may influence the way people think and behave. Yet since the way people think and behave reflects their own background and biases, it is at least as likely that the converse is true. (For a discussion of the role of values in research implementation, see Smith, this volume.)

Another example comes from the international debate on the education of children with special needs. Increasingly, parents of these children are demanding that they be educated in an ordinary school. They are not motivated primarily by research results, though research exists to support their arguments. Rather they are motivated by a drive to achieve the best, and most 'normal', education for their child. Tizard (1978) has argued convincingly that the function of research should not be to compare integration with separate provision for children with disabilities. That, he argues, is essentially a political decision. The function of research is instead to identify the circumstances in which certain policies can work, and the obstacles they are likely to meet.

Seeing policy development as a political exercise reveals the dilemma for research workers. There is no such person as an impartial, disinterested researcher, since all researchers are the product of their own social and political background. This, even more than their frequently small, unrepresentative samples and their occasionally misleading analyses of their results, is why they have no legitimate claim to any direct influence in the development of policy.

Conclusions

Publication of results which challenge existing policy and practice is a legitimate and necessary task for educational research. It is also a fairly simple task. Teachers are entitled to expect more immediate and more practical benefits from their participation in research than a challenge to the *status quo*. One response is to disseminate examples of 'good practice'. The trouble here is that good practice in one context may be utterly unrealistic and inappropriate in another. The fact that School A is running a highly successful tutorial programme, for example, does not mean that the same programme will be effective in School B, half a mile down the road.

This raises some difficult questions both about innovation and about dissemination. In some models of action research both can be built into the research design, though this does not overcome the underlying political constraints that concern the present chapter (for further discussion of the dissemination of research findings see Sylva, Desforges and McConkey, this volume).

I have argued, then, that applied research in education has two functions. First, it must provide a critique of current practice. Such research may contribute to theoretical and ideological debate, for example on the status of IQ or the concept of maladjustment. It may also focus on specific aspects of policy or practice, for example the implementation of the 1981 Education Act or a decision to establish off-site units for disruptive pupils. This kind of research lies essentially in the field which I described as policy development at the start of the chapter. I have argued that this is frequently used to legitimise existing or proposed policies, but that it is seldom used in the formation of policy.

The second function of applied research in education is in the area of policy implementation. This includes projects which evaluate existing methods and which explore appropriate means to achieve agreed ends. The researchers may or may not be entirely happy about the agreed ends. In either case it is their job to describe observed and/

or predicted consequences of the policy, irrespective of whether these are harmful or beneficial. If the consequences are harmful, the research should suggest how the effects may be mitigated. This model denies researchers the enjoyable self-indulgence of attacking existing policy or practice without proposing a practical alternative. It gives them a more limited role. This accepts the reality that research is seldom used in the formation of policy and, by increasing the researchers' responsibility to the subjects of the research, places them in a collegial relationship with one another.

Acknowledgements

Financial support from the Department of Education and Science, the New Zealand Education Department, the New Zealand Educational Institute and the Mental Health Foundation of New Zealand is gratefully acknowledged. I am also grateful to the Social Sciences Research Fund Committee of New Zealand for permission to use brief extracts from an article published in their 1983 *Seminar Series on Social Research*.

References

Aitken, M., Bennett, N. and Hesketh, J. (1981) Teaching styles and pupil progress: a re-analysis, *British Journal of Educational Psychology*, *51*, 170-86

Bennett, N. (1976) *Teaching Styles and Pupil Progress*, London: Open Books

Galloway, D. (1983) Issues in the planning, interpretation and dissemination of recent research on teacher stress in J.A. Johnston and T. Scotney (eds), *Seminar Series on Social Research: 1983 Proceedings*, Wellington, NZ: Social Sciences Research Fund Committee

——— (1985) *Schools, Pupils and Special Educational Needs*, London: Croom Helm

——— Ball, T., Blomfield, D. and Seyd, R. (1982) *Schools and Disruptive Pupils*, London: Longman

——— and Barrett, B. (1984) Off-site centres for disruptive secondary school pupils in New Zealand, *Educational Research*, *26*, 106–10

——— Boswell, K., Panckhurst, F., Boswell, C. and Green, J. (1985) Sources of satisfaction and dissatisfaction for teachers in New Zealand primary schools, *Educational Research* (in press)

Radical Statistics Education Group (1982) *Reading Between the Numbers: A Critical Guide to Educational Research*, London: BSSR Publications

Rutter, M., Maughan, B., Mortimore, P. and Ouston, J. (1979) *Fifteen Thousand Hours: Secondary Schools and their Effects on Pupils*, London: Open Books

Tizard, J. (1978) Research in special education, *Special Education Forward Trend*, *5(3)*, 23–6

PART THREE: PROFESSIONAL TRAINING

This section deals with child development research in relation to the training of professionals who will subsequently be involved in the care and education of children. Such professionals may operate in the home or in the school and may be primarily concerned with ordinary children or with those who have special educational needs or developmental problems.

Charles Desforges considers research on child development in relation to teacher training and argues that not only has research had relatively little impact upon teaching practice but that existing research on child development has not addressed educationally relevant problems. Kay Mogford looks at the role of child development research in the training of speech therapists and in particular the way in which research-based knowledge can be presented and combined with clinical experience, so that the two elements of training are mutually complementary. Like Charles Desforges, she argues that too little research has been undertaken which is of direct relevance to the problems of clinicians working with children or their caretakers. Roy McConkey sets out to explore a possible solution to the problem of initiating research which is relevant to practice. He argues for a restructuring of the research-practice division, and in particular a redefinition of roles so that a single individual, with appropriate practical experience, can be responsible for organising research which is explicitly concerned with the needs of practitioners. For McConkey the solution lies in recognising that practice is where research problems originate, not simply the final resting place of results produced by psychologists with different interests, trying to solve unrelated problems.

10 DEVELOPMENTAL PSYCHOLOGY APPLIED TO TEACHER TRAINING

Charles Desforges

Introduction

It is not surprising that developmental psychologists should express an interest in teaching and education, nor that they should find a ready demand for their ideas among educational practitioners. There is a broad common interest between those who study, and those who seek to train and develop, psychological processes. Their mutual interest lies in the problems associated with the acquisition, organisation, retention, elaboration and use of knowledge, skills, attitudes and values.

Those who study developmental processes in young children seem to have a special passion for generating educational messages. Intimate contact with the workings of young minds appears to coincide with a belief in children's potential. When this is compared with a knowledge of, and concern about, the products of schooling, the contrast frequently provokes the publication of appeals for desperate remedies (Piaget 1971a; Furth and Wachs 1974; Donaldson 1978; Duckworth 1979).

In parallel with psychologists' interest in education, educators have consistently afforded developmental psychology a place in educational theory (Tibble 1971; Taylor 1973). This is not the place to consider the general nature of educational theory, except to comment that at least some aspects of it must be value-laden, since the essential process of education is intended to be directed towards the attainment of valued ends (see Smith, this volume). The definition of these ends and the specification of the means by which they might be attained are informed by a wide range of considerations including conceptions of the nature of man and society, conceptions of the forces which shaped educational organisations, and theories of how institutions and individuals work. Developmental studies are strongly implicated in this list.

Fundamental Issues

Whilst in this light the place of developmental psychology seems assured in the student teacher's curriculum, there are many problems in translating from the essentially descriptive findings of psychology to the prescriptive business of education. These issues have long been recognised (James 1899; Dewey 1904; Münsterberg 1912; Piaget 1971a) but have rarely been given the exhaustive treatment they merit before being used in teacher education (Desforges 1981).

The first thing that must be established is the quality of the informing psychological theory. If educational practices are genuinely to be founded on psychology, then the theory must be sound. Münsterberg (1912:94) observed: 'There is nothing more reckless than to take fragments of an unsafe new doctrine and turn them into practical remedies.' Piaget emphasised the importance of resting educational principles, said to emanate from child study, on scientifically valid foundations. Whilst recognising some consonance between his educational principles and those of Rousseau, Piaget none the less emphasised that Rousseau's view was '. . . no more than a sociological belief or a polemical weapon . . .' (1971a:140) and that 'what Rousseau lacked in order to constitute a science of education was a psychology of mental development' (p. 141). It is the claim to scientific validity which underpins the developmentalist's right to a hearing on educational matters.

Unfortunately, there is no body of developmental theory which is not open to fundamental reservation. For example, extensive criticisms of Piaget's theory are available (Brainerd 1978; Donaldson 1978; Siegel and Brainerd 1978; Desforges 1979). The flaws have been considered to be of such magnitude that it has been thought premature and misleading to apply Piaget's theory to education (Sullivan 1967; Ammon 1977; Brown and Desforges 1977; Lawton and Hooper 1978; Desforges and Brown 1979). Piaget's theory dominates contemporary developmental studies and, since 'new doctrines' have yet to emerge from his critics, this must provoke considerable caution in applications of his work.

Since it is in the nature of science to contest theories, this could lead to a complete embargo on the educational applications of much developmental theory. As a way of avoiding this conclusion, it has been suggested (Hilgard 1964) that educators are practical people who must deal with facts and that conflicting theories are rarely about facts, but about interpretations of facts. So long as theoreticians agree on the facts, then the practitioner can work on the basis of secure knowledge. 'Whilst eventually the correct interpretation might make some difference, it often makes little difference at the present stage of technology.' (Hilgard 1964:403) Thus navigators do not suspend their calculations whilst they await the resolution of theoretical debates about the origins of the universe.

Although the above example is an impeccable instance of Hilgard's view on the practical utility of contested theory, it might not be applicable to conflicts in contemporary social science. For one thing, educational prescriptions rarely arise from the notional facts of a body of knowledge. Rather, they arise from interpretations. The educational prescriptions emanating from Piaget's work do not arise from the largely uncontested facts that, at particular ages, most children fail specific archetypal tasks. On the contrary, the prescriptions arise precisely from Piaget's contested interpretations of his observations. For example, Piaget's critics confirm his observations that children under the age of seven typically respond differently from adults on the whole range of tasks known in Piagetian terms as 'tests of conservation'. Piaget's interpretation is that these children lack the internalised operation of conservation and this is taken to be just one symptom of their being 'pre-operational'. From this it has been argued that for such children the curriculum should be dominated by direct sensory experience (Furth and Wachs 1974; Wadsworth 1978; Ginsburg and Opper 1979). However, Piaget's critics – whilst endorsing his observations – reject the interpretation. Children's performance limitations on these tasks have been variously attributed to memory limitations (Case 1974), the level of experience with specific task content (Engelman 1971) or inexperience in interpreting the social demands of the task (Rose and Blank 1974). Some of these interpretations have been associated with educational prescriptions at odds with the Piagetian approach (Engelman 1971; Case 1978). These authors do not assume that young children lack logical operations and do not limit pedagogies to direct sensory experience as *the* essential educational medium for young children.

Rather than searching for a solution to the problems of contested or condemned theory, as a basis for educational innovation, both psychologists and educationalists have tended to ignore the issues. For example, whilst Skinner's theory of language development was criticised by Chomsky (1959) and, whilst behaviourism generally has been criticised as naïve in cognitive terms (Broadbent 1958) and untenable epistemologically (Piaget 1971b), both find extensive use in contemporary educational practice and teacher education syllabuses.

Whatever the quality of particular theories, there remains the overriding and general problem of the nature of the link between schooling and developmental studies. Piaget (1971:145) asserted: 'That schooling should be adapted to the child is something that everyone has constantly urged.' This is simply not true. It is safer to say that no one has argued that schooling should be deliberately maladapted to the child. The practicalities of avoiding such maladaption depend, in general terms, on what the nature of child development is taken to be.

For those theorists who believe that development is merely the associative products of learning, there are no special assumptions in applying developmental psychology to schooling. Special assumptions become necessary only when the claim is made that there is a natural course to human development or that there are natural limitations to human learning at certain stages. This claim is often advanced and, since it takes a variety of forms, it is necessary to examine its implications.

Taken at its most general, the view of the superiority of natural propensities is well expressed by Smith (1975:2) who asserts that children know how to learn and that 'A fundamental problem for any instructor is to avoid interfering with natural processes of comprehension and learning.' The educational implication of this is that 'There is only one reliable way to improve instruction, and that is to assist the instructor in understanding children . . .' (p. 245) A similar view is often deployed by popularisers of Piaget's work (Yardley 1970; Ginsburg and Opper 1979). Occasionally, a debilitating natural decline is posited. Bereiter and Scardamalia (1977), for example, have taken the view that there is a natural decline in spontaneous curiosity. In establishing the educational relevance of such views, it is necessary to ask whether the postulated 'natural processes' are indeed natural or whether they are themselves the products of schooling, or the knock-on effects of schooling mediated by parents.

Even if a natural order were established, its application to instruction depends on whether Nature were to be considered ideal, less than ideal, or simply immutable. It is interesting that Smith (1975) views children's natural ways of knowing as self-evident and good, whilst Bereiter and Scardamalia (1977) view children's natural decline in curiosity as simply an immutable fact. It is clear that divining educational implications from developmental studies involves value judgements on whether natural development (when established) should set the limits to which schooling might aspire.

There is a third stance on the form of development and its limitations which has its origins neither in an appeal to the superiority of Nature nor, initially at least, in the analysis of psychological processes. This is the stance initiated by Piaget. Arising from his rejection, on epistemological grounds, of empiricism and rationalism as accounts of the growth of understanding and his adoption of a constructivist stance, Piaget's view of the impact of experience on the processes of equilibration was that it necessarily yielded cognitive structures of particular and temporarily limiting forms. Piaget's view of development is thus not based on a naïve view of the wisdom or otherwise of Nature. He observed '... let there be no misunderstanding. Memory, passive obedience, imitation of the adult, and the receptive factors in general are all as natural to the child as spontaneous activity.' (1971a:137-8)

Piaget's theory has had enormous prominence in teacher education. This is not the place to describe or evaluate the work (see Brown and Desforges (1979) for such a treatment). The concern here is to raise, in principle, the kinds of problems peculiar to the application of Piaget's work to schooling, and hence to evaluate its place in teacher education. Instructional implications have been taken to arise from the functional aspect of the theory (that is the description of the dynamics of development) and from the formal aspect of the theory (that is the description of the sequential stages of underlying competence).

Piaget's view of the dynamics of development (most notably his conception of equilibration) arises out of his position as a constructivist. Before applying this notion to education, it would be necessary to be convinced on epistemological grounds of the necessity of adopting this model. Piaget's own view was that equilibration was an unnecessary concept when contemplating teaching school subjects '... whose contents have been invented or even developed by adults' (1971a:26). However, there are some school subjects 'whose contents depend more on a process of research and discovery during the course of which the human intelligence affirms its own existence' (1971a:26). In these latter subjects, and Piaget quoted physics and mathematics as examples, the operation of the learner's own processes of equilibration were considered crucial.

In applying the stage model to education, different problems are met. The validity of the model would have to be established. This is extremely difficult since the theory is one of underlying competence. Even if the theory were considered valid, there are massive technical problems in translating descriptions of competence into taxonomies for analysing children's available structures (as revealed by their task-specific performances) and related taxonomies for sequencing curriculum tasks. Considerable effort has been put into such work (Shayer and Adey 1981) but the fundamental issues set out above seem to have been totally ignored (Desforges 1981).

Current Applications

In the contemporary application of developmental psychology to teacher education, all the above fundamental issues seem to be largely ignored. Time constraints must account in good measure for the manner in which developmental studies are met by student teachers. Teacher education curriculums are very crowded. The most obvious impact of developmental psychology is in the form of textbooks. Typically students are required to purchase introductory texts in which are set out rendered down versions of psychological theories and their conjectured implications (see Child (1973), for a very popular example). Frequently, texts introducing only developmental psychology are recommended (see Brown (1976), for example) or texts linking developmental psychology to the curriculum are offered (see Fontana (1978), for example). Even at best, introductory texts written for teachers do little justice to the quality, complexity and subtlety of the psychologist's understanding of development and appear to do no justice whatsoever to the business of schooling (Desforges and McNamara 1977). They appear to contain no model of the reader as learner-teacher; they are first and last guides to the psychological literature. Little effort is made to provide a serious rationale to the reader justifying either the content or organisation of the book. In the popular work of Fontana (1978), for example, he notes that the division of his book into two parts (developmental psychology followed by curriculum study) '... needs no lengthy justification. This provides a conceptual framework for prescriptions to be presented with coherence.' (p. xiv) He leaves questions about relevance, significance and validity of the developmental theories unexamined.

Other authors of texts on developmental psychology claim to provide perspectives within which teachers might interpret and understand children's behaviour. The explicit claim is that the perspectives which psychologists so readily criticise within their own profession might prove useful as a heuristic with which to view classroom life. This approach passes on to the teacher the problems of translation discussed earlier. It avoids the question of whether the teacher's practical problems, goals and processes can be conceptualised within the terms offered, or whether they must be necessarily limited thereby (Desforges and McNamara 1977). It ignores the old adage that a perspective is not only a way of seeing – it is also a way of not seeing. Whilst no one would argue against the proposition that student teachers should learn to understand children, the techniques adopted by contemporary authors are educationally amorphous and question-begging.

Whilst the above problems are not introduced to the reader of such texts, it seems inconceivable that the authors do not recognise them. However, by avoiding the issues, very strong claims may be made for the educational utility of developmental psychology. It is claimed implicitly that developmentalists have generated descriptions of natural sequences and that these should be used to inform decisions about the aims of education and the means of schooling. Prescriptions are given for the design of learning environments, for techniques of diagnosis and assessment, and for the methods of teaching (see Harris, J., this volume, for a discussion of these issues in relation to special schools).

Whilst the textbook is the most evident mode of introducing student teachers to developmental psychology, it is not the only contact attempted. Students are sometimes required to undertake a child-study, with the objective of understanding the dynamics of a particular child. Alternatively, and increasingly, students meet bold statements of developmental theory (usually Piagetian) in the introductions to school schemes (see, for example, Nuffield (1974)). Whether in child studies or in the rationales to commercial schemes, the relevance of a development perspective is taken to be self-evident. Whilst not spelt out, it is implied that developmental psychology adds the gloss of objective, even scientific, knowledge to justify teaching procedures.

The Impact of Developmental Psychology on Teaching

Many authorities in the field of educational psychology express considerable dismay and disappointment at the lack of impact of psychological studies on teaching behaviour (Ausubel and Robinson 1969; Atkinson 1976; Glaser 1978, for example). Ausubel and Robinson note, despite favourable responses on the part of teachers on psychology courses, that 'the behaviour of those same teachers observed later in the classroom, has typically shown distressingly little influence of the principles and theories which they had presumably learned' (p.iii). Some blame the quality of the psychology (Atkinson 1976), others blame the quality of psychology teaching (Jeffreys 1975; Povey and Hill 1975). None offers any evidence in support of the various conclusions.

In stark contrast to the view of no effect, King (1978) has suggested that much of the ideology of teachers in the first school is propped up by their studies in developmental psychology. Their ideology, according to King, revolves around the notion of 'child centred' education and involves attention to children's readiness to learn, their progress through stages, their inherent lack of malice and their subjective ways of knowing. All these, argues King, frame the design of the early years' curriculum, including content and teaching methods. It has been suggested that this massive impact of developmental psychology is responsible for much of what is wrong with first school teaching (Alexander 1984). The view of crucial impact, like the view of nil impact, is based on no substantive evidence. King (1978), for example, observed and interviewed only three teachers. His study, whilst provocative, provides little basis on which to discern the impact of developmental psychology and none whatsoever on which to damn it. Relevant evidence seems to be unavailable.

It would appear that those who wish to influence teaching processes must do so, at least in part, by influencing how teachers think and by endeavouring to understand teachers' existing theories and concepts as they relate to their classroom activities. However, research on teachers' thinking is largely undeveloped and it seems beset by methodological problems (Calderhead 1984). The only research which would directly inform the issue of the impact of teachers' training would, as a minimum, have to link teachers' thinking to teachers' behaviour and thence to their children's learning. Such research is virtually non-existent.

Future Directions

The present use of developmental psychology in teacher education is characterised by ignorance. It has been argued above that we are ignorant of the problems of translation from descriptive science to prescriptive action and we are ignorant of the effects of current approaches to teaching developmental psychology to student teachers. More fundamentally, developmental psychology is, at best, vague about processes of development. In respect of the crucial educational task of managing learning, there are important gaps in our knowledge regarding (a) the relationship between operational development and progress in curriculum subjects, and (b) the processes of transition from task to task or cognitive stage to cognitive stage. What we do not know here is precisely what a practitioner would need to know in order to optimise learning (Desforges, in press). We are also remarkably ignorant of the conditions and constraints under which teachers work. The practicalities of translating from theory to practice are largely ignored (Kuhn 1979). Finally, we are generally ignorant of the effect of schooling as a factor in development. In respect of cognitive growth, for example, the matter has received only the most general and trivial treatment (Brown and Desforges 1979). If developmental psychology is to be used with integrity in the education of teachers, each of these issues must become the subject of a great deal of work.

There is a case for demanding that teachers address the problem of what it means to 'understand children'. Since this problem is broached in a wide variety of contexts (literature, common sense, philosophy, psychology, for example) there is some possibility that psychologists might be given a hearing, but no special voice. In this respect, psychological theory and findings should be presented – warts and all. If teachers learned nothing of immediate practical use in these lessons they might at least learn to pause and reflect on the complexity of the job. But if this were the only claim for the utility of developmental psychology, it amounts to an impertinence, since it implies that teachers do not have enough to think about in respect of their profession and offers no assurance that reflection on complexity might lead to improved practice.

To move towards making respectable claims for a hearing in teacher education, it seems important that more developmentalists address themselves directly to educationally relevant questions. Most generally, this would involve understanding schooling as a developmental factor and understanding it as a manipulable variable. For example, what range of schooling conditions can be manipulated to produce developmentally significant effects which are, also, educationally valued effects? Understanding schooling, as a preliminary to prescribing for schooling, would have enormous impact on the design of practicable applications work. Much developmental psychology describes the notional limitations of children but offers prescriptions for teachers implying that the teachers' material and psychological resources are limitless. Modern theories of how classrooms work (Doyle 1980) indicate that this is not the case. Interestingly, Doyle's theory contains no developmental dimension.

In offering developmental work to student teachers it seems crucial to have a model (or at least a sense of audience) of the student as learner-teacher. What would such an audience's knowledge be? What would be their concerns, preoccupations and problems? What key questions of educational import would guide and frame communications from the psychologists? These seem obvious issues. They also seem to be generally ignored.

Conclusion

There seems to be a huge gap between aspiration and actuality in the use of developmental psychology in teacher education. Part of the hiatus arises from a limited empirical base, both in educationally relevant developmental studies and developmentally relevant educational studies. This is unlikely to be closed without extensive re-conception of research work in this field. The rest of the gap is a communication problem arising from an aberrant sense of audience and purpose in addressing and justifying the messages of developmental psychology for teachers. This problem seems to have defeated – or not concerned – writers in the past. It should concern us now.

References

Alexander, R.J. (1984) *Primary Teaching*, London: Holt Rinehart and Winston
Ammon, P.R. (1977) Cognitive development and early childhood education in H. Hom and P. Robinson (eds), *Psychological Processes in Early Education*, New York: Academic Press
Atkinson, R.C. (1976) Adaptive instructional systems; some attempts to optimise the learning process in D. Klahr (ed.), *Cognition and Instruction*, Hillsdale,

NJ: Lawrence Erlbaum Associates

Ausubel, D.P. and Robinson, F.G. (1969) *School Learning: An Introduction to Educational Psychology*, New York: Holt Rinehart and Winston

Bereiter, C. and Scardamalia, M. (1977) *The Limits of Natural Development*, Ontario: Ontario Institute for Studies in Education (mimeo)

Brainerd, C. (1978) *Piaget's Theory of Intelligence*, Oxford: Pergamon Press

Broadbent, D.E. (1958) *Perception and Communication*, Oxford: Pergamon Press

Brown, G. (1976) *Child Development*, London: Open Books

Brown, G. and Desforges, C. (1977) Piagetian psychology and education: time for revision, *British Journal of Educational Psychology*, *47*, 7-17

— (1979) *Piaget's Theory: A Psychological Critique*, London: Routledge and Kegan Paul

Brown, M. (1978) Cognitive development and the learning of mathematics in A. Floyd (ed.), *Cognitive Development in the School Years*, London: Croom Helm

Calderhead, J. (1984) *Teachers' Decision Making*, Slough: NFER

Case, R. (1974) Structures and strictures: some functional limitations on the course of cognitive growth, *Cognitive Psychology*, *6*, 544-73

— (1978) Piaget and beyond: towards a developmentally based theory and technology of instruction in R. Glaser (ed.), *Advances in Instructional Psychology*, Vol. 1, Hillsdale, NJ: Lawrence Erlbaum Associates

Child, D. (1973) *Psychology and the Teacher*, London: Holt-Blond

Chomsky, N. (1959) Review of Skinner's 'verbal behaviour', *Language*, *35*, 26-58

Desforges, C.W. (in press) Training for the management of learning in the primary school in H. Francis (ed.), *Psychology and Teacher Education*, Falmer: Falmer Press

— (1981) Linking theories of cognition and cognitive development to educational practice, Unpublished PhD thesis, University of Lancaster

Desforges, C. and Brown, G. (1979) The educational utility of Piaget: a reply to Shayer, *British Journal of Educational Psychology*, *49*, 277-81

Desforges, C. and McNamara. D. (1977) One man's heuristic is another man's blindfold, *British Journal of Teacher Education*, *3(1)*, 27-39

Dewey, J. (1904) The relation of theory to practice in education reprinted in R. Archambolt (ed.), *John Dewey on Education*, Chicago: University of Chicago Press (1974)

Donaldson, M. (1978) *Children's Minds*, London: Fontana

Doyle, W. (1980) *Student Mediating Responses in Teacher Effectiveness*, Denton, Texas: North Texas State University

Duckworth, E. (1979) Either we're too early and they can't learn it or we're too late and they know it already: the dilemma of 'applying Piaget', *Harvard Educational Review*, *49*, (3), 297-312

Engelman, S. (1971) Does the Piagetian approach imply instruction? in D.R. Green, M.P. Ford and G.B. Flamer (eds), *Measurement and Piaget*, New York: McGraw Hill

Fontana, D. (1978) *The Education of the Young Child*, London: Open Books

Furth, H. and Wachs, H. (1974) *Thinking Goes to School*, New York, Oxford University Press

Glaser, R. (1978) *Advances in Instructional Psychology*, Vol. 1, Hillsdale, NJ: Lawrence Erlbaum Associates

Ginsburg, H. and Opper, S. (1979) *Piaget's Theory of Intellectual Development*, 2nd edn, Englewood Cliffs, NJ: Prentice Hall

Hilgard, E.R. (1964) Twenty years of learning theory in relation to education in E.R. Hilgard (ed.), *Theories of Learning and Instruction*, Chicago: National Society for the Study of Education

James, W. (1899) *Talks to Teachers on Psychology: And to Students on Some of Life's Ideals*, London: Longman

Jeffreys, D. (1975) How psychology fails the teacher, *British Journal of Teacher Education, 1(1),* 63-9

King, R. (1978) *All Things Bright and Beautiful,* London: Wiley

Kuhn, D. (1979) The application of Piaget's theory of cognitive development to education, *Harvard Educational Review, 49(3),* 340-60

Lawton, J.T. and Hooper, F.H. (1978) Piagetian theory and early childhood education: a critical analysis in L.S. Siegel and C.J. Brainerd (eds), *Alternatives to Piaget: Critical Essays on the Theory,* New York: Academic Press

Münsterberg, H. (1912) *Psychology and the Teacher,* New York: Appleton

Nuffield Foundation (1974) *Science 5-13,* London: MacDonald

Piaget, J. (1971a) *Science Education and the Psychology of the Child,* London: Longman

— (1971b) *Structuralism,* London: Routledge and Kegan Paul

Povey, R. and Hill, E. (1975) Can pre-school children form concepts? *Educational Research, 17(3),* 180–93

Rose, S.A. and Blank, M. (1974) The potency of context in children's cognition: an illustration through conservation, *Child Development, 45,* 499-502

Shayer, M. and Adey, P. (1981) *Towards a Science of Science Teaching,* London: Heinemann

Siegel, L.S. and Brainerd, C.J. (1978) *Alternatives to Piaget: Critical Essays on the Theory,* New York: Academic Press

Smith, F. (1975) *Comprehension and Learning,* New York: Holt Rinehart and Winston

Sullivan, E. (1967) Piaget and the school curriculum, *Bulletin of the Ontario Institute for Studies in Education,* Ontario

Taylor, W. (1973) *Research Perspectives in Education,* London: Routledge and Kegan Paul

Tibble, J.W. (1971) *An Introduction to the Study of Education,* London: Routledge and Kegan Paul

Wadsworth, B.J. (1978) *Piaget for the Classroom Teacher,* London: Longman

Yardley, A. (1970) *Discovering the Physical World,* London: Evans

11 EVOLVING CLINICAL PRACTICE FROM RESEARCH FINDINGS: THE PROBLEM OF PROFESSIONAL EDUCATION

Kay Mogford

Introduction

It is possible to characterise two distinct approaches to the education of practitioners in a remedial profession such as clinical child psychology or speech therapy. Though they are not effectively mutually exclusive, both these approaches are only partial solutions to the problem that practice must inevitably be undertaken before there is a comprehensive body of knowledge on which intervention can be based.

The two available options are:

(1) to teach directly techniques for the assessment of clients' difficulties and a series of steps and measures needed for intervention. The greater part of the teaching effort is expended in inculcating skills and in assessing students' competence. A certain amount of background on normal functioning and development may be taught as part of an intervention rationale;

(2) to teach knowledge of normal processes and characteristics of clinical populations as they are currently understood from research studies. The greater part of this knowledge will not have been collected in a form that yields the kind of insights that are directly relevant to individual case-based intervention. Practical opportunities are provided for individual students, with peer groups, tutors and clinical supervisors to apply this knowledge to actual clinical problems, and students are encouraged to participate in assessing the adequacy of these solutions.

The first option is a relatively 'safe' one for both client and potential practitioner, giving a sense of security to the inexperienced. However, it assumes that the techniques that are taught can be adequately specified and described and are both effective and desirable. Even where these assumptions can be justified, this approach leaves little room for professional development, nor does it ensure that practitioners can respond flexibly to the individual needs of clients or tackle novel situations effectively when they arise. It also makes it unlikely that there will be a framework available to suggest why interventions may sometimes be unsuccessful and from which alternative strategies may be derived when necessary. The first approach can also prove intellectually frustrating for the practitioner unless techniques are adequately justified and derived from satisfactory scientific principles. The second approach should, in theory, allow practitioners to develop methods suitable for individual needs and circumstances. Where alternative solutions to a clinical problem are suggested, this can provide fertile ground for further research, in which practitioners themselves may take an active part, to establish which solution may be most productive in a given set of circumstances.

For those concerned with clinically-based intervention, most professional education is probably a blend of these two approaches. However, with growing provision for graduate training of those entering remedial professions, there is a tendency to emphasise the second approach. This is not without dangers. The second approach places the burden on individual students to digest and incorporate the academic component of training into a form which is applicable to their practical activity. It is unlikely that all students will be able to accomplish this without special facilitatory opportunities being made available in collaboration with academic tutors and other members of the profession. There needs to be a continual interplay between the academic and practical aspects of the learning experience if the student is to feel that one has relevance for the other. Unless students can see the relevance of academic studies to developing intervention, they may feel unprepared for clinical work. They then fall back upon accepted and traditional solutions, which are passed, by observational learning, from one generation of practitioners to another. Alternatively, attractively packaged and accessible techniques may be adopted and applied uncritically to a wide range of disabilities, when this may not be appropriate. This problem is one which not only faces students in initial training but is also relevant to the continuing professional development of qualified practitioners. Most professional practice is probably evolved from an amalgam of these sources. However, clinical practice is not simply a collection of therapeutic techniques applied in a skilled manner. It involves interacting with clients in a sensitive and responsive manner and developing intervention strategies which clients will accept and which suit the individual's particular social circumstances. A large part of remedial intervention is concerned with making decisions on alternative strategies. These should be based on an informed view of the nature of a client's difficulties, the likely outcomes of particular approaches and an ability to weigh up and judge the appropriateness of possible courses of action. To do this requires a broad understanding of the nature of clients and their behaviour. In designing a course component in child development and child psychology for a multidisciplinary degree course for a remedial profession, there is the need to select both content and methods of instruction, but the clinical relevance of the course content will be only one of the constraints operating on selection.

In this chapter there will be a brief and practical account of linking research and practice in child development and developmental psychology for the training of speech therapists. It is written from the personal experience of the author who has been, at various times, a speech therapy student, a practising speech therapist and a developmental psychologist involved in applied research. Her experience in teaching undergraduate speech therapists includes teaching child development and developmental psychology in a Polytechnic and University, as well as being involved in the teaching of developmental speech pathology and clinical tutoring. There may be alternative and more radical solutions to the problems of this particular instance of professional preparation but it seems unlikely that these will be found unless the current state of vocational preparation is described and set out in a form that can be reflected upon. Apart from a brief consideration of the needs of speech therapists in relation to the whole field of psychology in Purser (1982), at the present time there appears to be no comprehensive account to which to refer. Although some of the demands that need to be satisfied in course content and teaching methods are undoubtedly specific to the profession of speech therapy, others will be shared by other types of professional preparation. There will be no attempt here to evaluate the adequacy of research in child development for the task, since many of the issues which relate specifically to language acquisition are discussed in other chapters. (See especially the contributions of Gregory, Harris, J. and Masidlover, this volume.) The main argument will be that one of the aims of current professional preparation is, and should be, to equip practitioners to be recruited into the ranks of research workers. This will help to ensure a body of knowledge that is directly applicable to clinical work. However, it is suggested that this development will not take place without active support from those already involved in research in child psychology and other contributing disciplines and from the institutions that provide postgraduate research training and financial support for research (see McConkey, this volume, for a more detailed discussion of these issues).

Aims and Problems in the Education of Speech Therapists

Some of the problems currently faced both by students in initial training and by practising members of the profession, in evolving effective clinical procedures, arise from the need to synthesise approaches that have been borrowed from the parent disciplines of linguistics, psychology and medicine.

The assumptions and frameworks that these disciplines provide for the study of language disability are not always compatible. In addition, the institutional contexts in which speech therapy has been traditionally practised are not necessarily the best for encouraging the kind of interactions that are optimal for language assessment and for promoting language development or recovery from an acquired disability. At the present time, there is a great deal more to be learned about the reasons for language learning failure in children and methods of intervention. Intervention is currently invariably based on models of normal language development (Winitz 1983) and attempts to simulate simplified, but basically 'ideal', language learning environments. There is a lot more to learn about the value of different methods of language intervention. The state of knowledge is constantly changing, as are the frameworks for studying language.

In initial training, constraints are imposed on what can be taught and what is taught by the multiple demands made on teaching and learning time and the number of aims that need to be satisfied in any given course component. In some instances, the facilities offered by institutions and the traditions of teaching in institutions tend to discourage teaching methods that would help to overcome the separation of academic and practical elements of training courses.

To understand some of the constraints imposed on course design and the needs that must be satisfied by a child psychology course component, it is necessary to consider briefly the work of the speech therapist and the development of current methods of training.

The Work of the Speech Therapist

Despite the apparently unsatisfactory title adopted by the profession in Great Britain, it is now generally understood that speech therapists are employed to help solve problems experienced by both adults and children, problems that go beyond the narrow focus of 'speech' and include the broader field of communication. Although speech therapists are most frequently employed by the National Health Service, the work of the speech therapist is not carried out exclusively in medical settings, nor do medical explanations of communication disorders predominate. Work with children is often carried out in non-medical settings and the majority of child clients live at home with their own family and attend schools in their local community.

Although speech therapists may work with other medical and paramedical personnel, at the point at which they practise they are largely concerned with psychological issues surrounding language learning, including attitude and behavioural change. Their work with children involves an understanding of child development, children's language and communication. Developmental psychology is the discipline that provides the most insight into creating optimum language learning situations. Intervention is concerned with changing the behaviour of the client, either directly, through therapist-client interaction, or indirectly through changing the attitudes and behaviour of caretakers and teachers who communicate with the child. Speech therapists therefore need a sophisticated knowledge of language development, as well as an understanding of how this process may be altered under a variety of social circumstances and as a result of various organic disabilities which affect language acquisition either directly or indirectly. They also require an understanding of the family and its dynamics and relationships, since they may be involved in assessing the contribution of any disturbances in family relationships to communication disorders and, in intervention, may attempt to change patterns of interaction and relationships in the family. An understanding of the school and the classroom, as well as of educational practices, is essential since this is an important setting in which demands are made on a child's language skills for learning and in which language is both acquired and used. It is also the context in which intervention is often undertaken. Since language development reflects and influences so many aspects of a child's development, it follows that a speech therapist cannot operate without a broadly-based understanding of normal child development and the conditions that facilitate or hinder development. This background is essential for the assessment of disabilities, for explaining developmental language difficulties, and also as a basis for making decisions on when and how to intervene and for devising appropriate forms of intervention. Vocational preparation must not only provide an adequate account of the present state of knowledge (or the lack of it) but also provide students with the means to assess new contributions to the field in the future.

The major task facing anyone designing a course in child development and developmental psychology for speech therapists is one of selection. There is a wide range of possible topics that are relevant, if not essential. Often this includes areas of child psychology with a long history of research and a very extensive literature. In presenting material this necessarily involves the need to summarise and involves inevitable simplification. It is also critical that students develop a realistic attitude to the limitations of the research from which this 'knowledge' is derived and an appreciation of the strengths and weakness of different methodologies. This means that some work must be examined in depth.

Selection of the material to be taught must also take into consideration the experience and characteristics of the students themselves. The majority of students enter vocational courses at 18 years of age, after completing advanced level studies. Most students have three good passes at 'A' level or equivalent; usually at least one of these is a science subject. The majority of students are female, frequently coming from relatively advantaged families with professionally qualified parents. The students will have little shared cultural experience with many of their potential clients. A few students are more mature women who enter the profession after rearing their own children. For the most part, however, the students have limited practical experience of children, and enter undergraduate work as part of a further education course to continue their education as well as to receive a vocational preparation. Courses need to consider the academic development of the students as well as the professional demands to be made on them. Since practical experience of children and family life may be limited for the majority of students, the course needs to fill this gap in experience. There is also the need to develop understanding of clients' circumstances and sympathy for different experiences and views of the world.

The Development of Current Methods of Vocational Preparation

The academic qualifications of the students reflect the fact that there is now an all-graduate entry to the profession. This has occurred in the last few years, and reflects a change that began in the early 1960s. From 1948 to 1964 all speech therapists underwent a three-year training and took the Diploma which was examined by the profession's professional body, the College of Speech Therapists. The first degree course for the vocational education of speech therapists was set up in the University of Newcastle-upon-Tyne in 1964. This began the move from diploma training to degree course. The trend was reinforced by the recommendations of the report on *Speech Therapy Services*, made by the Committee set up by the DES in 1969 which was chaired by Randolf Quirk (hereafter Quirk Report). This recommended the phasing out of diploma courses and the establishment of vocational education at undergraduate level. This has now been accomplished with the exception of a modified diploma course for graduates in related disciplines. The degree courses, which are offered in universities, polytechnics and institutions of higher education, all give both academic and practical training. Graduates are recognised as eligible for employment without further postgraduate training.

It is important to recognise that following the recommendations of the Quirk Report, degree courses were specifically designed by the profession to change the nature of the vocational preparation and ultimately to raise the level of professional skill and clinical effectiveness. This involved changing a pattern of practical training, which relied almost entirely on observation of working therapists and clinical practice under supervision. Using this method of practical training meant that there was rarely any need to commit to print either the rationale for particular methods of working or an account of methods themselves. Methods were passed from one generation of therapists to another through the mechanism of observation. Professional 'folklore' could go unchallenged. The change to education at degree level is seen as the principal means of evolving clinical practice that is based on scientifically evaluated methods and which reflects the most advanced understanding of the relevant scientific disciplines involved. The aim of this education is to produce students with the inclination and ability to question current practices, to draw out the practical implications of the available research, and to apply their understanding to the practical problems with which they are presented.

The immediate consequence of these endeavours has been to increase the academic component of initial training. In the tradition of higher education, students have been exposed to theoretical issues and controversies in all areas of study in order to develop their critical abilities regarding the limits of knowledge and the methodological problems of extending this knowledge. An explicitly stated aim of speech therapy education, again recommended by Quirk, is that students should be trained in basic research methods and statistics. All courses now include these elements and several courses include small-scale, individual research projects as part of the final examination for an honours degree.

Practical training is usually interspersed between blocks of academic work or runs concurrently with academic courses. Although some alternative methods of training have been introduced, a significant part of practical training remains as work under the supervision of a therapist. However, the role of supervising therapists has now changed and they receive some form of training for this task. Clinical skills are no longer learned simply by direct observation. Supervisors are no longer primarily models for trainees, or assessors of clinical competence, but teachers with a more catholic interpretation of their role.

For the most part, however, there is a separation between the academic and practical aspects of the course. These elements usually take place in different institutions and are carried out by different personnel. Because of the emphasis in academic teaching on examining the findings of relevant research, there may be no direct relationship between what is taught and the practical intervention required. The students are encouraged to make an intellectual leap, though in theory they will be supported and encouraged by both academic and practical teachers.

To summarise, the general aims of current degree courses are as follows:

1. To provide an academic education appropriate to the abilities of entrants.
2. To provide opportunities to develop the practical skills for professional practice.
3. To provide basic training in research skills to equip students to proceed to research training at a higher level, should they so wish.

Courses in Developmental Psychology

These aims must also be satisfied by a course in Child Development and Developmental Psychology. What is taught, and the teaching methods used, will not be the same as in other academic courses in developmental psychology. In more traditional academic courses, teachers are often free to teach what interests them most as well as that which arises from their own research activities. In a course that is related to clinical training, what is taught will be partially dictated by clinical relevance and topics for study must include certain essentials. Methods of teaching must take into consideration the need to develop certain skills (observing, assessing and handling children) that are rarely a feature of traditional academic courses in child psychology. Academic institutions may lack adequate facilities to support this practical teaching, particularly the provision of well-designed observation rooms, with one-way viewing screens. These need to be adequately equipped with audiovisual recording facilities that are maintained by appropriate technical personnel. However, to make good use of these facilities, relationships need to be developed and sustained with schools, families and community services so that it is possible for students to study children that represent different developmental stages and come from a range of social backgrounds. Although it is preferable for children to be observed in more natural circumstances, these facilities can make possible a wider range of group teaching situations, with a smaller investment in student travelling and more effective use of tutor's time, particularly if interdisciplinary teaching is undertaken.

To provide this mixture of practical and academic elements, courses for speech therapists usually contain the following elements:

(1)   Descriptive accounts of the course of development. This is usually backed up with practical experience of observation and teaching of different forms and uses of observational methods. A study of an individual child, with no major developmental difficulties, is usually carried out, either in a nursery class, day nursery or in the child's own home. This may continue over a sufficient period of time so that significant developments can be noted and studied. Recording the child's communication and language is obviously encouraged. This experience may be supplemented by video-recordings and observation of children at particular stages of development, or recorded sequences of particular aspects of development such as play, feeding or motor development, as well as children attempting particular tasks or assessments. Case studies of children with communication disorders are then undertaken to apply the observational skills acquired earlier in the course.

(2)   Processes of Development. This usually involves looking at the

environmental and maturational influences on development. The interrelations of different aspects of development may be stressed. This involves looking at the way language and language development interact with areas of development that are singled out for particular study. For example, in the author's course particular attention is paid to the roles of language and communication in socialisation and to the relationship between language development and play. Cross-cultural and historical material is also included to provide a perspective on possible variations in children's experiences and child-rearing philosophies. The consequences of different types of disabilities for development are considered. This has two functions: to prepare students for work with children who are disabled, and to give insight into the developmental process, particularly in relation to language acquisition. The study of child language may be included in the course on child development but usually forms the basis of a separate course.

(3) Theoretical aspects of development. The purpose of teaching some theories of child development is to provide an integrative framework; they give an essential basis for understanding the problems that developmental psychologists have chosen to study. It could also be argued that there are pure (non-vocational) educational reasons for introducing students to more informed versions of theories that have, in a distorted form, had an impact on their own development and education. Since, in practice, therapists will need to share the perspective of other people who are intimately involved in shaping children's lives, they need to understand some of the ideas that may influence these significant adults in their thinking on child development, rearing and education.

(4) Experiential Learning. This part of a course will be aimed at developing practical skills in interacting with children and is normally, at least in part, a spin-off from the activities described in (1) above. However, it can also be used to develop empathy and understanding of clients and to enlarge students' experience and cultural perspectives. For example, it can help students to appreciate the daily tasks of parents and teachers as well as to gain 'a child's eye' view of the world. This kind of experience is not easy to provide in an academic setting. Descriptive research studies are useful to enlarge students' experience. Recent studies that have proved valuable in this respect are those by Blatchford, Battle and Mays (1982) and Cleave, Jowett and Bate (1982) because they include descriptive case study accounts of different children's experience of their first day at school

or nursery school and the settling-in experience. Studies which elicit a particular view of a situation and report responses verbatim are also useful. The work of John and Elizabeth Newson (1963, 1968, 1976), which reports the everyday dilemmas of parents in Nottingham and their views on child rearing, can be mentioned in this connection, as well as the work of their associates Hewett (1970) and Gregory (1976) who used a similar method with parents of children with disabilities. The experiences of families as 'consumers' of professional services can also be made available from the books written by parents about these experiences. For example, for speech therapists, Elizabeth Browning's book (1972) is essential reading. Other, less conventional, sources include films and novels, which portray a particular view of the child's or adult's experiences. Children's creative and imaginary activities that have been observed by students provide material for discussion, and the experiences which students recall from their own childhood can help to heighten sensitivity to the way children experience their world.

Integrating Academic and Practical Experiences

Whatever the particular content of a course, it has to be transformed by each student into a resource that can be called upon in clinical decision-making or in developing clinical activities. This demands more than a superficial acquaintance with facts. Although the learning effort and motivation must come from the student, the implications of the knowledge need to be drawn out in a collective effort. This can be done through group discussion or through supervision by clinicians and clinical tutors. In most training establishments the link between the academic work-place and the clinical context is maintained by the clinical tutor, usually a lecturer with a professional qualification, who visits students in their clinical practice and who is available for consultation about actual clinical problems. It is obviously an advantage if the clinical tutors are themselves teachers of the academic course. Not only does this facilitate the choice of clinically relevant material but it also means they are familiar with the knowledge that is potentially available to students. It is particularly helpful when those teaching developmental psychology are also qualified and experienced as speech therapists. If clinical supervisors are to play an active part in integrating academic studies in the practical arena, some practical mechanism must be devised to keep them informed of the academic course content, and study facilities should be available to them so that they can ensure they share at least some of the academic course content with their students.

The clinical supervision of speech therapy students is a neglected topic in the United Kingdom, and literature concerning this topic is only now beginning to appear in journals (McGovern and Wirz 1980; Pletts 1981). In the United States, where the numbers of students in comparable vocational education is estimated at 44,000 (Oratio 1977), this topic has received rather more attention in the literature over a longer period. Most of this work has concentrated on the nature of the student's interaction with clients or on interactions with supervisors. Relatively little attention has been paid to the content of academic courses on which clinical practice is based. However, it has been pointed out that there is little research directly applicable to clinical interaction. Recently, there has been some research work in the United Kingdom, involving co-operation between developmental psychologists and teachers that might be used as a model for research based on therapist/client interaction. Wood and colleagues have examined, with nursery teachers (Wood, McMahon and Cranstoun 1980) and teachers of the hearing impaired (Wood and Wood 1984), how the actual style of interaction matches up to their educational aims. Teachers were actively involved in both collecting and evaluating data.

It was pointed out earlier that not all the work of a speech therapist concerns direct interaction with patients. Work that aims to promote language development concerns influencing the language learning environment provided by parents and teachers. Some recent work by McConkey has concerned different methods that might be used to share knowledge of language with parents and teachers. This has been developed from studies of language learning with non-disabled children and has also involved the relevant practitioners (McConkey and O'Connor 1981). Thus, there are some models for co-operative investigation that address issues directly relevant to practice. Modifications of this research have been involved in training speech therapy students by this author and shared with supervising therapists as a technique to be used in student training. The methods used by Wood and Wood (1984) have appeared effective not only in developing conversational skills but also as an objective means for self-evaluation. By directly manipulating the interactive situation, students have a vivid demonstration of their own contribution to their client's communicative competence.

A further difficulty that arises in evolving clinical practice from research findings involves the research methods themselves. Barlow and Hersen (1984) outline a number of difficulties that come directly from the group comparison approach. They point out that group results are not readily translated or generalised by the practising clinician. Although they are writing in particular about the evaluation of intervention, the same point could be made about research that examines the characteristics or abilities of groups sharing a particular disability or social disadavantage. It can be difficult to assess the relevance of these studies to the individual patient. Barlow and Hersen recommend the single case study as a method that is particularly relevant to applied research. In the meantime there is a danger that studies of groups that merely share one disadvantage are likely to play a part in encouraging and perpetuating stereotypes, or set up expectations which may lead to self-fulfilling prophecies.

Conclusion

If professional training for speech therapists and other related remedial professions is to be approached from a sound, relevant and comprehensive knowledge base, then more research needs to be directed towards problems that are essentially clinical. Although there have been some recent examples of this kind of research by developmental psychologists, there seems no reason, in this specialist area, why researchers should not be recruited from among practitioners. This is the avowed objective of current degree courses for speech therapists. It is a paradox that in attempting to relate research and practice more closely, academic teaching and practice have drifted further apart with greater emphasis on research methods and theoretical issues. One way to resolve the difficulty has already been suggested; that is, to recruit researchers from practitioners (see McConkey, this volume). This involves a recognition that therapists have the basic training from which research skills can be developed. The establishment of a joint honours degree in Speech and Psychology at the University of Newcastle-upon-Tyne, with joint recognition by the College of Speech Therapists and British Psychological Society, may be a small step towards this recognition and may create some precedent for students from speech therapy degree courses to proceed to postgraduate research in psychology departments. Already there are some postgraduate research opportunities in departments which undertake initial training and these may be taken up by psychologists. However, it is likely to be some time before there are sufficient experienced research workers able to attract financial resources and make an impact on the body of available knowledge. As well as the need to develop suitable methodology, there is also room for more partnership in research. Without the commitment to training practitioners for research at the postgraduate level, both for graduates with some research training, and for non-graduate but experienced practitioners, clinical practice is unlikely to evolve more effectively. Commitment precedes the provision of means. Some part-time courses are already available at polytechnics and universities, for working practitioners to develop a research orientation and basic research skills. Employers also need to recognise that time and support for research activities can ultimately benefit the service through improvements in training. These developments are beginning in a small way, but it is 15 years since Quirk and associates suggested that speech therapists had a unique contribution to make to the understanding of human communication and its disorders. They recommended that there should be greater provision, for those willing and able to do so, to divide their careers between clinical work and research. In addition to a more generous recognition of the right of practitioners for access to research facilities and skills, there should also be more readiness by practitioners to accept that developmental psychologists, and those with academic training and research experience in other disciplines, can make a useful contribution to evolving more effective clinical practices if they are allowed access to the clinical context. There may be both practical and ethical difficulties to overcome but – with sufficient commitment to the outcome – there could be a productive collaboration.

References

Barlow, D.H. and Hersen, M. (1984) *Single Case Experimental Designs: Strategies for Studying Behaviour Change*, 2nd edn, Oxford: Pergamon Press

Blatchford, P., Battle, S. and Mays, J. (1982) *The First Transition: Home to Preschool*, Windsor: NFER-Nelson

Browning, E. (1972) *I Can't See What You're Saying*, London: Elek

Cleave, S., Jowett, S. and Bate, M. (1982) *And So to School: A Study of Continuity from Pre-school to Infant school*, Windsor: NFER-Nelson

Gregory, S. (1976) *The Deaf Child and His Family*, London: Allen and Unwin

Hewett, S. (1970) *The Family and the Handicapped Child*, London: Allen and Unwin

McConkey, R. (1981) Sharing knowledge of language with children and parents, *British Journal of Disorders of Communication*, *16(1)*, 3

McConkey, R. and O'Connor, M. (1981) Spreading the word: the implementation of findings from language research in P. Mittler, (ed.), *Frontiers of Knowledge in Mental Retardation: Social, Educational and Behavioural Aspects*, Vol. 1, Baltimore: University Park Press

McGovern, M.A. and Wirz, S.L. (1980) The use of videotape in the training of speech therapy students: the development of an observation schedule, *British Journal of Disorders of Communication*, *15(2)*, 65-74

Newson, E. and Newson, J. (1963) *Patterns of Infant Care in an Urban Community*, London: Allen and Unwin

— (1968) *Four years Old in an Urban Community*, London: Allen and Unwin

— (1976) *Seven Years Old in the Home Environment*, London: Allen and Unwin

Oratio, A.R. (1977) *Supervision in Speech Pathology*, Baltimore: University Park Press

Pletts, M. (1981) Principles and practice of clinical teaching: a need for structure, *British Journal of Disorders of Communication*, *16(2)*, 129-34

Purser, H. (1982) *Psychology for Speech Therapists*, London: British Psychology Society and the Macmillan Press

Quirk, R. (1972) *Speech Therapy Services*, Report of the Committee of Inquiry, London: HMSO

Winitz, H. (1983) Use and abuse of the developmental approach in H. Winitz (ed.), *Treating Language Disorders*, Baltimore: University Park Press

Wood, D., McMahon, L. and Cranstoun, Y. (1980) *Working with Under Fives*, Oxford Pre-school Research Project, London: Grant McIntyre

Wood, H.A. and Wood, D.J. (1984) An experimental evaluation of the effects of five styles of teacher conversation on the language of hearing-impaired children, *Journal of Child Psychology and Psychiatry*, *25(1)*, 45-62

12 SERVICE-BASED RESEARCH

Roy McConkey

Introduction

We live in the age of the specialist: our domestic and industrial technologies demand it. The washing-machine engineer does not mend colour television sets and the computer mechanic is unable to solve a programming fault. Education, health and social services have not escaped this phenomenon; indeed some would say they revel in it. Not only do they have a plethora of different professions, but within each one there are sub-specialities – medicine and teaching supply the most obvious examples, but others such as psychology and nursing have their share, too.

Given this prevailing ethos it is not surprising that many professions, including psychology, have created a speciality of research in their particular disciplines with conditions of employment, status rewards and systems of funding that are quite different from those of practitioners.

Consequences of Specialisms

The growth of specialisms is no accident. They are a testimony to human inadequacy in coping with burgeoning knowledge. Although the result is that each specialist knows more and more about less and less, there can be no doubt that higher standards in education and health care have been generated. But we must not underestimate the costs involved; and I do not just mean in monetary terms even though the financial burden has been considerable.

Specialisms bring with them a nasty side-effect which Cunningham (1983) diagnoses as 'expertosis'; a disease with symptoms similar to myxomatosis – 'the head swells and the sufferer goes blind'. Self-imposed isolation and paranoia may follow, suggests Midwinter (1977): 'they [the specialists] have become bureaucratised, defensive about manning and function, haunted by false fears of "dilution", jittery about evaluation and open accountability, jargon-plagued, status-conscious and sheltering in a pother of insecurity behind a barricade of mystiques'. Possibly an exaggeration but I am sure you will be able to think of some specialisms – or at least 'specialists' – for whom this description is apt.

The predisposing influence is our faith in professionalism, whose central tenet, according to Tizard, Mortimore and Burchell (1981:104), 'is the belief that because of the professional's specialist knowledge, critical comment on his work cannot be made by laymen'. If you substitute the words *researcher* and *practitioner* for *professional* and *layman* – and then alternate their order – you will discover one potent reason for the gap between research and practice. Neither of the specialisms accepts the right of the other to make critical comments on their work. Perhaps Midwinter wasn't exaggerating after all.

I am not hopeful of bridging this gap. It cannot be done quickly and it will never be done completely. But I like to think of myself as a realistic optimist – which, I realise, is some people's definition of a pessimist. Hence in this chapter I shall outline some ways in which a *rapprochement* might come about between the systems in which researchers and practitioners operate; I shall argue that this should be achieved primarily through the expansion of service-based research.

This process can only begin when we acknowledge our short-comings. As a professional researcher it would be presumptuous of me to expound the failings of practitioners; that could only result in mutual recrimination. Rather I shall identify four features prevalent in current research that increase its isolation from practice and blunt its effectiveness in adding to our knowledge about child development. I believe there is a particular onus on researchers to change. We are hardly worthy of the name we bear if we are unwilling to search for other ways.

Farewell Lone Ranger

> Psychology like the social sciences (and arts subjects) seems to have accepted a rather romantic notion of the lone researcher developing an original approach in splendid isolation. (Watts 1984)

The cowboy hero of my childhood was the Lone Ranger. The anonymous masked hero who came to help the troubled and afflicted but disappeared just as quickly as he came when the job was done. The parallel with researchers is too close for comfort, except that our trusty friend is no longer an Indian named Tonto but a computer package known as SPSS (Statistical Package for the Social Sciences).

The image of the lone researcher is set during undergraduate training, when each student has to find a different topic for their dissertation, and is further reinforced by our Master and Doctoral degrees. But the most enduring influence is the way professional research is financed. Government monies, be they from research councils or departments, are nearly always channelled to individuals working in universities, polytechnics or specialist research centres, and many charitable trusts, such as Leverhulme, prefer to do this too. The system has its benefits – ready access to computer and library facilities, a saving on salary costs and impartiality, in the sense that the country as a whole should benefit, rather than one region or service. But the price is that researchers have been isolated from practitioners and, more critically, they have evolved different perceptions of their responsibilities and hence their criteria of success; for instance, number of papers published rather than clients helped.

Of course, the system does not preclude researchers working alongside practitioners; fortunately we have various examples of how this can come about, but even the more successful researcher-practitioner partnerships could hardly claim that gains reflected the energy expended. Three difficulties are common.

First, the system does not provide enough time. Bruner (1980:201), reflecting on his experience in the Oxford Pre-school Project, writes: 'collaborative research between a university-based research group and practitioners in the community requires an investment of time and resources that is difficult to come by in the lives of both'. The short-term funding of most research projects further compounds this difficulty.

The second concerns the failure of an 'outsider' to make an impact within an ongoing service system. This is vividly portrayed in Georgiades and Phillimore's (1975:315) 'myth of the hero-innovator' whom they portray as:

a knight in shining armour, who, loins girded with new technology and beliefs, will assault his organizational fortress and institute changes both in himself and others at a stroke. Such a view is ingenuous. The fact of the matter is that organizations such as schools and hospitals will, like dragons, eat hero-innovators for breakfast.

Thirdly, Shipman (1977:177) warns of the 'false dawn' he

observed during his experiences 'inside' a school's council curriculum project that was located in a university but which worked closely with teachers from 38 schools. He writes of the latter:

> the pioneers and enthusiasts they attract can make the innovation work, can produce results that make early evaluations positive . . . but the spread of an innovation involves increasing the number of teachers who lack the skills and enthusiasm of the pioneer. The result is that an apparently successful innovation in the hands of a few can fail when generally adapted and diluted.

Research that is conceived and executed outside of a system remains a foreign body and, while it may cause some irritation and even inflammation, the system's defences can often overpower it. There is no shortage of examples, but the following will suffice. In 1955 Jack Tizard, as an experiment, took children from the wards of a hospital for the mentally subnormal and rehoused them as a family group in an ordinary house called 'Brooklands'. The resultant gains in their development were quickly apparent – far in excess of their counterparts who remained in hospitals. Even so by 1970 there were still 6,000 children in hospitals and, although a policy of no further admissions was then instituted, it will not be until the 1990s that all children have alternative placements (Mittler 1984).

The failure of research findings to influence service-providers is probably only matched by their scepticism both of researchers and the usefulness of their research. Baumeister and Hillsinger (1984) invited the directors of 272 public residential institutions for the mentally retarded throughout the United States to rate the activities of the psychologists in their employment, both in terms of importance to the service and the preparedness of psychologists to undertake appropriate tasks. Not only was research rated the *least* important but the rating given to preparedness was equally low and just marginally higher than the lowest rating of all – their preparedness to administrate!

I realise that not all researchers will want or need to work alongside practitioners. The present system suits them well enough because it is built largely to their specifications. But for those researchers and practitioners who want to merge their roles, even in a small way, new systems will have to be invented. When money is scarce, this means change rather than creation and one dominant feature of our health, social and educational systems is that they do not easily change. The Lone Ranger could be with us for some time yet.

An End to Experimenting?

> For its rigour and precision, laboratory research came to be viewed as 'better' than other methods, independent of the importance of the question being addressed. (Morrison, Lord and Keating, 1984)

Research and experimenting are synonymous in many people's minds. Vasta (1979:15) asserts in his introductory textbook on research methods for studying children that 'the heart of the scientific method is the experiment. Psychologists employ other methods of research, such as naturalistic observation techniques but the experiment is clearly the most popular and useful research approach.' Although we might question his evidence for usefulness, the rise in popularity of experiments since the 1960s has been well-documented. Doyle (1971) examined the contents of twelve journals in the field of mental handicap between 1959 and 1970. The most striking trend was a considerable increase in experimental studies from 14 per cent to 39 per cent. This was balanced by a drop in training, rehabilitation and educational studies – 17 per cent in 1959 to only 5 per cent in 1970.

Super's (1982) analysis of articles published during the 50-year history of the journal *Child Development* showed a similar shift in the 1960s, with a marked increase in authors based in universities rather than services.

The rise of experimentalism, as Sears (1975) has termed it, helped to make the study of children respectable in the eyes of the parent discipline (psychology) and led to the establishment of lectureships and training courses in developmental psychology. These in turn have served further to reinforce the movement which gave them birth. Nor can we ignore the valuable contribution which the experimental approach has made to our understanding of children, a shining example being the insights gained into the perceptual and cognitive development of neonates and infants. But the very success of experimentalism has both blinded research sponsors to other methodolgies and further divorced researchers from practitioners.

Taking the latter first, experimentalists have invented a plethora of sophisticated measuring procedures, research designs and statistical analyses that are neither easily communicated nor readily comprehended even by researchers working in fields of enquiry. Moreover, those practitioners who attempt their own research, of necessity using simpler procedures, are made to feel that their work is naïve and inferior, irrespective of its outcome.

Secondly, the primary technique of the experimenter – the control of variables through selection or exclusion of 'subjects' – is denied the practitioner. Consequently, they perceive opportunities for doing 'proper' research as severely limited and often incompatible with their existing responsibilities. A particular instance is the use of 'no treatment' control groups in the validation of clinical or educational interventions. For practitioners to withhold knowingly, either a time-honoured procedure (albeit one that is ineffective) or a new one that appears promising, leaves them open to the charge of neglect if their clients – even just one client – *appear* to suffer.

But there is a more fundamental antipathy within services towards the idea of experimentation. By definition, they are there to help the more vulnerable people of our society, those who cannot help themselves. The idea of exposing them to unknown effects, inherent in every experiment, involves the risk of public and professional condemnation. The safer strategy is to let the *status quo* prevail. Precedent protects even if it does inhibit progress.

Rethinking for Researchers

The exaltation of experimentalism within developmental psychology is not without its internal critics. 'Recent research', wrote Morrison, Lord and Keating (1984:11), 'ironically most from the laboratory itself, is leading some developmental psychologists to question the generality and accuracy of recent conclusions about human development, conclusions drawn largely from research conducted in laboratory settings with heavy emphasis on the experimental method.'

Three stark failures can be identified.

First, as Donaldson (1978) admirably illustrated in her book *Children's Minds*, results obtained in laboratory settings with arbitrary, experimenter-designed tasks may grossly underestimate children's competence to deal with real world problems in familiar contexts.

Second, Jack Tizard (1976) long advocated the need to complement our studies of the enduring or the developmental characteristics of persons with an examination of organisational structures and their effects upon the behaviour of the individual 'actors'. In his research with children residing in residential homes he demonstrated that their competences were markedly affected by the differing characteristics of institutions – the formal and informal command networks, the different patterns of behaviour of staff, the facilities available, and so on. The research task, as he saw it, was 'to analyse why these differences occur – for they are not arbitrary or idiosyncratic – and to find ways of modifying them as appropriate' (ibid.:232). That cannot be done in a laboratory.

The most damning criticism of all is the charge levelled by McCall (1977:333) that developmental psychologists 'rarely actually collect or analyse truly developmental data' because of their 'veneration of manipulative experimental methods'. This results in a preoccupation with *'can'* questions (can exposure to television violence increase the incidence of aggressive behaviour?) rather than *'does'* questions (under typical natural circumstances does television influence playground aggression?); a preference for identifying continuities in children's performance rather than investigating changes and their antecedents; and above all a penchant for cross-sectional assessments that merely describe age *differences* rather than longitudinal studies that will help us to discern developmental transitions and the factors influencing them. He does not underestimate the difficulties inherent in these 'new' methods, and he offers some suggestions for surmounting them, but the essential challenge – as he and others have argued – is not technical but attitudinal. Developmental researchers must break free of the mentality inherited from the physical sciences – that they can *prove* the causes of new behaviours, when at best they can only establish probabilities. In acknowledging this a greater value is then placed on other research methods – especially naturalistic descriptions and longitudinal studies – because the data they generate will help to strengthen or weaken the competing explanations; each approach is inadequate by itself but each can make a vital contribution to the conclusion.

Forsaking the familiar for the unknown is as risky for the researcher as it is for the practitioner. Precedent protects them too, even if it does inhibit progress.

Tell Me The Story Simply

It took us in our project nearly two years to discover that the essence of dissemination was not in disseminating a product but a process, helping them [practitioners] to see more dispassionately, rather than broadcasting what *we* had seen. (Bruner 1980)

A researcher's first priority – some would say only priority – is to share his or her findings with other researchers. Mittler (1975:18) draws a parallel between journal articles and the language of legal documents:

> It is not that the people who write these documents are incapable of writing plain English but that what they have to communicate is beset with so many technicalities that there must be no danger of misinterpretation, no loopholes for ambiguities and irrelevancies to slip through.

Even the most ardent practitioner will struggle hard to find practical significance amid a literature preoccupied with statistical significance.

Parallel publishing is a possible solution, with researchers writing articles specially for practitioners – outlining their results with the minimum of technical jargon and emphasising the implications for practice. For instance, Belbin (1979), in recalling how the Industrial Training Research Unit was anxious to get its work used, decided to divert its attention 'to the industrial journals and magazines most likely to be read by their prospective users, rather than learned journals *even though this might result in loss of academic status*' (my italics). Publication in 'reputable' journals is not just about sharing results; it is a vital part of a researcher's career advancement. What then have researchers to gain from writing articles in practitioners' magazines?

But Bruner (1980) raises a more fundamental issue when he questions whether 'dissemination' of research findings *per se* can ever make headway against received wisdom and common-sense practice. He continues, 'there is an increasingly educated population emerging who want to do better *themselves*. They do not want to be made to feel helpless or ignorant by experts; they are interested in cultivating skills.' Yet the collaborative work this entails between researchers and practitioners 'rarely results in the elegant paper so favoured by learned journals' (ibid.:215). He also notes that research councils are not in the business of training practitioners and that there are few research centres in Britain and elsewhere concerned with the transformation of research findings into practitioner skills.

There is, however, a still wider audience which researchers have failed to address – parents, policy-makers and the public at large. McCall and Stocking (1982) view this lack of communication as more than 'benign neglect'. 'The schism between researchers and communicators reflect real differences in values, criteria and procedures, magnified by the fact that each profession perceives the other to be more extreme than is actually the case.' They instance researchers' complaints about their control over the final product and the accuracy and tone of media portrayals. The solution they, and others, advocate is for researchers to work alongside journalists and television producers. Indeed, Gallagher (1981:389) urged a reallocation of resources 'from the specific task of gathering knowledge to the communication task of informing those in the public domain of what we have to say on important issues'. Our 'deafening silence' makes us ever more vulnerable to cut-backs in resources.

Here, too, a change of attitude is needed among researchers, best summarised by Zigler and Muenchow (1984:420) when they wrote:

In addition to sharing our knowledge, we must also learn how to listen and how to compromise, even in those instances where we are reasonably certain of the idea we wish to sell . . . We must rid ourselves of a mystique held by too many, namely, that impacting social policy is too far afield, too Byzantine, and too self-defiling to be engaged in by self-respecting psychologists.

Effective communication involves give and take.

The Question is More Important than the Answer

The reason that problem-oriented activity . . . is not widely undertaken in psychological research or in professional practice, is not, I suggest, because it has been tried and found unprofitable. Rather it is that academic and professional traditions are based on a different conception of what constitutes the core of psychological study. (Tizard 1976)

'Why do you want to know that?' It is ironic that researchers, who are usually adept at finding answers, encounter difficulties in justifying their choice of research topic. I well remember my own feeble attempts to explain my doctoral research to (rightly) cynical instructors from centres for mentally handicapped adults and I remember thinking that if only they were psychologists, then they would understand. But even if we answer the sceptic confidently and unequivocally, there still remains a value judgement as to whether that question, rather than another, is worthy of all the time and effort involved in discovering an answer. The worth of an answer is determined by the quality of the question posed. So how do researchers formulate their questions?

Masters (1984:855) makes a useful, if somewhat gross distinction between 'knowledge-driven' and 'decision-driven' research. The former is

> formulated from a consideration of contemporary theory and research, concerning a question already of relevance within the discipline, with little (if any) regard for the broader social ramifications of the research. Decision-driven research, on the other hand, stems from a consideration of the decisions facing someone; a policy-maker on some level or another; and comprises the conversion of a socially important question into a research endeavour.

These definitions encapsulate the essential contrasts that traditionally have been drawn between pure or basic research versus applied or applicable research. Yet the debate as to whether these are alternatives or the poles of a continuum has done little to resolve, and may even have bolstered, the marked bias towards knowledge-driven research in developmental psychology. For example, Morrison *et al.* (1984) argued that 'the fundamental aspects of an applied perspective – the focus on substantive and meaningful questions, analysis of complex issues and promotion of inter-disciplinary approaches . . . are not at present integral features of the current scientific ethos'.

I think it is instructive to ask why that should be so, for I have yet to meet a psychologist – no matter how pure – who does not believe in the relevance of the discipline to human well-being. Why do we not engage in more decision-driven research?

Tizard (1976) provides a philosophical answer. Current psychological theory is preoccupied with a study of supposedly general laws governing the behaviour of a species rather than the study of rules governing the behaviour of individuals in differing environments. Watts (1984) is rather more pragmatic. Research aimed at solving practical problems has, from the outset, to be designed in consultation and collaboration with the decision-makers who can implement the solution. This requires negotiation, trust and shared responsibility, none of which is easily attained if the researchers and the decision-makers' loyalties are to different systems. (See also Galloway, this volume.)

Moreover, Belbin (1979) has strong doubts as to whether 'good research men' can make the grade as applied researchers. 'Pure research fosters a loner approach but development requires a person who can interest others, secure their participation, draw on external resources, discover needs and opportunities and overcome all kinds of practical and organisational impediments which stand in the way of successful application.' Among the personal attributes she instances are – 'toughness, diplomacy, ability to communicate in the vernacular and a willingness to take calculated risks'. Not the criteria usually employed when interviewing PhD candidates.

Finally, there is a widespread consensus that research training in undergraduate and postgraduate courses for psychologists must be drastically revised, with less emphasis on methods and statistics and more on the study of existing social service systems (Shadish 1984); ways of instituting organisational change (Georgiades and Phillimore 1975) and influencing policy formulation (Zigler and Muenchow 1984) and, perhaps most crucially of all, in-depth practical experience of children in natural settings (Morrison *et al.* 1984). Sadly, the dearth of suitable trainers to promote such a curriculum is an unresolved problem.

All in all, although we may talk glibly of redressing the balance between pure and applied research, I conclude that the odds are so heavily loaded in favour of knowledge-driven research that to attain even a small increase in applicable research will require a commitment to change that will prove too uncomfortable for many, if not most, research sponsors.

Rather, as Tizard (1976) and Watts (1984) hint, our energies might be better directed – at least in the first instance – at enabling practising professional psychologists to tackle significant problems that are within their field of competence. They certainly know the questions that most need answering.

Introducing Change

The foregoing review of developmental research has been brief and selective but, I hope, not overly biased. The recent upsurge of articles about research policy and policy research in the bulletins of both the British and American Psychological Societies is some indication of a widespread concern among the profession.

I admit to dwelling on the shortcomings in our past research endeavours, not in a spirit of recrimination but rather to highlight the tasks we have yet to complete. These can be summarised as follows:

1. A better appreciation of children's development in natural surroundings under ordinary circumstances.
2. The effect which differing environments have on children's development and how they can be modified so as to maximise their impact on children's well-being.
3. To share, in a more meaningful way, our approach to studying children and the knowledge we have gained with the many other professionals involved with children and also with parents and policy-makers.
4. A more effective participation by researchers in formulating policies for the child and family services offered by our society.

I realise that there will be many developmental researchers who, for different reasons, do not personally share these goals or my interpretation of them. I shall not pretend that I could convince them otherwise, nor am I sure that I would want to.

The study of child development is far too complex to be confined to these four tasks. Hence I accept, with Masters (1984), that for the next decade or so, university-based, knowledge-driven, experimental type research will continue to dominate in developmental psychology. I do not doubt that there could be pressures for change from within the system – most notably if grant-awarding bodies changed their priorities – but I pin my hopes on change emanating from outside the present research system, primarily through the growth of service-based research teams.

Service-based Research

I envisage not just a change in location for researchers, but rather a new style of research, one that possibly should be called by another name. None seems immediately suitable, though the term 'development', in the research and development sense, seems to come closest. An interim job description for this new type of research might read as follows (cf. Belbin 1979).

–   A commitment to developing both the policy and the practice of the services to which they belong. This will entail regular monitoring of clients' needs, along with short- and long-term evaluation of services provided.

- An involvement in developing the skills of staff and parents, so that new insights can be translated into ongoing practice in the negotiated manner advocated by Bruner (1980).
- The collection and analysis of objective and accurate information regarding particular problems facing the service that will inform the development of solutions. Such data may have to be culled from census returns, economic reports, retrospective analysis of clients' records and opinion poll-type surveys.

This listing is not meant to be exhaustive or exemplary but it is intended to convey a flavour of the breadth of opportunities with which service-based researchers will have to contend. It is certainly not a job for young people straight from university or for a junior member of staff. Indeed, the combination of qualities needed to make such posts successful could make one despair of their feasibility. In no particular order of priority, the following seem to be the most necessary attributes.

- Familiarity with most aspects of their service, preferably through previous experience as a practitioner in the service or in one similar to it.
- Experience in using a range of research methodologies and a willingness to learn about new ones with which they are unfamiliar.
- They should have sufficient status within the organisation to have direct access to, or involvement in, the formulation of service policies.
- They must be good communicators – willing to listen and able to convey complex ideas or issues in layman's terms.
- They must be relieved of all, or nearly all, their responsibilities for ongoing service delivery to clients so that they can devote themselves to the new role.

Although this combination of qualities may be rare in any applicant, I take comfort from knowing that people can 'grow into' a job.

Making It A Reality

So how might this new type of research come about? To be frank, I don't know, although I do have some ideas about possibilities. Our personal and social services systems are so diverse that no one way will suit them all. That is why I am wary of the idea, floated by a number of eminent commentators, of a new profession. For instance, Bruner (1980: 217) speculates that 'there may be coming into being a new profession concerned precisely with turning knowledge about human development into skills for cultivating its development'. Yet on past experience our penchant for creating new specialisms is hardly conducive to bridge-building. If anything, our goal must be to blur the demarcation lines and to foster an overlap of responsibilities.

Instead, my suggestions centre around empowering practitioners – especially professional psychologists working with children and families – to become researchers/developers within their services. But let me make quite clear that there is no presumption that every professional psychologist has to adopt this role. Even if only 1 in 100 were to do so, a sufficient start could be made. I believe that service-based research and development could take place at a number of different levels, in the sense of extra resources needed; some examples follow below. But more important to my mind are the 'enabling conditions' needed to sustain this innovation and I shall describe those which appear to be essential. Finally, four illustrations will be given of the type of work which these researchers might undertake.

Where There's A Will, There's A Way

The following suggestions range from those in which research/development form *part* of the practitioner's ongoing responsibilities to those in which it becomes a whole-time job either in the short term (for example, three months to six months) or longer (up to five years).

- Practitioners could structure their ongoing work – or aspects of it – so that the information collected could be pooled, systematically analysed and shared with other colleagues (Gillham 1978; Salkovskis 1984).
- A reallocation of responsibilities within a department could result in the creation of a development post – even a part-time one –that could be filled on rotation or for stated periods of time, to undertake specific projects.

- Services such as LEAs or area Health Authorities or Social Services could be persuaded to apportion some of their budget to research and development. This may mean a reallocation of existing monies rather than deploying extra money. Can we demonstrate that it will be money well spent?
- Voluntary organisations could establish a trust fund, made up of donations from firms and individuals which then qualify for additional tax rebates. My research post is funded in this way.
- Services organisations could apply for grants from central government departments and, arguably, even research councils to fund their research personnel. Other possibilities include international agencies, such as EEC and UNESCO, and charitable trusts, such as Leverhulme and the Ford Foundation.

In these latter two instances, research and development staff could be appointed from experienced staff within the service, preferably on secondment or by an 'outside' person with relevant expertise, for example, a university researcher. In the latter instance, they could be given the brief of developing the research skills of designated staff within the organisation.

Enabling Conditions

Over and above finding the right person for the job (see p. 247), there are a number of enabling conditions which will make these developments likely.

Training. The research components of professional training courses need revision. As Salkovskis (1984: 377) has argued in the context of clinical psychology, 'The university and MRC-based models of groups (and research assistant implemented) research should give way, in clinical courses, to appropriate applied (and applicable) models, with an emphasis on generalizability'. Equally, in-service training opportunities and possibly a new type of research degree will be necessary. 'The national interest would surely be served if more able people were attracted into development by offering them higher degrees, with their own identifiable titles, for distinguished work in this field.' (Belbin 1979:243) One could expect a new type of conference paper to emerge, and also research articles, which would in turn further promote practitioners' skills.

Support Groups. In the early stages, it is likely that this work will have more than its fair share of difficulties which may cause doubts and uncertainties for the researcher, an inclination to give up or to compromise wrongly. The presence of a support group from within the organisation or across organisations is then essential; as Smetherham (1981:96) argues:

> one can more readily make the often necessary acknowledgements of uncertainty in one's own work and conjecture about this, with the relative freedom from anxiety that only operational confidence allows. Without it, it seems equally likely that one will become liable to confuse the uncertainties of research issues with personal/ professional uncertainties.

More pragmatically, support networks across organisations can result in the sharing of techniques, methodologies and resources; they also allow for replications across different settings. These networks could evolve out of existing ones, for example, those provided by professional organisations such as the British Psychological Society; they could also be formed on a regional or interest basis.

Priorities. 'I believe it is a prerequisite of progress to be clear what kind of research the NHS needs and why.' (Watts 1984) Watts is right but the trick is knowing how to arrive at agreed priorities for developments within a service. These, after all, are value judgements and Eysenck (1957:108) warns that, 'scientists, especially when they leave the particular field in which they have specialised, are just as ordinary, pig-headed and unreasonable as anybody else and their unusually high intelligence only makes their prejudices all the more dangerous'. Shadish (1984:725) is equally scathing: 'policy researchers have failed to understand the ideologies implicit in their own work. As a result they have proposed solutions that are inconsistent with the social system that must implement them.' Hence innovations fail.

Short of stating the obvious need for debate and compromise, I find it difficult to suggest other strategies, as this is an unresolved problem within my own work. However, I did take heart from a comment made by Georgiades and Phillimore (1975:317): 'Often the best supporters of innovation and change are among the ranks of people just below the top, where the personal commitment to the present is less and where the drive for achievement may be higher than at the very top.'

Illustrations

I end by giving four illustrations of the type of research which practitioners could readily engage in, even as part of their ongoing commitments. I make no apology for their applied nature and I certainly would not claim that they *will* inform our theories of child development. But I am not conceding that they *could* not. In fact, many of us would echo Belbin's (1979) assertion that innovative development is a great stiumulator of research and the generator of new knowledge. At the very least, practitioner-based research should be granted the same indulgence long enjoyed by 'pure' researchers, namely, that no one can predict what important insights will emerge from research.

Descriptive Surveys. These might range from the relatively straightforward analysis of referrals and outcomes (for example, McConkey and O'Connell 1982) to what Clarke and Clarke (1973) call 'social follow-ups', documenting the long-term outcomes of a clinically defined group. In this category, I would also include the naturalistic descriptions of children's behaviour advocated by McCall (1977). As he notes, longitudinal descriptive studies could reveal details of variabilities in behaviours, suggest antecedents to change, and point out the most salient measurements. Practitioners are in the best position to collect such data provided they have time to analyse it.

Evaluation of Therapies. Barlow, Hayes and Nelson (1984) have explained how single case, between-subject replication designs can be used by practitioners to validate and test the generalisability of their interventions and thereby contribute to psychological theory. In many instances the skills are little different from those which a good, systematic clinician would be using (Shapiro 1970).

Developing Training Resources. Tangible resource material, such as teaching packages and videos, can have a powerful effect on service development; for instance, the Portage model of home-based interventions with mentally handicapped children (Wilcox 1981; Wolfendale, this volume). Not only is the final product important, but the *process* leading to its creation (for example, forming resource groups of teachers, try-outs of materials, differential successes) can provide a valuable insight into the critical elements of instituting changes and the robustness of these across settings and people (Curtis and Blatchford 1981). There is a particular dearth of resource materials for use in parent education (McConkey 1985; Harris, P., this volume).

Monitoring Services.   Watts (1984:42) rightly bemoans the dearth of research to aid the planning of services – 'identifying the number of patients who might need a proposed service and the kind of problems they would present . . . very few clinical psychologists come out of training courses knowing how to do it'.

Equally, we have little tradition of evaluating our existing services (for example, through consumer reaction surveys), which may account for some of the difficulties in setting the priorities for change which I mentioned earlier.

We have much to learn, too, about changing systems. Burden (1978) provides one example of how attempts by trainee educational psychologists and teachers to improve the overall reading standards of pupils in one school involved changes in various levels of the school system. He concluded that

> only by viewing such problems within the wider context of the institutions and environments in which they occur can the psychologist be in the best position to discover where the real problem lies and help to provide *from within these environments* themselves, the kind of strategies that are likely to be most effective in achieving satisfactory solutions for all concerned. (p. 131; his italics)

Redressing the Balance

My emphasis on the need for, and the possible style of, service-based research does, I admit, distance it from the bulk of current research in child psychology. That is unavoidable when the intention is to 'redress the balance' or to study hitherto ignored influences on children's development (Morrison, *et al.* 1984).

In essence, my argument is that the divide between research and practice is a systems problem. Researchers have evolved a system which favours 'theory-driven', experimental studies, instigated by staff based in higher education or specialist research centres and one which ensures communication of findings within the system but rarely beyond it. Yet, as I have tried to illustrate, these are but reflections of the values inherent in the system – scientific rigour, control of subjects, indisputable proof, learned papers, sound theories, unbiased experimenters – values that are not shared by most practitioners in their work within service systems. Indeed the values prized by services may be the antithesis of these.

We must also remember that increases in our understanding of children's development and ways of nurturing it are *not* dependent on these values alone. Rather, we must rediscover the value of describing developmental transitions and environmental effects; of evaluating interventions in the lives of children and families; of monitoring services and attuning them to clients' needs and of formulating and testing our policies in dialogue with colleagues from other professions. I believe these 'new' research values are more easily nurtured in service settings but I hope that the growth of productive research endeavours from services will elicit complementary reactions from those employed in traditional research systems, which will at some point in the future make possible a merging of their roles. Of course, the sooner it can start, the better it will be for our understanding of how best to promote the well-being of all our children.

References

Barlow, D.H., Hayes, S.C. and Nelson, R.O. (1984) *The Scientist–Practitioner: Research and Accountability in Clinical and Educational Settings*, New York: Pergamon

Baumeister, A.A. and Hillsinger, L.B. (1984) Role of psychologists in public institutions for the mentally retarded revisited, *Professional Psychology*, *15*, 134–41

Belbin, A. (1979) Applicable psychology and some national problems, *Bulletin of the British Psychological Society*, *32*, 241–3

Bruner, J. (1980) *Under Five in Britain*, London: Grant McIntyre

Burden, R. (1978) Schools' systems analysis: A project-centred approach in Gillham, B. (ed.), *Reconstructing Educational Psychology*, London: Croom Helm

Clarke, A.M. and Clarke, A.D.B. (1973) *Mental Retardation and Behavioural Research*, London: Churchill-Livingstone

Cunningham, C.C. (1983) Early support and intervention: the HARC infant project in P. Mittler and H. McConachie (eds), *Parents, Professionals and Mentally Handicapped People: Approaches to Partnership*, London: Croom Helm

Curtis, A. and Blatchford, P. (1981) *Meeting the Needs of Socially Handicapped Children: The Background to My World*, Windsor: NFER-Nelson

Donaldson, M. (1978) *Children's Minds*, London: Fontana

Doyle, C.E. (1971) cited in Clarke and Clarke, *Mental Retardation*

Eysenck, H.J. (1957) *Sense and Nonsense in Psychology*, London: Penguin

Gallagher, J.J. (1981) Transforming research to policy in the field of language studies in P. Mittler (ed.), *Frontiers of Knowledge in Mental Retardation*, Vol. 1, Baltimore: University Park Press

Georgiades, N.J. and Phillimore, L. (1975) The myth of the hero-innovator and alternative strategies for organizational change in C. Kiernan and F.P. Woodford (eds), *Behaviour Modification with the Severely Retarded*, Amsterdam: Elsevier-Scientific

Gillham, B. (ed.) (1978) *Reconstructing Educational Psychology*, London: Croom Helm

McCall, R.B. (1977) Challenges to a science of developmental psychology, *Child Development*, *48*, 333–44

—— and Stocking, S.H. (1982) Between scientists and public: communicating psychological research through the mass media, *American Psychologist*, *37*, 985–95

McConkey, R. (1985) *Working with Parents: A Practical Guide for Teachers and Therapists*, London: Croom Helm/Cambridge, Mass., Brookline Books

—— and O'Connell, A. (1982) A national survey of child referrals to psychologists, *Irish Journal of Psychology*, 5, 85–95

Masters, J.C. (1984) Psychology, research, and social policy, *American Psychologist*, *39*, 851–82

Midwinter, E. (1977) The professional–lay relationship: a Victorian legacy, *Journal of Child Psychology and Psychiatry*, *18*, 101–13

Mittler, P. (1975) Research to practice in the field of handicap. Public lecture, London, Institute for Research into mental and multiple handicap

—— (1984) Quality of life and services for people with disabilities, *Bulletin of the British Psychological Society*, *37*, 218–25

Morrison, F.J., Lord, C. and Keating, D.P. (1984) *Applied Developmental Psychology*, Vol. 1, New York: Academic Press

Salkovskis, P.M. (1984) Psychological research by NHS clinical psychologists: an analysis and some suggestions, *Bulletin of the British Psychological Society*, *37*, 375–7

Sears, R.R. (1975) Your ancients revisited: a history of child development in E.M. Hetherington (ed.), *Review of Child Development Research*, Vol. 5, Chicago: University of Chicago Press

Shadish, W.R. (1984) Policy research: lessons from the implementation of deinstitutionalisation, *American Psychologist*, *39*, 725–38

Shapiro, M.B. (1970) Intensive assessment of the single case: an inductive–deductive approach in P. Mittler (ed.), *The Psychological Assessment of Mental and Physical Handicaps*, London: Methuen

Shipman, M.O. (1977) *Inside a Curriculum Project*, London: Methuen

Smetherham, D. (1981) Accomplishing evaluation: towards a methodology in C. Lacey and D. Lawton (eds), *Issues in Evaluation and Accountability*, London: Methuen

Super, C.M. (1982) cited in Morrison *et al.*, *Applied Developmental Psychology*

Tizard, B., Mortimer, J. and Burchell, B. (1981) *Involving Parents in Nursery and Infant Schools*, London: Grant McIntyre

Tizard, J. (1976) Psychology and social policy, *Bulletin of the British Psychological Society*, *29*, 225–34

Vasta, R. (1979) *Studying Children: An Introduction to Research Methods*, San Francisco: Freeman

Watts, F. (1984) Applicable psychological research in the NHS, *Bulletin of the British Psychological Society*, *37*, 41–2

Wilcox, P. (1981) The Portage project in America in G. Pugh, *Parents as Partners*, London: National Children's Bureau

Zigler, E. and Muenchow, S. (1984) How to influence social policy affecting children and families, *American Psychologist*, *39*, 415–20

As the different chapters in this book suggest, the relationship between research and practice is not a simple one. It is also an area which until recently has received relatively little attention from developmental psychologists. One very consistent conclusion reached by the contributors is that if research and practice are to benefit from a productive and reciprocal relationship greater attention must be given to the process by which the two kinds of activity are related. There is broad agreement that traditional ways of thinking about the role of academic researchers and professional psychologists have resulted in very little in the way of useful dialogue and that the direct impact of research upon practice has been negligible. It follows that if research and practice are to be mutually beneficial, the relationship which exists between researchers and practitioners must be renegotiated. Some would go further and argue that the distinction between different fields of activity has outlived its usefulness and ought to be replaced by alternative formulations which more accurately reflect the nature of the subject matter of psychology.

This overview is not an attempt to formulate solutions; these will only arise as efforts are made over a period of time to establish more effective links between research and practice. However, before it is possible to think of a solution, the problem must be clearly understood. It is hoped that this book will make some small contribution to this more modest objective. With this in mind, the main themes which emerge from the 14 chapters will be briefly summarised.

The Social Context of Research

The first and most significant theme is the recognition that research takes place within a social context, which places political and ideological constraints upon the research process, as well as attempts which may be made to use research findings to alleviate developmental problems through psychological intervention. Research cannot be considered as the unbiased pursuit of objective knowledge and intervention clearly implies a whole range of values about 'what ought to be'. Facts and theories from psychological research can only therefore provide a basis for initiating social change. The values which determine whether change is appropriate and what constitutes improvement may be informed by psychology but the criteria for making judgements must come from other sources. This in turn suggests that not only individual development but also the relationship between research and practice needs to be considered in terms of a wider ecological framework.

Theories are Context Specific

An ecological view of research-practice relations – provides a framework for discussing the second major theme to emerge. This is the view that research has specific social, political and academic functions and that the products of the research process, whether they be 'results' or 'theories', are subordinate to those functions. The contexts within which academic research and psychologically-based intervention occur are sufficiently different to raise serious problems for those who seek to base strategies for intervention upon the products of research. Academic theories do not automatically provide ways of understanding children which are appropriate to the development and introduction of innovations in practice. Such theories must be exposed to practical contexts so that their potential for guiding practice in that context can be established. Two changes which are contributing to this process of testing theories within practice settings are, first, the growing numbers of practitioners who are taking on board the role of researcher and, secondly, the growing popularity of collaborative research in which researcher and practitioner are forming working partnerships with the specific aim of carrying out research which is applicable to practice.

The Role of Personal Values

The third theme, again arising from the recognition of the wider social context in which research and practice are located, is concerned with the role of personal values. Personal values are most clearly implicated in the choice of objectives for intervention since – covertly or overtly – this involves making judgements about how other people will live their lives. Making personal judgements about other people is clearly necessary and is very much a part of the social world outside the realm of psychological intervention. However, there are dangers when the values which underlie specific decisions are not acknowledged and intervention objectives are based upon the assumption that research provides not only descriptions of the way things are but also the criteria for what ought to be. This endows psychology with a capacity for giving value judgements a spurious scientific legitimacy, and in doing so relieves those who are concerned with intervention from the responsibility of providing other, more relevant arguments, to justify their actions.

Questions About 'Normal' Development and 'Normal' Environments

The fourth theme which emerges from these chapters is the role of 'normality' as a construct within child development research. While psychologists are quick to emphasise that 'the normal child' or 'the normal environment' are abstractions which have evolved for academic and scientific ends, there continue to be numerous instances where these fundamental features of 'the normal child' and 'the normal environment' are overlooked. It has been stated that practice deals with different problems compared with research; one of the most obvious differences is that while research is generally concerned with description and generalisations from group data, intervention is concerned with recommendation for action in the case of individuals. The positive values which have become attached to normality (fed no doubt by much psychological research) include its 'naturalness' and its 'desirability'. However, as a number of the authors point out, for the purpose of intervention, normality needs to be operationalised in terms of specific behaviours or specific environmental conditions; but this procedure is doomed to failure for the simple reason that the normal child in a normal environment does not exist. Attempts to reconstruct normality for children with developmental disorders or those at risk from psychological or social deprivation will not succeed, not because of the severity of the problems encountered or the relative inadequacy of the strategies, but because the goal is both inappropriate and unattainable. Instead, what is needed is a research strategy which recognises the limitations of theories and methods of academic research but is also able to use them as a basis for initiating research within the field of psychological practice. Some of the chapters in this volume provide examples of how this has been achieved.

Awareness of Existing Abilities and Predispositions

The concern arising from attempts to establish too rigid a view of 'normality' as the goal of intervention has in turn led to an increased awareness and respect for the abilities of those who are the recipients of intervention; this is the fifth theme which emerges from these chapters. First, it has been suggested that because people (including parents, children, teachers and other professionals) actively manipulate the environment to achieve specific ends and impose structure and meaning on their experiences, those who would introduce change must first come to terms with what adults and children already know; their existing ways of understanding and the values they hold. Secondly, it is increasingly recognised that people form powerful environmental influences on those around them; a change in the behaviour of an individual is likely to have implications for others who normally come into contact with that individual and, to the extent that those others are encouraged to respond differently, so the environment for the first individual is changed. This reciprocal and open-ended view of human interactions suggests that, rather than attempting to introduce changes with immediate or short-term objectives, intervention would be more productive if it focused on ways of exploiting existing patterns of interaction between, for example, mothers and children or teachers and pupils so as to maximise opportunities for growth and development in the medium and long term. It also indicates the limitations of traditional models of evaluation, whereby attempts are made to link specific changes in the environment with specific behavioural outcomes. Instead researchers and practitioners are giving greater attention to the social processes which form the context of development in the belief that this may be a more appropriate focus for intervention.

Communicating with Practitioners and Policy-makers

The sixth and final theme which I wish to highlight in this overview concerns the importance of dissemination of innovations in practice both to practitioners and to policy-makers. No matter what new developments emerge from the changing relationship between research and practice, little will have been achieved if the products of collaboration are not made available to a wider audience.

A number of possibilities exist for the future. In this volume it has been suggested that research may become an integral part of practice and, as practitioners take on research responsibilities, so service provision will be systematically modified, and successful innovations disseminated to others working in similar settings. Another possibility is that successful research-based innovations for practice might be communicated to practitioners more effectively, either through intensive workshop courses or alternatively through mini-courses using complete video-taped presentations (McConkey 1983; McConkey and O'Connor 1983; Robson 1982). Thirdly, it has been suggested that in order to influence policy and practice, researchers and practitioners must pay special attention to existing institutional frameworks. At one level this involves relevant and well-informed teaching about research and practice in child development in universities and colleges, particularly when the audience is teachers or trainees for the health professions. At another level, it involves a willingness to seek representation on advisory bodies and committees which formulate and comment upon policy proposals at both local and national levels.

This overview has identified a number of issues and challenges which confront psychologists and other professionals who are concerned with forging new links between research and practice. Some of the preceding chapters have gone further in describing ways in which successful links have already been established. It is hoped that the book as a whole will encourage those working in child development not only to build upon these examples but to find additional ways of relating research and practice for the benefit of children and their families.

References

McConkey, R. (1983) Video courses for parents: a model of systematic dissemination, *Association of Child Psychology and Psychiatry Newsletter, 16*, 7–12
and O'Connor, M. (1983) Video-courses in the in-service training of social service staff, *Journal of Education for Teaching, 9(1)*, 46–54
Robson, C. (1982) *Language Development Through Structured Teaching*, Cardiff: Drake Educational Associates

CONTRIBUTORS

Moncrieff Cochran is an Associate Professor of Human Development and Family Studies in the College of Human Ecology at Cornell University and is currently Director of the United States component of the international Family Matters project. His current academic interests include social networks as family supports, the empowerment process, and public policies affecting families and children.

Charles Desforges is Senior Lecturer in the School of Education at the University of East Anglia and, as Director of the Early Years Sector, is responsible for training teachers for work in first schools. Before taking up his present position he taught in schools and carried out research at the University of Lancaster. He has published extensively in classroom learning, children's thinking and teachers' professional knowledge. He is currently directing a research project on teaching mathematics in first schools.

David Galloway is a lecturer in Education at University College, Cardiff. He is professionally qualified in residential child care, teaching and educational psychology. He was previously Senior Educational Psychologist in Sheffield where he was responsible for a research programme concerning truancy and disruptive behaviour in schools, funded by the DES. From 1980 to 1983 he was Senior Lecturer in Education at Victoria University of Wellington, New Zealand. While there he directed contract research programmes on provision for disruptive pupils and on stress and satisfaction in teaching. His publications include *Teaching and Counselling* (Longman 1981), *Schools and Disruptive Pupils* (Longman 1982, with D. Bull, D. Blomfield and R. Seyd), *Schools and Persistent Absentees* (Pergamon 1985) and *Schools, Pupils and Special Educational Needs* (Croom Helm 1985).

Susan Gregory is Research Fellow with the Deafness Research Group in the Department of Psychology, Nottingham University. She also teaches on the Masters Course on Child Development and Educational Psychology. Her research interests concern the development of young deaf children with particular emphasis on the role of

260

parents. She has published widely in the field of deafness including her book *The Deaf Child and His Family* (Allen and Unwin, 1976).

John Harris is a lecturer in Child Development in the Department of Education, University College Cardiff. His academic interests include language acquisition, cognitive development, and severe developmental disorder. He is currently involved in a research project on language teaching and language learning in special schools.

Pam Harris is lecturer in Psychology at the South Glamorgan Institute of Higher Education. Her research and publications have been concerned mainly with children in hospital, including a co-authored book (with D. Muller and L. Watley) on *Nursing Children: Psychology, Research and Practice* (Harper and Row 1985). She has lectured widely to parents and recently published a book (with Toni Arther) on entertaining young children at home.

Mark Masidlover is an Educational Psychologist working for Derbyshire County Council. He is seconded by his Local Authority to continue the development of the Derbyshire Language Scheme and to act as Tutor on a training course for Clinical and Educational Psychologists in the Child Development Research Unit at the University of Nottingham. His current interests include the assessment of communication skills in natural settings, the communication difficulties of autistic children, and the design and evaluation of staff training in assessment and remediation.

Roy McConkey is Senior Research Officer with St Michael's House, a Dublin-based organisation providing services to mentally handicapped people and their families. He is also a part-time lecturer in the Department of Psychology, University College and the Department of Remedial Linguistics, Trinity College, Dublin. His particular research interests are play and language intervention, parental involvement and community education about disability. He is co-author of several books giving practical advice to parents and staff; the latest being *Working With Parents: A Practical Guide for Teachers and Therapists* (Croom Helm 1985). He has also published articles in many professional journals.

Kay Mogford is currently Lecturer in the Department of Speech, University of Newcastle-upon-Tyne. She initially trained and gained experience as a Speech Therapist. Later, having graduated as a Psychologist, she joined the Child Development Research Unit, University of Nottingham as a Research Officer participating in an Action Research Project into methods of developing play and communication in young handicapped children. A subsequent research project involved a longitudinal study of the development of young deaf children. Current research interests include the language development and social interaction of twins and the use of play therapy techniques with language disordered children.

Leslie Smith has taught in secondary, further and adult education and is currently a lecturer in Education at the University of Lancaster. His main interests lie in psychological, philosophical and educational aspects of Piaget's work with papers published by the *British Journal of Psychology*, *Philosophy of the Social Sciences* and the Further Education Unit.

Kathy Sylva is a lecturer in Psychology in the Oxford University Department of Social and Administrative Studies. She has studied play in young children, especially its role in intellectual development. She was a member of the Oxford Pre-school Research Group and co-author (with Carolyn Roy and Marjorie Painter) of one of its research volumes: *Childwatching at Playgroup and Nursery School* (Grant McIntyre 1980). She is currently investigating the ways in which young children cope with the stress of hospitalisation. Her main interest is in the ways that a variety of settings – homes, schools, hospitals – affect the development of intellectual and coping skills. Recent books include *Play: Its Role in Development and Evaluation* (Penguin 1976, with Jerome Bruner and Alison Jolly) and *Child Development: A First Course* (Grant McIntyre 1982, with Ingrid Lunt).

Sheila Wolfendale has been a primary and remedial teacher, a college of education lecturer and an educational psychologist in several LEAs. She is currently a Principal Lecturer in educational psychology, and Course Tutor to the MSc in educational psychology, a postgraduate training course for educational psychologists. Author of many publications on learning difficulties and special needs, her books are: *Identification of Learning Difficulties – A Model for Intervention* (NARE, with Trevor Bryans); *Parental Participation in Children's Development and Education* (Gordon and Breach

1983); *Parental Involvement in Children's Reading* (Croom Helm 1985, co-edited with Keith Topping). She has been working actively within the area of parental involvement, with teachers and parents, exploring with them the potential of home–school links.

AUTHOR INDEX

Addington, J. 88, 95
Adelberg, T. 17, 32
Adey, P. 213, 219
Ainsworth, M.D. 37, 49
Aitkin, M. 193, 204
Aitman, J.B. 78, 94
Alexander, R.J. 215, 217
Ammon, P.R. 209, 217
Anyon, J. 14, 32
Apter, S. 76, 94
Archambolt, R. 218
Argyle, M. 5, 8
Arnold, H. 81, 96
Ashton, P. 113, 125
Atkinson, R.C. 215, 217
Ausubel, D.P. 215, 218

Baker-Miller, J. 13, 32
Ball, T. 194, 204
Balla, D. 170
Banet, B. 132, 142
Barlow, D.H. 232–3, 251–3
Barr, D. 13, 14, 32
Barrett, B. 196, 204
Barton, L. 33, 92, 94
Bate, M. 229, 233
Bates, E. 177, 188
Battle, S. 77, 95, 229, 233
Baumeister, A.A. 146, 152, 166, 238, 253
Belbin, A. 242, 245–6, 249, 251, 253
Bell, S. 37, 49
Bendall, S. 87–8, 95
Bender, M. 79, 95
Bennett, N. 103, 113, 125, 193, 204
Bereiter, C. 211, 218
Berger, P. 12–13, 32
Beveridge, M. 170, 174, 188–9
Bishop, J. 71
Blackstone, T. 73, 96
Blank, M. 210, 219
Blatchford, P. 229, 233, 252–3
Blomfield, D. 194, 204
Bloom, B.S. 111–12, 125
Bloom, L.M. 177, 180, 188–9
Blott, J.P. 156, 168
Blunden, R. 85, 96

Bobbitt, R.A. 156, 168
Bodmer, W.F. 104, 125
Bond, J.T. 134, 142
Booth, T. 96
Boswell, C. 199, 204
Boswell, K. 199, 204
Bower, G.H. 115, 125
Bower, T.G.R. 37, 49
Bracken, D. 79, 96
Bradley, M. 75, 95
Brainerd, C.J. 150, 166, 209, 218–19
Brassard, J. 17, 32
Breedlove, C. 134, 142
Brice-Heath, S. 160, 166
Bricker, D. 154, 166, 167
Bricker, W. 154, 166
Brimer, M.A. 182, 188
Brinker, R.P. 156, 166, 174–5, 188–9
Broadbent, D.E. 210, 218
Bronfenbrenner, U. 15–17, 32, 74–6, 95
Brooks, P.H. 146, 152, 166
Brown, R. 177, 183, 189
Brown, G. 147, 149–50, 166–8, 209, 212–13, 216, 218
Browning, E. 230, 233
Bruner, J. 107, 110, 121, 125, 135–6, 138–9, 141–2, 184, 190, 237, 241–2, 247–8, 253
Bryant, P. 129, 131, 142, 150–1, 167
Buium, N. 156, 166
Bullock, A. 74, 81, 95
Burchell, B. 236
Burden, R. 252–3
Burton, L.W. 49
Bushell, R. 81, 96
Butterworth, G. 165, 167, 169

Calculator, S. 174, 190
Calderhead, J. 215, 218
Cameron, R.J. 88, 95
Carl-Haywood, H. 189
Carpenter, R.L. 151, 167
Carter, A.L. 177, 189
Case, R. 116–17, 125, 210, 218

Chesaldine, S. 156, 167
Cheyne, W. 95
Child, D. 213, 218
Chomsky, N. 53, 81, 155, 167, 210, 218
Claparède, E. 103, 125
Clark, R. 171, 189
Clarke, A.D.B. 95, 251, 253
Clarke, A.M. 95, 251, 253
Cleave, S. 229, 233
Clift, P.S. 77, 95
Cochran, M. 4–5, 11–14, 16–17, 32–3, 75–6
Cockburn, A. 113, 125
Coggins, T.E. 152, 167
Cohen, L. 73, 79, 95
Collett, R. 60, 71
Conrad, R. 58, 71
Cotton, J.W. 126
Coupe, J. 155–6, 168
Court, S.D.M. 41, 49, 74, 95
Craft, M. 73, 79, 95
Cranstoun, Y. 231, 234
Crawley, S. 154, 168
Crockenberg, S. 32
Cromar, R. 152, 167
Cross, W.E. 15
Crutchfield, R.S. 53, 71
Crystal, D. 156, 167
Cummins, J. 151, 167
Cunningham, C.C. 89, 95, 235–53
Curtis, A. 252–3
Cyster, R. 77, 95

Dale, D.M.C. 67, 71
Daly, B. 88, 95
Davie, C.E. 76, 95
Davies, A. 142, 189
Davies, F. 113, 125
Davis, J. 77–8, 95
De 'Ath, E. 78, 96
De Haven, E. 175, 189
De La Cruz, F. 169
Dean, C. 28, 32
Derman, L. 113, 126
Desforges, C. 4, 6, 113, 125, 140, 147, 149–50, 162, 166–7, 172, 203, 207–9, 212–14, 216, 218
Dessent, T. 88, 95
Deuchar, M. 71
DeVries, R. 148–50, 167
Dewey, J. 128, 130, 137, 141, 209, 218
Dick, W. 107, 110, 115, 120, 125

Donachy, W. 74, 95
Donaldson, M. 37, 49, 97, 129, 142, 147–8, 167, 240, 208–9, 218, 253
Douglas, J. 39, 49
Doxiadis, S. 49
Doyle, C.E. 239, 253
Doyle, W. 217–18
Duckworth, E. 208, 218
Dunn, J. 37, 49
Dunn, L.L.M. 182, 188

Easley, J.A. 167, 169
Eisenberg, K. 182, 189
Elliott, J. 93, 95
Ellis, N. 190
Engelmann, S.E. 113, 116, 125, 210, 218
Engman, H. 32
Epstein, A.S. 134, 142
Eysenck, H.J. 250, 253
Ewing, A. 54, 67, 71
Ewing, E.C. 54, 67, 71

Ferguson, C.A. 189
Finch, A.J. 49
Fincham, F. 146–7, 167
Fischer, C. 32
Flamer, G.B. 125–6, 218
Flavell, J.H. 150, 167
Fletcher, P. 156, 167, 181, 189–90
Floyd, A. 218
Fokkema, S.D. 125
Fontana, D. 213, 218
Ford, D. 109, 126
Ford, M.C. 125–6
Ford, M.P. 218
Forehand, R. 40–1, 49
Fox, K. 32
Francis, H. 218
Freedman, P.P. 151, 167
Freire, P. 12–13, 27, 32–3
Froebel, F. 127–8, 130
Frohman, A. 85, 95
Fullbeck, C. 68–9, 71
Furth, H. 149, 167, 208, 210, 218

Gagne, R.M. 107, 109–10, 115, 120, 125
Gallagher, J.J. 243, 253
Gallagher, J.R. 167, 169
Galloway, D. 94, 101–2, 194, 196–7, 199–200, 204
Garcia, E. 175, 189

Gardner, D.E.M. 128–30, 142
Garman, M. 156, 167, 189–90
Gaussen, T. 87, 89, 95
George, A. 77, 95
Georgiades, N.J. 237, 245, 250, 253
Gesell, A. 88
Gibbs, T. 153–4, 167
Gillham, B. 248, 253–4
Ginsburg, H. 210–11, 218
Giroux, H. 15, 32
Glaser, R. 107, 110, 119, 125, 215,
    218
Gleidman, J. 92, 95
Glendenning, H.C. 56, 71
Glyn, T. 82, 95
Goldstein, S. 156, 168
Gordon, K. 156, 168
Grabe, S. 17, 32
Graham, J.T. 151, 167
Graham, L.W. 151, 167
Gray, J. 103, 126
Green, D.R. 125–6
Green, J. 199, 204
Greenfield, P.M. 138, 142
Gregory, S. 3, 11, 50, 52, 61, 63–5,
    68, 71, 222, 230, 233
Grieve, R. 97
Griffiths, A. 81, 95
Grimmett, S. 75, 96
Grotberg, E.H. 35, 39, 49
Grubb, W. 17, 32
Gunnarsson, L. 17, 32

Halford, G.S. 116, 126
Halkes, R. 126
Halliday, M.A.K. 177, 189
Halsey, A.H. 73, 95
Hamilton, D. 81, 95
Hannon, P. 81, 96
Hanson, M. 89, 96
Harris, J. 5, 11, 101, 143, 152, 155–
    7, 159–60, 167–8, 174, 189, 222
Harris, M. 138–9, 142
Harris, P. 5, 34, 252
Harris, S.L. 175, 189
Harrison, M. 34, 49
Hartman, M. 156, 168
Hayes, S.C. 251, 253
Heatherington, E.M. 254
Hegrenes, J.R. 156, 168
Henriques, J. 7–8, 143, 158, 164–5,
    168, 170
Hersen, M. 232–3
Hesketh, J. 193, 204

Hester, P. 91, 95
Hewett, S. 230, 233
Hewison, J. 81, 97
Hilgard, E.J. 115, 125
Hilgard, E.R. 209–10, 218
Hill, E. 215, 219
Hills, R. 77, 96
Hillsinger, L.B. 238, 253
Hipgrave, T. 90, 96
Hobbs, N. 76, 96
Hobsbaum, A. 182, 189
Hohmann, M. 132, 142
Holland, A. 190
Holley, B.J. 113, 125
Holloway, W. 7–8, 143, 168, 170
Hom, H. 217
Hood, L. 177, 180, 188–9
Hooper, F.H. 209, 219
House, B. 175, 190
Howlin, P. 156, 168
Hubbell, R.D. 174, 189
Hudson, W.D. 104, 126
Hughs, M. 40, 49, 76, 97
Hume, D. 104, 126
Hutt, S.J. 76, 95
Huttenlocher, J. 182, 189

Ingleby, D. 7–8, 143, 165, 168
Inhelder, B. 115–16, 126, 146, 169
Irvine, S.H. 160, 168
Irwin, O.C. 175, 189
Isaacs, N. 127
Isaacs, S. 127–9, 131, 135–7, 141–2

Jackson, A. 81, 95
James, W. 209, 218
Jeffree, D. 89, 96
Jeffreys, D. 215, 219
Jensen, A.R. 104, 126
Johnson, S. 81, 96
Johnston, J.A. 204
Jones, O.H.M. 156, 168
Jones, M.F. 188
Jowett, S. 229, 233

Kagan, S. 94, 97
Kahn, J.V. 154, 168
Kamii, C. 113, 126, 150–1, 168
Keating, D.P. 239–40, 254
Kendall, P.C. 49
Keniston, K. 18, 32
Keough, B. 168
Kerfoot, S. 88, 95
Kiernan, C. 150, 154–5, 159, 168,

254
Kineen, P. 113, 125
King, R. 215, 219
Klahr, D. 217
Klatzky, R.L. 126
Klein, N.K. 146, 149, 168
Klugman, E. 94, 97
Koch, R. 169
Kogan, K.L. 156, 168
Kohlberg, L. 150, 168
Krech, D. 53, 71
Kuczaj, S. 189
Kuhn, D. 216, 219
Kushlick, A. 87, 95
Kyle, J. 71

Lacey, C. 254
Lacey, R. 79, 96
Lamb, M. 18, 32
Laosa, L. 32
Lawrence, E. 127
Lawton, D. 254
Lawton, J.T. 209, 219
Lazerson, M. 17, 32
Lee, V. 190
Leeming, K. 155–6, 168
Lenneberg, E.H. 151, 168–9
Lenneberg, E. 169
Leopold, W.F. 177, 189
Lesgold, A.M. 125
Levine, M. 89, 96
Lewin, K. 76
Lewis, J. 17, 32
Lieven, E.V.M. 177, 189
Light, P. 165, 167, 169
Lightbrown, P. 177, 188
Lloyd, L.L. 169
Lock, A. 153, 168
Lord, C. 239–40, 254
Lyon, E. 96

McArthur, K. 68–9, 71
McCall, R.B. 241–2, 251, 254
McConkey, R. 6–7, 89, 96, 140,
    156, 167, 172, 203, 207, 223,
    231–2, 234–5, 251–2, 254, 258–9
McConochie, H. 90, 96, 253
McCormick, B. 61, 63, 71
MacDonald, J.D. 156, 168
McGovern, M.A. 231, 234
McKnight, G. 81, 97
McLanahan, S. 17, 32
McLean, J.E. 151, 153, 155, 168,
    170, 174, 179, 189

McMahon, L. 231, 234
McNamara, D. 213–14, 218
Mahoney, G. 154, 168
Marcus, S. 157, 169
Marshall, N.R. 156, 168
Masildover, M. 6, 101, 171, 222
Mason, M. 76, 95
Masters, J.C. 244, 246, 254
Maughan, B. 193, 204
Mayer, R. 150, 168
Mays, J. 229, 233
Meltzer, L. 89, 96
Metzl, M. 39–40, 49
Midwinter, E. 235, 254
Millar, G.A. 53, 71
Miller, J.F. 151, 155, 168–70, 179,
    189
Mittler, P. 90, 96, 155–6, 168–70,
    182, 189, 234, 238, 242, 253–4
Modgil, C. 167–8, 170
Modgil, S. 167–8, 170
Mogford, K. 6, 65, 71, 207, 220
Moody, S. 92, 94
Morgan, R. 96
Morrison, F.J. 239–40, 244–5, 252,
    254
Mortimore, J. 73, 96, 236, 254
Mortimore, P. 193, 204
Moyle, D. 81, 96
Muenchow, S. 243, 245
Müller, D.J. 167–8, 189
Münsterberg, H. 209, 219
Mussen, P.H. 169

Nelson, K. 155, 169, 174, 176–7,
    190
Nelson, R.O. 251, 253
Neuhaus, R. 12–13, 32
Newson, E. 35, 49, 90, 96, 230, 234
Newson, J. 35, 49, 230, 234
Nolan, M. 57, 59, 61, 68–9, 71–2
Norman, D. 112–13, 123, 126
Novak, G. 156, 170
Nunn, P. 129

Oates, J. 49
Ochs, E. 65, 72
O'Connell, A. 251, 254
O'Connor, M. 231, 234, 258–9
O'Dell, S. 40, 49
Oller, D.K. 154, 169, 176, 190
Olson, J.K. 119, 126
Olver, R.R. 138, 142
Open University 77, 96

Opper, S. 210–11, 218
Oratio, A.R. 231, 234
Ouston, J. 193, 204

Painter, M. 140, 142
Panckhurst, F. 199, 204
Peed, S. 40–1, 49
Pelligrino, J.W. 125
Percival, W. 77, 96
Peters, R.S. 104, 126
Peterson, P.L. 114, 126
Phillimore, L. 237, 245, 250, 253
Piaget, J. 37, 113, 115–16, 126–32,
    135, 137–8, 141, 145–8, 157–8,
    161, 169, 208–12, 214, 219
Pletts, M. 231, 234
Plowden, B. 73, 96, 119, 126
Pond, B. 81, 96
Potts, P. 92, 96
Povey, R. 215, 219
Pratt, C. 97
Prehm, H.J. 152, 169
Pringle, M.K. 35, 49, 79, 96
Pugh, G. 41, 49, 78, 85, 96, 254
Pullis, M. 154, 168
Purser, H. 222, 234
Pyke, G. 127
Pyke, M. 127

Quirk, R. 226–7, 233–4

Radford, J. 49
Raph, J. 168, 170
Rappoport, J. 13, 33
Ratner, N. 184, 190
Raynor, J. 73, 79, 95
Rees, N. 153, 169
Reeve, C.J. 82, 97
Reid, D.K. 146, 148, 169
Reif, F. 126
Resnick, L.B. 107, 109–10, 126
Revill, S. 85, 96
Reynell, J. 89, 173, 182, 190
Richards, M.P.M. 8, 49, 168
Richman, N. 39, 49
Riley, D 14, 32
Robinson, F.G. 215, 218
Robinson, P. 217
Robinson, W.P. 177, 190
Robson, C. 156, 169, 258–9
Robson, D. 81, 96
Rondal, J. 152, 169
Rose, D. 49
Rose, N. 7, 8

Rose, S.A. 210, 219
Roth, W. 92, 95
Roy, C. 140, 142
Rummelhart, D.E. 112–13, 126
Rutter, M. 193, 204
Ryan, J. 146, 151–2, 169
Ryan, W. 18, 33
Rynders, J. 156, 167

Safford, P.L. 146, 149, 168
Salkovskis, P.M. 248–9, 254
Samuel, J.C. 78, 94
Satterley, D. 103, 126
Scardamalia, M. 211, 218
Schaffer, H.R. 168
Schiefelbusch, R.L. 167–70, 189
Schieffelin, B.B. 65, 72
Schneider, D. 89, 96
Schofield, W. 81, 97
Schwebel, M. 168, 170
Schweinhart, L.J. 134, 142
Scotney, T. 204
Scott, M. 75, 96
Sears, R.R. 239, 254
Seibert, J.M. 154, 169, 176, 190
Seitz, S. 157, 169
Selman, R.L. 147, 149, 169
Seyd, R. 194, 204
Shadish, W.R. 245, 250, 254
Shapiro, M.B. 251, 254
Shayer, M. 213, 219
Shearer, D.E. 150, 159, 169
Shearer, M.S. 150, 159, 169
Shipman, M.O. 237, 254
Shipman, V. 74, 96
Siegel, L.S. 209, 219
Sigel, I. 32
Siegler, R.S. 116–17, 126
Sigston, A. 88, 95
Sinha, C. 7–8, 144, 159, 169
Skinner, B.F. 155, 210
Sloper, P. 89, 95
Smedslund, J. 147, 169
Smetherham, D. 250, 254
Smilansky, S. 135, 141
Smith, F. 211, 219
Smith, J. 87, 95
Smith, L. 7, 101, 103, 162, 202, 208
Snow, C.E. 189
Snyder-McLean, L.K. 151, 153, 155,
    168, 174, 179, 189
Solity, J. 82, 97
Solomon, B. 12, 33
Solso, R.L. 189

Southgate, V. 81, 96
Spiegel, B. 156, 168
Stayton, D. 37, 49
Steen, L.A. 106, 126
Stern, D. 40, 49
Stierer, B. 77, 96
Stocking, S.H. 242, 254
Strauss, S. 182, 189
Sullivan, E. 209, 219
Sullivan, M. 89, 96
Super, C.M. 239, 254
Sutton-Smith, B. 131, 142
Swann, W. 95, 155–6, 168
Sylva, K. 6, 101, 127, 131, 140–2, 144, 203

Tamburrini, J. 147, 170
Taylor, L. 79, 96
Taylor, T. 74, 96
Taylor, W. 208, 219
Tibble, J.W. 208, 219
Tizard, B. 40, 49, 76, 97, 236, 254
Tizard, J. 81, 97, 202, 204, 238, 240, 243–5, 254
Tjossem, T.D. 169
Tomlinson, S. 92, 94, 97
Topping, K. 79–82, 97
Torre, D. 32
Toulmin, S. 120, 126
Tucker, I. 57, 59, 61, 68–9, 72
Tumu, D.T. 126
Turner, 41–2
Turnure, J. 156, 167
Tyre, C. 84, 97

Urwin, C. 7–8, 143, 168, 170

Vanderslice, V. 14, 32, 33
Vasta, R. 239, 254
Venn, C. 7–8, 143, 168, 170
Vincent, E. 76, 95
Vorhaus, G. 97
Vygotsky, L.S. 138, 142, 148, 170

Wachs, H. 149, 167, 208, 210, 218
Wade, B. 79, 97
Wadsworth, B.J. 210, 219
Walberg, H.J. 126
Walker, S. 33
Walkerdine, V. 7–8, 143, 148, 157–8, 160–1, 168, 170
Walrond-Skinner, S. 79, 97

Warnock, M. 52, 72, 74, 78, 89, 97
Wasserman, R. 89, 96
Waterson, N. 189
Watts, F. 236, 244–5, 250, 252, 254
Weber, S. 85, 95
Wedell, K. 97
Weikhart, D.P. 132–4, 141–2
Weiner, S.L. 182, 189
Weisz, J.R. 145, 170
Wellman, B. 17, 33
Wells, G. 76, 97, 153, 170, 174, 181, 190
Welton, J. 74, 97, 106, 126
White, P.G. 82, 97
Whitehall, J.B. 57, 72
Whitehead, D. 93, 95
Whitehurst, G.J. 156, 170
Whitham, M. 13–14, 32–3
Wickens, D. 149, 170
Widemeyer, N. 17, 32
Wilcox, M.J. 174, 190
Wilcox, P. 251, 254
Wilkinson, B. 113, 125
Williams, K. 60, 67, 72
Willis, P. 14, 33
Wimberger, H.C. 156, 168
Winitz, H. 223, 234
Wirz, S.L. 231, 234
Wolfendale, S. 5–6, 11, 34, 36, 38, 40, 73, 75–6, 79–82, 89, 97, 251
Wolinsky, G.F. 146, 170
Woll, B. 71
Wollenburg, K. 85, 95
Wood, D. 138–9, 142, 174, 190, 231, 234
Wood, H. 174, 190, 231, 234
Woodford, C.P. 254
Woodhead, M. 73, 97
Woodward, W.M. 146, 148, 170
Woolever, F. 13, 32

Yardley, A. 211
Yeates, K.O. 145, 170
Yoder, D.E. 151, 155, 168, 170, 174, 179, 189–90
Young, P. 84, 97

Zeaman, D. 175, 190
Zigler, E. 94, 97, 145, 170, 254, 243, 245, 254
Zorn, G. 156, 170

SUBJECT INDEX

Assessment
  cognitive (Piaget) 146–8
  language 153–4
  parents role in assessment of
    children 88–90

Behaviour modification (training
  parents) 40–1

Child development
  courses for parents 41–8; *see also*
    parents: training courses
Child development research 35–7
  influence of research on parents
    38–9; *see also* parents
Children
  active learning 137–8
  developmental theories 143–4
  learning 103–24 *passim*; *see also*
    learning principles: learning
    propositions
  mentally handicapped children 84,
    143–66, 171–88; and Piaget's
    theory 145–51; language
    development 151–7;
    developmental processes 159,
    166
  play 136, 140–1
Children's thinking 128–9, 131,
  136–7, 140
  Piaget's theory 128, 130, 210
  theories 115–16
  theories and educational practice
    209–12, 214–15
Clinical practitioners and research in
  child pyschology 220–33
Clinically based intervention 221
Curriculum
  and development psychology
    209–12, 216
  and normal developmental
    sequences 158–9, 162–5, 176
    nursery/pre-school 132–3,
    136–7
  special schools 148–50,
    154–5, 162–3; influence of
    developmental theories 162–5

Deafness
  advice to parents 56–66 *passim*;
    see also parents
  advising services 51–2
  diagnosis 50
  families 51
  language acquisition of deaf
    children 53–5; spoken language
    58; normal communication
    61–5
  normal behaviour 67–9
  teachers 69; peripatetic teachers
    52
Derbyshire Language Scheme (DLS)
  6, 171–87
  dissemination 184–86; problems
    186
  eliciting contexts for language
    177
  evaluation of DLS 187
  modification of DLS 180
  original formulation of DLS
    173–4
  roles reversal as teaching
    technique 184
  teachers role 175, 183
  teaching comprehension 182–4
  teaching syntax 178, 180–1
  training courses 186–7
Developmental psychology
  clinical 220–1
  developmental processes 159, 166
  influence on school curriculum
    209–12, 216
  influence on special educational
    practice 157–65 *passim*;
    normal development as a
    curriculum aim 158; *see also*
    special schools
  influence on special school
    curriculum 160
  influence on teachers 214–15
  needs of teachers 217
  normal development and mental
    handicap 158, 171, 172
  role in teacher education 208,
    213–16; textbooks for teachers
    213–14
  role in training of speech

therapists 227–9
role in training remedial
    professions 220
Disruptive pupils
    in off-site units 195–7
    in on-site units 194–5
Ecological approach 17–18, 76,
    256
Empowerment 4, 12–16, 26–8
    and human development 14
    and resistance 15
    definition 15
    state versus process 13–14, 28

Family Matters Project (FMP)
    11–30 *passim*
    ecological perspective 17–18
    effects of FMP 22–5; contacts
        between home and school 24;
        on children 25; on mothers
        22–4
    issues 25; determination of needs
        29–30; empowerment of
        parents 26; family differences
        30–1
    participants 16
    processes 19–27 *passim*

Hume's rule 104

Instruction
    instructional psychology 105–7
    meta theory 105, 123 *passim*;
        normative principles 111–13,
        121; permissive principles
        108–25 *passim*; prescriptive
        principles 108–23 *passim*;
        proscriptive principles 108–22
        passim
    theories 118–22
    see also learning theories
Isaacs, Susan 127–30

Language development
    assessment 153–4
    curriculum 154–5; limitations of
        normal developmental sequence
        177–8
    deaf children 53–4, 61; advice for
        parents 56–66 *passim*; normal
        communication 61, 63, 64, 65
    deep structure 55
    disorders 223
    intervention 231; communication
        oriented approach 174–5;

competing aims 179; evaluation
    179; limitations of normal
    developmental data 177–8, *see
    also* language development:
    teaching Derbyshire Language
    Scheme
'normal' language development
    151, 171
pre-linguistic period 65
special schools 151–7
surface structure 55
syntax 178–81 *passim*
teaching 155–7, 176, 180–1, *see
    also* language development:
    intervention; comprehension
    activities 182–4
training speech therapists 223–4
Learning theories 115, 120, 121
    mastery learning 111
    learning principles 108–23 *passim*
    learning propositions 103–24
        passim
    see also instruction

Malting House School 127–31
    passim, 137

Nuffield Foundation 214, 219
Nursery schools/pre-schools 127–9,
    130–3
    adults role 135–7, 140
    high/scope 131–8; evaluation
        133–5

Oxford Pre-School Research
    Group 139–41

Parents
    and children's reading 79–82;
        behavioural approaches 82;
        features of research projects
        81–2; listening approaches 81;
        paired reading 82; planning
        83; results 83–4; take-up 80;
        training 82
    deaf children 56–66; advice from
        professionals 56–70 *passim*;
        advice on language 56–66
        passim, *see also* language
        development; process of giving
        advice 66; professional
        expectations 60–3
    empowerment 4, 26–7
    Family Matters Projects 18–19,
        20, 28; effects of Family

Matters Project 22–3, 24–8
functions of parents 36–7
influence on children's
    development 34–6, 76
intervention: behaviour
    modification 40; by
    professionals 39–40;
    partnership with professionals
    78–9, 88, definitions 90–1, *see
    also* assessment parents and
    children's reading, deaf children,
    portage, courses for parents,
    empowerment
knowledge of children's
    development 38
rights 75, 79, 89
role in children's assessment
    88–90
role in children's education 73–4,
    76–7
training courses 41, 48; feedback
    44–7; course organisation
    43–4
see also mothers, families
Piaget's theory
impact on educational practice
    209–13
impact on nursery/pre-school
    education 130–1, 138
influence on special education
    (mentally handicapped
    children) 145–51; assessment
    146–8; curriculum 148–50;
    teaching strategies 150
Play 136, 140–1
Portage 85–8, 251
evaluation 87–8
use 86

Research
and government policy 94,
    191–204, 238; policy
    development 191–2, 195, 203,
    251; policy implementation
    192, 195, 203–4; role of
    researcher 197, 202–4
and practice 3–8, 70, 203;
    academic teaching 232;
    collaborative research 256;
    characteristics of recipients of
    intervention 257; characteristics
    of researcher-practitioners
    245–7; clinical practice 220–1,
    232–3; descriptive surveys
    251; developing training

courses 251; dissemination of
    research findings 140–1,
    242–3, 258; educational
    settings 209–11, 215–17;
    evaluation of therapies 251;
    experimental methodology
    239–41; language intervention
    179; monitoring services 252;
    normal development and
    intervention in special schools
    161–3, 165, 171; parental
    involvement 92, 93; *see also*
    parents; personal values 256;
    pure versus applicable research
    244–5; practitioners
    involvement in research
    138–40, 233, 248–52;
    recommendations for change
    246; relationship between
    researchers and practitioners
    236–8, 255; research aims,
    243, research questions 244;
    researchers role 236–7;
    support for researcher
    practitioner 249; specialists
    235–6; systems approach 252;
    training researcher practitioners
    207, 245, 249; values 250,
    253; views of normality 61–4,
    67–9, 257
applied 203
implications for practice 191,
    201–4
influence on parents 38–9; *see
    also* parents
political context of research 201
social context of research 193,
    195, 201–3, 255–6
service based research 235–52
    passim, see also researched
    practice

Schools
developmental psychology 208,
    212, 214–15, 216–17;
    developmental theories 209–
    10; Piagetian theory 210–13
off-site units 195–7
on-site units 194–5
stress, health and job satisfaction
    in teaching 198–9
see also nursery schools/
    pre-school special schools
Special Schools 101, 143, 160–5
curriculum 160–5

influence of developmental
theories 157
language development in special
schools 151-7
Piaget's theory 145-51
role of developmental processes
159
teaching normal development
160-5
Speech therapy
characteristics of trainee speech
therapists 225
conditions of employment of
speech therapists 223-4
education and training of speech
therapists 223-33 *passim*
knowledge of developmental
psychology 224-5
knowledge of language
development 224, 231
responsibilities of speech
therapists 224
training 225-31; aims 227;
clinical supervision 231;
collaboration in research 231;

in developmental psychology
227-9; integrating academic
and practical elements of
training 230; Quirk Report
226, 233; recent history 225-7

Teachers
and developmental psychology
208, 213-16
educational practice 144
stress, health and job satisfaction
198-9
Teaching Kits/programmes (in special
schools) 162-3, 165; *see also*
Portage
training courses for parents 41-8;
see also parents
training psychologists 245
training researcher-practitioners
249
training speech therapists 225-31;
see also speech therapy

Values 112-13, 122, 256